T0418492

Who Am I?

Who Am I?

Understanding Identity and the Many Ways We Define Ourselves

Christine L. B. Selby

An Imprint of ABC-CLIO, LLC
Santa Barbara, California • Denver, Colorado

Copyright © 2022 by ABC-CLIO, LLC

All rights reserved. No part of this publication may be reproduced, stored in a retrieval system, or transmitted, in any form or by any means, electronic, mechanical, photocopying, recording, or otherwise, except for the inclusion of brief quotations in a review, without prior permission in writing from the publisher.

Library of Congress Cataloging-in-Publication Data

Names: Selby, Christine L. B., author.
Title: Who am I? : understanding identity and the many ways we define ourselves / Christine L. B. Selby.
Description: Santa Barbara, California : Greenwood, [2022] | Includes bibliographical references and index.
Identifiers: LCCN 2021025261 (print) | LCCN 2021025262 (ebook) | ISBN 9781440872044 (hardcover ; alk. paper) | ISBN 9781440872051 (ebook)
Subjects: LCSH: Identity (Psychology) | Self. | Self-perception.
Classification: LCC BF697 .S42125 2022 (print) | LCC BF697 (ebook) | DDC 158.1—dc23
LC record available at https://lccn.loc.gov/2021025261
LC ebook record available at https://lccn.loc.gov/2021025262

ISBN: 978-1-4408-7204-4 (print)
         978-1-4408-7205-1 (ebook)

26 25 24 23 22   1 2 3 4 5

This book is also available as an eBook.

Greenwood
An Imprint of ABC-CLIO, LLC

ABC-CLIO, LLC
147 Castilian Drive
Santa Barbara, California 93117
www.abc-clio.com

This book is printed on acid-free paper ∞

Manufactured in the United States of America

This book is dedicated to the first person (LKH)
who truly accepted me as is
and to those who seek to understand themselves
while finding that kind of acceptance.

Contents

Preface		ix
Acknowledgments		xiii
Part One	**Defining Identity**	1
Chapter 1	What Is Identity and Its Different Components?	3
Chapter 2	Types of Identity	15
Chapter 3	Theories of Identity Development	35
Part Two	**For Better or for Worse: The Factors That Affect Identity**	59
Chapter 4	Biopsychosocial Factors across the Life Span	61
Chapter 5	Fitting In versus Individualism	93
Chapter 6	Signs and Impacts of a Well-Developed Identity	107
Chapter 7	Signs and Impacts of a Poorly Developed Identity	123
Part Three	**Identity and Challenges of the Twenty-First Century**	139
Chapter 8	Millennials and Generation Z	141
Chapter 9	Technology and Social Media	157
Chapter 10	Local Factors	169
Chapter 11	Global Factors	181

Part Four   Case Studies   211

Sources for Further Information   233

Glossary   239

Bibliography   251

Index   269

Preface

Who Am I? Understanding Identity and the Many Ways We Define Ourselves explores the theories and factors that influence our respective answers to the question, Who are you? There are easy answers to this question, including things such as what you do in and outside of your home, where you grew up and where you live, what your likes and dislikes are, and so on. More difficult answers to this question involve your core beliefs and values that drive each decision you make. I do think we often give lip service to identifying our core beliefs and values; most people will say things like, "I'm helpful, kind, trustworthy," and so on. But the question that remains, in my opinion, is how do you truly live your life? Do the choices you make, small and large, truly reflect those beliefs and values? Do your actions do the same? Answering those questions requires a much deeper dive into truly understanding one's self and one's identity.

This book is intended to provide a brief examination of the theories that explain how and why our identity develops, the different terminology used in the context of *self* and *identity* that has great overlap and important distinctions, and the contemporary issues that, undoubtedly and beyond our control, affect who we are and who we become.

The book is organized into four parts. Part 1, "Defining Identity," includes three chapters that explain what identity is and the terms we use to describe identity, different types of identity, and a few of the theories that describe identity development. Chapter 1 explores the basics with respect to constructs such as self-concept, self-esteem, and self-knowledge, with emphasis on how these concepts help us understand ourselves as well as how others may see us. Chapter 2 explores many of the different types of identity, such as personal identity, social identity, racial identity, gender identity, and professional identity. There are many other types of identity not included in this chapter because one could likely write an entire book on the different types of identity. Those covered here are those most commonly discussed in other writings on identity. The focus of chapter 3 turns to a few of the theories that describe how our respective identities are formed. There are many other theorists who have contributed to this knowledge base; however, those selected here include a combination of historical and currently relevant theories (e.g., Erik Erikson's theory of psychosocial development) and contemporary theories that have seen a great deal of research supporting their respective tenets (e.g., Richard Ryan and Edward Deci's self-determination theory).

Part 2, "For Better or for Worse: The Factors That Affect Identity," includes four chapters that explore the factors that affect us at different stages in our lives, whether we are motivated by fitting in or being individualistic, and what a well-developed or poorly developed identity "looks like." Chapter 4 takes a life span approach to examining the impact of various factors during important periods in our lives: childhood, teenage years, and adulthood. Chapter 5 explores what it means to "fit in" or conform and what it means to maintain a sense of individualism. These concepts are explored at the individual as well as cultural levels. Chapter 6 focuses on the signs of a well-developed identity and the impact that knowing who you truly are has on one's life. Chapter 7 examines the antithesis of chapter 6 by identifying what a poorly develop identity looks like and what impact that may have on an individual's life.

Part 3, "Identity and Challenges in the Twenty-First Century," include four chapters that examine the differences between the various generations and how various forms of media (particularly social media) as well as local and global factors affect how we view ourselves and the world around us. Chapter 8 explores the similarities and differences between the various generations, including Generation Z (or iGen), millennials, Generation X, and baby boomers, with a particular focus on understanding the millennial generation and Generation Z. Chapter 9 examines how the rapid development and expansion of technology and social media impact how we see ourselves and others. Chapters 10 and 11 explore local and global factors, respectively. Chapter 10 takes a look at how the economic challenges of this century impact employment stability for individuals and their families and examines the issues of bullying and diversity. Chapter 11 takes a broader approach and examines climate-related concerns and threats of terrorism and how these issues may impact our understanding of who we are.

Part 4, using the moniker "Case Studies," includes ten different scenarios involving various aspects of identity and the factors that can influence our identity. Readers are presented with a description of various real-life inspired situations and a brief analysis of what identity-related factors are involved. The first scenario describes a twenty-year-old college female who is dealing with pressures to conform and has foreclosed on her identity. Scenario two involves an eighteen-year-old high school male who is dealing with a diffused identity. Scenario three illustrates a nineteen-year-old female college

Preface

sophomore who is identified as being in the moratorium identity status. Scenario four involves a twenty-four-year-old male college graduate who is identity achieved and appears to reflect fidelity to his identity. Scenario five describes a twenty-five-year-old Latino male who is developing his racial and ethnic identity. Scenario 6 examines a young man's struggle to reconcile his sexual identity. Scenario 7 describes a female high school senior who has a high degree of athletic identity and how that impacts her life and well-being. Scenario 8 discusses a sixteen-year-old male who is a junior in high school and is grappling with his adoptive identity. Scenario 9 involves a ten-year-old who was born a biological female but feels strongly like a male and is therefore exploring his gender identity. Scenario 10 describes a twenty-two-year-old female who has begun her graduate-level professional education and may have foreclosed on her identity, and is struggling with the imposter phenomenon.

Finally, this book includes a resource section that contains links and descriptions to various sources of information related to various topics in this book, a glossary of terms used throughout the book that may be unfamiliar to readers, and a bibliography of sources from which information included in this book was gleaned.

I hope you enjoy learning more about what it means to have an identity, how one's identity is formed, and the various factors that influence the development of our individual identities. I also hope that you explore how the material in this book applies to your own sense of who you are.

Acknowledgments

My formal interest in the concept of identity extends back to my college years. That is when I was first introduced to psychologists and philosophers who contemplated and researched what it means to have an identity, what constitutes the real versus false selves, and why living from one's real self is important for one's overall well-being. I have the late Larry K. Hamilton to thank for introducing me to many of these important thinkers. More importantly, I have him to thank for accepting me as I was—no matter what that looked like. His unconditional acceptance led me to conclude for myself and for my psychotherapy patients that there are very few things more powerful than being truly accepted as you are, without judgment or qualification. In my husband, I found such a person. It is difficult to write that without becoming tearful, as no matter what, he has shown time and time again that he accepts me, loves me, and tolerates the not so great parts of me because he knows who I truly am and loves me unconditionally. Thank you for that extraordinary gift, Brian.

My sons must be included on this list of acknowledgments. Both are now young men, and I have had the great privilege of helping them learn how to navigate and understand the world around them. And perhaps more importantly, I have been able to witness who they have become and how they have expressed themselves throughout the years in ways with which I did not always agree. The beauty is that I do not have to agree. Their choices are their own, and it is clear when they make them that they both do so thoughtfully (and, of course, sometimes impulsively!). On more than one occasion, they have changed course when they realized on their own, or after discussion with others, that the path they were headed down was not what was best for them. I truly could not be more proud of them both and who they are.

I have, to date, written four books for ABC-CLIO; this book makes five. The process by which each book was conceptualized, edited, and ultimately published has been truly enjoyable. Each book was written with the assistance of my editor, Maxine Taylor. She has been and continues to be a fervent cheerleader. Her support allowed this book to materialize after I suggested it, given my long-standing interest in and passion about all issues identity. Without her support and belief in me as a writer, she would not have been able to "sell" this book to the decision-makers at ABC-CLIO, who ultimately agreed that a book on identity was worth devoting resources to. As I have stated in the acknowledgment sections of previous books, this book is in its current form because of her excellent guidance. Thank you, Maxine, for helping me to hone my writing voice and to ABC-CLIO for committing resources to the production of this book.

There are numerous others who have undoubtedly influenced me, my writing, and my interests. The influence of some is unseen, and therefore they remain unnamed but nevertheless deserve my thanks. We do not always recognize when we are influenced (positively or negatively) by those who ultimately shape us. The influence of others is clearer and includes colleagues and family: Justine Reel, Rachelle Smith, Robert Buntrock, and Gloria Buntrock (posthumously). There are many others, too numerous to include here, who have influenced me. If you have ever crossed paths with me in any meaningful way, you are among those counted here. Thank you.

PART 1

Defining Identity

Each of us has our own unique identity. The question, of course, is whether you know yourself well enough to understand and describe your identity. As will be discussed in the chapters within part 1, exploring what it means to have an identity and a thorough understanding of one's experiences can help individuals more fully understand who and what they are. Moreover, there are myriad ways of describing one's identity. In chapter 2, over ten types of identity will be described. There are far more than this, but we will review some of the more common types. Chapter 3 describes various psychological theories about how our identities develop. Although there are numerous theories on how identity develops, including theories that were developed in the 1800s, we will focus on some historical theories developed in the twentieth century and more contemporary theories developed in the late twentieth century.

CHAPTER ONE

What Is Identity and Its Different Components?

Identity is composed of our values and beliefs that help direct the decisions we make, both small (e.g., What do I want to eat for lunch?) and large (e.g., What should I do for a living?). Of course, our identities are not formed in a vacuum, meaning that we are influenced a great deal by outside forces, including family and friends, culture and consumerism, dating relationships, and so on. This chapter alludes to the impact of some of these outside forces; however, it ultimately focuses on describing elements that contribute to our understanding and enactment of our individual selves. As such, we will focus, here, on a discussion of what identity means and explore related concepts, including the self, self-concept, self-esteem, and self-control.

Identity

Whereas the self can be discovered by asking the question, Who am I? (with accompanying questions such as, Am I good enough?), one's identity can be discovered by answering the question, What am I? Answers to this question may be many for a single person, and the question is often answered by identifying the specific roles one has, such as being someone's child, employee, religious faithful, romantic partner, and pet owner. The things that define our identity are things to which we have committed. These commitments help to guide our behavior, thoughts, and feelings. Of course, we may be committed to some things more strongly than others. For example, if a person has to choose between focusing on their work or focusing on their family, whatever they decide certainly does not mean they are not at all committed to the facet of themselves they did not choose; however, it does mean that they are to some degree *less* committed.

When we identify roles that matter to us, we commit energy and resources to being in that role, staying in that role, and being the best version of ourselves we can be while in that role. Some adolescents, for example, may struggle to conjure and sustain motivation for performing well in school, but they may devote most unscheduled time to ensuring they are selected to be part of a particular athletic team, club, or other group. Many adults devote exceptional time, energy, and financial resources to becoming part of a particular profession (i.e., professional identity; see chapter 2) that requires a commitment of ongoing resources to stay a member of that profession.

Principal identity and *generalized core identity* are terms used to describe the most, or one of the most, important aspects of one's identity. For example, when you think about your own identity or when you meet someone for the first time and attempt to describe yourself and who you are, what comes to mind first? your job or your major? your status as a member of a particular family? your athletic status? your religious beliefs? When you imagine no longer having that aspect of your identity (e.g., you lose your job, you realize you no longer believe the tenets of the religion you were raised in, your competitive athletic career ends), how do you feel about that? If you have lost a salient aspect of your identity, or you imagine what it might be like to lose that part of you, you likely feel a constellation of emotions, such as sadness, anger, or confusion, and you may experience what is often referred to as an *existential crisis*. You may question your purpose in life, or you may have the experience of feeling "lost." Sometimes experiencing such a crisis leads to diagnosable mental health issues, such as clinical anxiety or depression. It is important to note that each of us will experience a loss to our identity differently.

What seems to be most predictive of how someone may react to this type of loss has to do with how important that loss was to one's identity and the extent to which other aspects of one's identity are also important. For example, when an athlete only or principally defines themselves as an athlete and their status as an athlete is threatened by injury or having been benched for some reason or their athletic career has ended due to a career-ending injury or having "aged out" of their sport, there is a very good chance that athlete will experience a significant disruption to their identity, their sense of purpose, and possibly their mental health. On the other hand, for an athlete who defines themselves as an athlete but who also strongly identifies with being a student, parent, or employee, the loss of that one aspect of their identity, while disruptive, will not likely have as much of an impact compared to the person whose identity solely rests on one aspect of their life.

Understanding and describing identity is an interdisciplinary endeavor that has been a long-standing focus of attention for psychologists, sociologists, and philosophers. It is generally agreed that our identities partly

What Is Identity and Its Different Components?

develop via social interactions because our identities often include elements of the groups to which we belong (e.g., family, school, sport, religion) and because social interactions provide us with information about which aspects of our respective identities are rewarded or accepted and which ones are rejected. This can have a significant impact on which aspects of our identity we decide to keep salient and devote time and energy to and which aspects of our identity we wish would go away or change. As such, identity development is complex and dynamic. Who we are today is not the same as who were as young children or who we will become as an older adult. This is largely due to the ongoing experiences we have, our perceptions of those experiences, others' reactions to us based on our behaviors and expressed beliefs, and the aging process itself.

What is also the case, however, is that despite these changes throughout our development, most of us recognize ourselves in childhood stories that no longer truly represent who we are. For example, you may remember how difficult it was for you to make friends or how you thought you would never do well in school when you were a child. Many can look back on that time in their lives and think, "I have a lot of friends now, and I find it pretty easy to make new ones," or "I'm a really good student and get good grades in college." What tends not to happen is that you think, "Was that really me?" Okay, you may think that, but not in the sense of not recognizing that the child was you. More likely than not, you can connect the dots of your life from then to now and know that you are you. That child was you. You have simply changed, developed, or evolved into the person you are now.

The focus of this book, as seen in its title, is identity. The term *identity* certainly includes how you see yourself, but it mostly refers to what you show others. It can also include how you think others see you. The term *self*, on the other hand, refers to your own perception of who you are and what comprises you as a person. The terms *identity* and *self* will be used throughout this book. Regardless of the term used by this author or to describe some aspect of self or identity identified by researchers or theorists, the use of either term always points to some element of who you are, whether you show that aspect of yourself to others, whether you are aware of that aspect of who you are, or whether or not you like the sum total of who you are.

How We Define, Feel about, and Regulate Our Self

The self is typically conceptualized as pertaining to who we are as a whole person, which includes our connection to our body. Erik Erikson (see also chapter 3) conceptualized the experience of one's self as feeling "at home in one's body" and an existential knowing of what you are doing and why you are doing what you do. Each person's understanding of their self is believed to reflect a fairly stable sense of who one is that transcends environmental influences and the people we are around. This is typically reflected in statements such as, "Well, this is just who I am," and "I can't help it; I've always been this way." Our sense of self includes our beliefs about ourselves, which is referred to as our *self-concept*, our evaluation of ourselves, which is primarily reflected in *self-esteem*; and the degree to which we are able to resist acting on impulse or pure desire, which is reflected in the construct called *self-control*.

Self-Concept: How We Define Our Self

The term *self-concept* is undoubtedly one that many readers are familiar with. It refers to the beliefs we have about ourselves that help us understand who we are as individuals. Like many things in the field of psychology, the definition is correct, but the construct is far more complex than the brief description suggests. Some have linked the construct of self-concept specifically to the construct of identity. For example, in the early 1980s, Viktor Gecas suggested that the content of "self-conceptions" can be understood in terms of "identities." He also made the distinction between the self-concept and self-evaluation. He noted that whereas the self-concept is about facets of ourselves that make up who we are, self-evaluation, which consists of self-esteem (discussed later in this chapter), refers to what we think or feel about these aspects of ourselves. Moreover, he also noted that an important distinction can be made between the "self" and "self-concept." Gecas stated that the self is a process whereby a person thinks about and examines who they are, what they believe, what they think about others and experiences, and so on. Self-concept, on the other hand, is the result or outcome of engaging in this self-reflexive process. After turning inward and engaging in the process of examining one's beliefs, attitudes, values, and ideas, we come up with what amounts to a definition of who we are. The self-concept refers to the descriptors we use to describe ourselves to ourselves and others.

Self-concept is believed to be composed of self-schemas connected with our past (who we were), current (who we are), and future selves (who we will be). *Schema* is a term used in the area of cognitive psychology. It refers to mental representations of concepts we encounter throughout our lives. As we have more and more experiences, our schemas change because we come to realize our previous schema may have been too narrow or wholly inaccurate. For example, very young children can struggle to tell the difference between a small dog and a cat and therefore have a narrow and ultimately inaccurate schema for dogs (or cats). The child may think a cat is always small or a dog is always big. When they are very young, the child fails to denote important distinctions, such as the sound a cat or dog makes, how they move their tail, and what their ears and faces look like. So, too, do we create schemas about ourselves, such as what it means to be someone's child, student, dating partner, and so on.

What Is Identity and Its Different Components?

Researchers believe that just as we try to organize information about the world around us into categories, such as dog/cat or male/female/non-binary, we also attempt to organize the information we encounter about ourselves. As these individual schemas about ourselves develop and become part of our self-concept (e.g., I am a good student; I am part of the ____ family; I am a member of ____ team/club), they become increasingly resistant to change, particularly when we encounter information inconsistent with how we already see ourselves. For example, when someone has, as part of their self-concept, the schema of what it means to be a good student and subsequently declares one's self a good student, they will struggle to incorporate information suggesting that they are not a good student. Such a person who repeatedly fails exams in a class is not likely to change this part of their self-concept; rather, they are more likely to look for other explanations for this seemingly erroneous information, even if that explanation is fabricated. They may, for example, believe the test was unfair or that the teacher is bad at their job. They may struggle to accept that they are not as good a student as they thought, even if only in one subject area.

Regardless of how a self-concept is formed and what ultimately comprises one person's self-concept compared to another's, the self-concept is believed to serve an organizational function. The self-concept provides a framework that becomes familiar and guides our behavior so that we can behave, or at least believe we behave, consistently. The self-concept is like a motivation guidebook that helps us determine how to act so that we behave according to who we believe we are. In this way, we can be consistent or, at minimum, give ourselves the illusion of consistency. If we believe we are a nice person, for example, niceness is part of our self-concept. Therefore, we will behave in ways that are objectively nice (e.g., holding the door open for someone, giving money to a homeless person), or we may rationalize or explain to ourselves or others why a not nice behavior (e.g., insulting someone's choice of clothing) can be viewed as nice (e.g., declaring that you were helping them by telling them their clothes are "not right" or "unattractive" so that they can then fix that). Either way, the self-concept helps us to make sense of what we do (or do not do) and gives us direction on how to act so that we maintain our sense of consistency.

Self-Concept Clarity

Some researchers and theorists have suggested that while each of us has an idea of who we are, that self-based perception may or may not be accurate (see, e.g., Carl Rogers's ideas about self-concept in chapter 3). When someone asks us who we are, we may or may not be able to easily describe ourselves, and even if we can, we cannot be sure, without sufficient self-examination, whether our description of ourselves truly reflects who we are. *Self-concept clarity* is a term used to describe a self-concept that is very clearly defined. The individual who has high self-concept clarity knows who they are and is confident in what they know about themselves.

Having a high degree of self-concept clarity also means that we are internally consistent at a singular point in time and across time. This means that our internal thoughts, feelings, beliefs, values, and so on fit well together and tend not to change from one situation to the next, and they do not contradict one another. In addition, over time, we behave consistently compared to previous behaviors precisely because we confidently know who we are, and each facet of ourselves fits together to create a coherent sense of self.

Some readers may have had the experience that they believe something about themselves that is challenged by another person. For example, you may believe yourself to be fairly perceptive. You believe you are able to accurately read situations and what others may be experiencing in various situations. What if someone said to you, "No. You're actually not perceptive at all"? How would you respond? Those with low self-concept clarity are likely to find themselves questioning their own perception of themselves. They may experience anxiety about who is right and how they can go about figuring that out. Depending on who contradicted them, the person may spend a great deal of time ruminating about who is right. This may lead to a cascade of questions about one's self and whether they truly know who they are. This is not necessarily a bad thing. Self-reflection and self-questioning are important parts of truly getting to know one's self; however, they can also lead to self-doubt and difficulty in trusting one's self.

Someone with high self-concept clarity might reflect on the contradictory statement and ask the person, "What makes you say that?" and then reflect on the person's answer. If they truly have high self-concept clarity, they will likely come to the reasonable conclusion that they know themselves well and better than anyone else. They know their own mind, their intentions, and their beliefs and values, and they know that what others perceive in them may very well be based on not having all the information. Of course, from the outside looking in, we cannot know for sure whether the person truly knows themselves or is deluding themselves into thinking they know themselves. However, if we know and interact with someone over time, that person's degree of true self-concept clarity will become evident. We will notice that they feel, act, and behave in ways that are consistent and reflect what we know about the person. They will not be easily swayed from a particular viewpoint because they know themselves well enough to know that their viewpoint truly reflects who they are and what they value.

Research examining self-concept clarity has consistently revealed that higher levels of self-concept clarity are associated with higher levels of self-esteem. This means, of course, that the more one truly knows about one's self and that the self-concept they have constructed is indeed accurate and

What Is Identity and Its Different Components?

consistent the more likely one is to feel good about themselves. There is a strong likelihood that this correlation exists because the better one knows one's self the more likely they are to act in ways that truly reflect who they are. This then leads to feeling good about one's self, as one's actions are clearly precipitated by a crystal clear understanding of what one wants and needs.

Research conducted in the 1990s revealed that those with low self-concept clarity were found to be more passive, and when making decisions, they had a tendency to not rely on their self to inform their process. This body of research also revealed that in addition to having lower levels of self-esteem, those with low self-concept clarity tend to be more neurotic (i.e., having an automatic, usually unconscious, response to experiences that causes deep-seated anxiety or distress), low levels of agreeableness (i.e., being more likely to act in selfish ways and less likely to empathize with others), and low con-scientiousness (i.e., being less invested in doing something well and being less likely to take obligations and responsibilities seriously).

Independent Self-Concept and Interdependent Self-Concept

Two other aspects of self-concept that reflect the more cultural aspects of collectivism and individualism (see chapter 5 for more information) are the *interdependent self-concept* and the *independent self-concept*. The interdependent self-concept refers to a self-concept that is mostly composed of the norms and expectations of groups, including the opinions of other people. Those with this type of self-concept place more weight on their close relationships and memberships in various groups, making these relationships and groups central to their understanding of themselves. By contrast, someone with an independent self-concept places greater importance on internal traits, abilities, beliefs, and values when defining themselves. One indicator of which type of self-concept someone has is how they answer the question, "Who am I?" Those with an interdependent self-concept are more likely to describe themselves in terms of their roles within a group (e.g., "I am a daughter"; "I am a member of my school's choir"), whereas those with an independent self-concept are more likely to rely on identifying what makes them unique in comparison to others (e.g., "I am a good soccer player"; "I am excellent at math").

Researchers examining these two types of self-concept have found, unsurprisingly, that an interdependent self-concept is more likely to be found among those living in collectivist cultures (e.g., Japan), and an independent self-concept is more likely to be found among those living in more individualist cultures (e.g., the United States). Researchers have also found that the interdependent and independent self-concepts are not mutually exclusive. That is, it is possible to have high levels, low levels, or some mixture of both types of self-concept. In addition, advances in genetic- and neuroscience-related research have revealed that the type of one's self-concept is likely inherited and that the brain functions differently depending on which type of self-concept is most dominant.

Self-Esteem: How We Feel about Our Self

Self-esteem represents how much you appreciate and like yourself. This is akin to Carl Rogers's concept of positive self-regard (see chapter 3), which he describes as the experience of valuing one's self. Self-esteem is conceptualized to be an umbrella term that reflects how we feel about ourselves in terms of self-worth and how we evaluate ourselves (e.g., positively, negatively). Self-esteem has been linked to numerous other facets of one's life. For example, knowing one's level of self-esteem can predict with reasonable accuracy how happy you are with your level of academic achievement, how satisfied you are in your interpersonal relationships, and whether or not you are likely to engage in criminal behavior. Although not entirely the same, other terms in psychology that reflect the notion of how you feel about yourself include *self-worth*, *self-regard*, and *self-respect*. Generally speaking, those with higher levels of self-esteem do not require others to affirm they are a good, likeable, and capable person. Such individuals developed the ability to trust that they are all of those things, which usually means that early on in their lives others viewed them positively (see "Person-Centered Theory: Carl Rogers" in chapter 3); they internalized these views and made them their own. Whereas many of us develop self-esteem and can reasonably maintain it without the need for consistent reassurance from others or experiences that affirm our self-esteem, some people feel an insatiable need to seek out opportunities to reaffirm their positive views of themselves.

Roy Baumeister, a social psychologist, noted that *terror management theory* helps to explain some people's pursuit of self-esteem at any cost. Terror management theory was alluded to in the second chapter of anthropologist Ernest Becker's Pulitzer Prize–winning book *The Denial of Death*. He titled this chapter "The Terror of Death." In this chapter and throughout the book, Becker suggests that most of our behaviors as human beings can be understood as myriad efforts to deny our inevitable end: death.

Psychologists Tom Pyszczynski, Jeff Greenberg, and Sheldon Solomon developed terror management theory in the 1990s. They contend that all human behavior is ultimately motivated by self-preservation or staying alive. They stated that even motives that may not appear to be influenced by avoiding death are in one way or another linked to avoiding death. They referred to this pursuit as the "prime directive." With respect to self-esteem, these psychologists summarized previous research they contended is consistent with terror management theory: higher levels of self-esteem are associated with lower levels of anxiety and anxiety-related illnesses, both physical and

What Is Identity and Its Different Components?

psychological. Moreover, they noted that threats to self-esteem lead to feelings of anxiety and subsequent defensiveness. Successfully defending one's self-esteem buffers against feelings of failure and other threats to one's self-esteem.

Roy Baumeister noted that most people are not literally threatened with death in an ongoing way (although, of course, some people are), but anything we do in an effort to avoid experiencing even a hint of our ultimate demise is consistent with terror management theory and ties into our quest for self-esteem. Those who seek to maximize their self-esteem by pursuing every avenue through which their self-esteem will be enhanced are conceptualized via terror management theory as attempting to "obliterate thoughts and fears of death" and that one's self esteem is considered to be "an artificial defense mechanism that helps people forget about death."

Terror management theory and its contention that all human behavior is ultimately motivated by a desire to avoid being reminded of one's death dovetails with what Roy Baumeister called the "self-esteem maximizer." The self-esteem maximizer is someone who does whatever they need to do to avoid a loss of self-esteem. Thus, any threat to one's self-esteem (i.e., anything that might make themselves look or feel bad) must be avoided at all costs by the self-esteem maximizer. Such a person will avoid the people and situations that are likely to result in their experiencing a loss of self-esteem, and if they nonetheless find themselves in such a situation, they are prone to rationalization and will find an excuse that explains to themselves and others why an event or person may have made them look bad. Essentially, they are trying to save face. Therefore, someone motivated by terror management who may be a self-esteem maximizer likely does not have a well-developed, stable sense of self-esteem because they require consistent reassurance and avoid circumstances that might disabuse them of their positive views of themselves.

Self-Control: How We Regulate Our Self

Self-control is another aspect of the self and one's identity. It refers to one's ability to control one's self regardless of temptation or impulse. Self-control is considered to be a higher cognitive function that requires the use of the frontal cortex of the brain, which allows one to pursue and achieve one's goals. For example, if you plan to go to college, some measure of self-control will be necessary to study for exams and write papers by the due date despite your desire to socialize with others or engage in more enjoyable activities.

One of the most famous tests of self-control was conducted in the 1970s by Walter Mischel and Ebbe Ebbesen at Stanford University and is colloquially known as the "Marshmallow Test." The original study used either a marshmallow or a pretzel (the child got to choose) as a reward for waiting for something they wanted (i.e., delay of gratification). In this experiment, an initial treat was placed in front of the child, who was aged from three to six years old, and the child was instructed that they could eat the treat immediately; however, if they waited a while (fifteen minutes), they would be rewarded with a second treat. The experimenters concluded that in order to delay such a reward, it is not enough for the child to merely not think about the reward; they also had to actively manage their frustration with not having the reward immediately. They noted that some children hid their head in their arms, made up songs, prayed, or, in at least one case, fell asleep. Overall, Walter Mischel and colleagues found the opposite of what they expected. They ultimately found that having the reward present did not help the child wait for a future reward. In fact, they concluded that the presence of the initial reward was frustrating to the children and resulted in a decrease in the children's ability to delay gratification.

Subsequent follow-up studies conducted by Walter Mischel and colleagues were designed to determine whether certain characteristics revealed later in the children's lives, when they were much older, were predictable based on their ability or inability to delay gratification in the original experiment. They found correlations between an early ability to delay gratification with later levels of competence, higher scores on standardized tests, and specific activity levels in certain areas of the brain when they were in the middle-aged adult years. Other researchers who studied this phenomenon concluded that other factors likely impact a child's ability to delay gratification, including the child's belief in whether they will actually get a later reward, the quality of their home environment, and their early cognitive capacity.

Another term often used synonymously with self-control is *willpower*. Willpower refers to our ability to keep our desire for a future goal in mind when we are confronted by and ultimately attempt to resist short-term temptations. For example, you may have an exam the next day that you really need to study for, but all your friends are going out. You have a decision to make: go out and have fun (short-term goal) or resist that particular temptation and focus on studying so you can perform well on the exam, which will contribute to a better grade in the course and help you complete your diploma or degree (long-term goal).

The ability to consistently exert this type of self-control, or willpower, has been consistently linked to better overall health, fewer problems with substances and criminal behavior, and increased financial security. When considering each of these things in terms of their association with higher self-control, the connection seems clear. If you are able to prioritize your health, you are less likely to engage in unhealthy behaviors (e.g., not exercising, eating foods high in fat or sugar) or to engage in risky behaviors (e.g., using addictive substances, engaging in criminal acts) and are more likely to save or invest one's money (e.g., financial security). Each of these outcomes requires the ability to inhibit one's self from engaging in something that

What Is Identity and Its Different Components?

might provide short-term pleasure in favor of longer-term goals, such as having enough money for retirement, being healthy into one's older adulthood years, and so on. It turns out, however, that willpower (i.e., self-control) is not unlimited. This helps to explain why some people may struggle more than others with engaging in self-control and delaying gratification.

Willpower depletion is the term used to describe what happens to us when we can no longer resist temptation. The notion is that we have a limited supply of willpower on a day-to-day basis. If we use a lot of willpower to get through the day, then when confronted by yet another situation in which we need to exert self-control, we literally may not be able to because we have effectively run out of willpower. Researchers over the years have demonstrated this phenomenon when asking participants to resist some sort of temptation, thereby exerting some type of self-control. When they do, compared to those who did not have to use their willpower, they were less able to control themselves on a later task. For example, one study asked participants to either feel and express their emotions or suppress them while watching an emotional film. When both groups of people were later asked to suppress their laughter when exposed to something intended to make them laugh, those who had not previously had to suppress their emotions were more successful compared to those who were instructed to suppress their emotions on the previous task.

Willpower depletion can help to explain why it can be a challenge to start a difficult task, such as exercising or resisting a type of food that you are trying to eat less of. If we have had a challenging day already, summoning the power of self-control to inhibit behaviors we are trying to avoid or engaging in behaviors that are difficult can feel like climbing Mount Everest. Researchers who have attempted to determine why willpower depletion occurs have concluded that it does not reflect physical fatigue; rather, it has to do with which parts of the brain are used to inhibit behavior, how much they are used, and what happens when we have to use those areas of the brain yet again. These researchers have suggested that when we reach our limit of exerting self-control, our brains start to work and process information differently. Moreover, additional studies have found that our brains may be literally starved in the periods of willpower depletion. Animal and human studies have revealed similar results: engaging in self-control requires metabolizing glucose (i.e., blood sugar), which is important for adequate brain functioning. When study participants engaged in a task requiring self-control, they burned through glucose at a much higher rate compared to those not engaged in self-control. The good news is that there are some things we can do to help stave off willpower depletion or at least mitigate it so that it does not have as much of a negative impact.

Some researchers found that those who feel compelled to engage in self-control based on others' expectations reached depletion more quickly than those who were exerting self-control for intrinsic reasons (i.e., personal reasons). In addition, another group of researchers found that some of the willpower depletion was mitigated when study participants were exposed to something designed to make them feel good (e.g., a funny show, receiving an unexpected gift), suggesting that these people were able to exert additional self-control that they might not have otherwise been able to without the mood-enhancing experience. Another piece of good news is that there are some strategies that can help reduce one's degree of willpower depletion, thereby strengthening one's ability to engage in self-control.

Actively avoiding temptation is one way to help maintain one's self-control. As previously discussed, Walter Mischel noted, in the context of the Marshmallow Test, that kids who were able to manage their frustration with the presence of a treat and ultimately did not eat it employed strategies designed to help them avoid the temptation altogether—one child reportedly found a way to fall asleep! Another strategy that can be helpful essentially involves planning ahead when you know or anticipate that you might be in a tempting situation. The term for this strategy is *implementation intention*, which involves thinking about how one might be tempted in the future and coming up with a concrete response ahead of time. For example, if you are trying to quit smoking and know you will be around others who smoke, it can be helpful to determine precisely what you will say or do if someone offers you a cigarette. This strategy is powerful enough that it can override one's willpower depletion.

Finally, another strategy for strengthening one's self-control is to think of self-control or willpower like a muscle you would like to strengthen. Most readers likely know that you cannot get strong muscles overnight and that it is possible to overdo exercise to the point that you can fatigue your muscles and even injure them. The most effective way to strengthen one's muscle is to engage in activities over time that challenge your muscles until they strengthen. Researchers say the same can be done with self-control. Intentionally encountering situations in which self-control will be required, but not too much, can, over time, strengthen your ability to resist temptation when the stakes are high and a good deal of self-control or willpower is required.

Although being terms that can be defined in a sentence or two, *self* and *identity* are highly complex concepts. There are myriad factors that affect how one's self and one's identity develop, including the interactions we have with important others, especially early in life; the culture in which we grew up and live; and our internal experiences, which include our interpretations of the experiences we have throughout our lives. The remainder of this book will examine many of these factors. The remainder of part 1, however, will focus on specific types of identity (e.g., athletic identity, professional identity) and some of the theories that help to explain how our identities develop.

CHAPTER TWO

Types of Identity

This chapter focuses on the various ways in which we might identify ourselves and is by no means all-inclusive. It focuses on the aspects of identity that have garnered substantial theoretical or research attention. This chapter begins with a description of personal identity, which is more difficult to define than one might imagine. The remainder of the chapter focuses on other aspects of identity, presented in alphabetical order that arguably can be part of one's personal identity. Careful readers and those who have already reflected on the concept of identity will notice that many of these aspects of identity intermingle and can affect other aspects of identity, such as the degree to which one's racial or ethnic identity affects one's professional identity or how one's sexual identity might be influenced by one's disability identity.

Personal Identity

Personal identity is seemingly a simple concept, but it has baffled psychologists and philosophers in terms of how to best define or describe what personal identity actually is. They speak of reductionism and nonreductionism and ask whether or not one's identity is the same thing as one's soul, and they have contemplated whether one's personal identity is physical or nonphysical. We will not be diving into such complex philosophical and esoteric pursuits. We will discuss personal identity from the perspective of who you are, or who you think you are, as well as whether or not someone is the same person at different times in their life.

Of course, saying that someone is exactly the same person now as they were when they were a young child may be disingenuous. Throughout our lives, we have myriad new experiences, we physically change, our values and beliefs may change, and so on. But do those changes constitute a shift in who you truly are? Many will argue yes, and others will argue no; still others may say, "It depends." Regardless, personal identity is considered to be who you are and how you would characterize yourself at any given point in time. Some of the descriptors you use about yourself may take the form of "I am a kind person," "I am family oriented," or "I am a silly person." Other characterizations may include "I am Muslim," "I am bisexual," or "I am an athlete." Statements like the last three will be further discussed in the following sections that describe specific types of identity (i.e., religious identity, sexual identity, athletic identity) and therefore can also be considered aspects of one's personal identity.

Another term that may be used to describe personal identity is *self-concept* (see also chapter 1). Self-concept refers to the ideas and beliefs you have about who you are. These ideas and beliefs come not only from your thoughts and feelings about yourself but also from how others in your life respond to you. The potential issue with the notion of self-concept (discussed further in the "Person-Centered Theory" section in chapter 3) is that your perception of who you are may or may not accurately reflect who you truly are. It is not uncommon for people to really want to be like a certain type of person or to have certain specific qualities. We therefore may believe that we have them even if we do not. So, our self-concept might include descriptors such as "I am a caring person," "I am funny," or "I am very talented at ____"; however, in reality, you may or may not be any of those things. This gets at the heart of why so many people have tried to definitively determine what personal identity really is and how we can know for sure whether one's personal identity is what we think it is. If we cannot rely on ourselves (or other people for that matter) to describe who we are, then how do we know?

Some readers may recall an issue that garnered a great deal of national and international attention in 2015. It involved a woman who identified as Black who was president of her local NAACP chapter and who was an instructor of Africana studies at a local university. The wrinkle was, and continues to be, that she was born White and is the biological child of White parents. She later acknowledged this when pressed on her background and heritage but insisted that, despite this, she identified as Black. Some have denounced her claims as a way of seeking attention and in terms of Black cultural appropriation. Others who support her have said that her identification with Black culture is heartfelt and genuine.

Regardless of the veracity of this woman's claims about herself, she clearly has included being Black as part of her personal identity. We do not know whether she held these same perceptions of herself when she was a child. However, in the view of many philosophers, whether she did or did not may not matter in terms of personal identity. In fact, one way to define *personal identity* acknowledges that we change over time and that who we were as a

Types of Identity 17

child is likely not the same person we are now; our sense of who we are has evolved. This means that we can connect the dots from birth to death in terms of personal identity, even if the descriptors we use about ourselves in kindergarten are not at all the same as those we may use at the end of our lives. This may seem to suggest that we are not the same person from one time to the next; however, if you consider this in terms of how your childhood version of yourself changed into your adult self, you are likely to agree that you are still you—just not exactly the same. For example, as a child, you may have sworn that you were going to be a firefighter when you grew up, but now you are studying to become a lawyer or have become an electrician. You may not remember the exact moment you changed your mind, but you recognize that, yes, the child version of you wanted to be a firefighter; however, as you gained more life experience and learned about what was possible for you, you found a career interest that fit with your adult self.

Though the question of how to truly define personal identity remains murky, my guess is that most readers will feel confident that they mostly know who they are right now and, thus, know their current personal identity.

Adoptive Identity

Note: I will make the distinction between adopted and biological parents by using the term *parents* for the adopted parents and added *biological* when referring to one's biological parents.

All adoptions involve the termination of the parental rights of one or both biological parents and the transfer of those rights to one or two other adult parents. However, not all adoptions occur under the same conditions, which can render the development of a child's adoptive identity very different from one adoptee to the next.

Harold Grotevant and Lynn Von Korff refer to four different "worlds" of adoption that help to illuminate the differences. These worlds are domestic adoption of an infant, domestic adoption of a child from the public welfare system, international adoption, and kinship adoption. In addition to the varying circumstances in which an adoption can take place, adoptees also have varying amounts of information about their biological parents and biological families. This can range from little to no knowledge about the biological parents to knowing who the biological parents are and having regular contact with them. Moreover, a child may have been born to an unfit set of biological parents, to young biological parents who are not ready for the responsibility of raising a child, to biological parents who live in poverty and cannot afford to care for the child, to biological parents who had raised the child for a period of time only to lose parental rights due to abuse or neglect of the child, and so on. All of these factors contribute to the nature of a person's adoptive identity.

As will be seen throughout this book, each of us has our own unique identity based on numerous factors, which include our life experiences and our understanding of those experiences. We may ask ourselves questions such as Who am I? Am I more like my mom or my dad? What values and beliefs are important to me? Adopted persons will ask those questions as well, but they may also wonder about other things, such as Who are my biological parents? Am I like them? Where was I born? What were my early days like? What genetics did I inherit? These questions may or may not be easily answered and can affect an adopted person's overall and adoptive identities.

Grotevant and Von Korff noted that each of us has aspects of our identity that we have some measure of control over. Those things over which we have less or little control (e.g., race or ethnicity, adoption) are called *assigned identities*; they are aspects of our identity that we have, ideally, come to terms with because we cannot change them. That is, we need to figure out the degree to which we are okay with this assigned aspect of our identity and what it means to us. For these assigned aspects of our identity, the question is not whether you want them to be part of your identity but rather what does that part of your identity mean to you? How salient will that part of your identity be to how you think about yourself and how you relate to others? For some, considering their adoptive status may mean questioning whether their adopted family is their "real" family. For many, the answer is clear, but others may struggle with this, particularly those who have memories of their biological parent(s).

When considering one's own adoption or when interacting with someone who is adopted, Grotevant and Von Korff caution that one size does not fit all. That is, one person's experience with their own adoption is not likely to be the same as another person's. Some may consistently struggle with understanding how adoption fits in with their understanding of who they are, whereas others may resolve whatever questions they have relatively early in life and may not give their adoption much thought thereafter. Grotevant and Von Korff further note that although researchers may conclude what is more or less optimal for adoptive identity development, the path toward healthy adoptive identity development will vary widely from one person to the next.

When there are problems with someone's adoptive identity, Grotevant and Von Korff state that this is usually due to the adoptee's lack of complete and accurate knowledge about themselves, the nature of their adoption, knowledge about and contact with biological relatives, and so on. Although some adoptees may never get the information they crave, it is possible for this aspect of one's identity to develop in a healthy way via interactions with others from a similar background—whether cultural or adoptive. This can give the adopted person an indirect way to learn more about themselves and how their adopted status affects (or does not affect) how they interact with the world around them.

Types of Identity

Athletic Identity

Athletic identity is a concept that was identified in the early 1990s by Britton Brewer, Judy Van Raalte, and Darwyn Linder. They defined this construct as "the degree to which an individual identifies with the athlete role." The stronger the athletic identity, the more likely the person will also strongly endorse statements such as "I spend more time thinking about sport than anything else" or "Sport is the only important thing in my life." It is not uncommon for competitive athletes to closely identify with the athlete role, which can be beneficial but can also have its problems.

Some researchers have shown that committing to any role, including the role of an athlete, is beneficial because it helps the individual understand who they are. Moreover, individuals who identify strongly with the athlete role may be more likely to see benefits in their sport-related performance. Having a limited or singular focus in terms of their identity can mean they are more likely to devote all, or nearly all, of their resources (e.g., time, money, energy) to that particular role. Therefore, it is likely that successful athletes have a strong athletic identity and may, in fact, identify exclusively with the athlete role. There are, however, potential downsides to identifying too strongly with the athlete role, particularly when that role is threatened.

Competitive athletes often have lives that revolve around their sport. How they think about themselves, their degree of self-worth, and their level of self-esteem may derive from this singular identity. If they are no longer able to participate in their sport, they may experience a drop in emotional well-being, especially if they do not have any other sources of self-worth, such as "student," "employee," or "partner." For example, a recent study conducted by George Sanders and colleagues examined the level of athletic identity and degree of depression-related symptoms in over three hundred retired footballers (i.e., soccer players). They reported that just over 15 percent of participants could be classified as clinically depressed. These depressed athletes had, on average, retired more recently compared to others in the study and had higher levels of athletic identity. Another study conducted by Leslie Podlog and numerous colleagues indicated that those with a higher degree of athletic identity were more likely to "over adhere" (i.e., do more than is recommended) to rehabilitation recommendations, presumably in an effort to get back to their sport sooner, and were more likely to prematurely return to sport. This means that athletes who highly identify with the athlete role were more likely to rush their postinjury rehabilitation and return to their sports before their bodies were truly ready, thereby risking further injury.

Other researchers have examined the impact of retirement from sport and have found that those with a higher athletic identity are more likely to have difficulty in their post–competitive sport adjustment. A study from several decades ago found that athletes retiring from sport who had something else to which they could direct their energy (i.e., something other than sport that they were interested in) adjusted to retirement from sport more smoothly compared to those who did not have another commitment or interest. A more recent study conducted in 2017 by Zarina Giannone and colleagues studied the retirement experiences of those leaving varsity sports. They found that those who had a higher level of athletic identity were more likely to experience higher levels of anxiety symptoms and depressive symptoms. They concluded that the extent to which an athlete identifies with their athletic role is a risk factor for a decline in overall well-being and mental health when they retire from sport.

Cultural Identity

Cultural identity is, in the simplest terms, the sense someone has of belonging to a clearly defined group that has norms and expectations associated with it. Therefore, the term *culture* refers to a particular way of living or doing things associated with a particular group. When we think of culture, we often think of nationality or ethnicity; however, it can also refer to religion, social class, athletic teams, specific generations, specific families, and so on. *Cultural identity* can be defined as how one thinks and feels about belonging to a particular group and therefore can be signaled by the language one speaks, the country in which one lives, the types of foods one eats, the type or color of clothing one wears, the customs performed, and so on. All human beings have a cultural identity. It just may not be as obvious as that reflected by one's racial or ethnic heritage.

One way to think about one's own cultural identity is to consider the specific groups one is part of and then the norms and customs associated with that group. Another important aspect is to then consider whether you align yourself with or identify with a particular group. You may live in a particular country or a particular region of a country but not identify with it. So, the group(s) of which you consider yourself to be a member may or may not be the group(s) with which you have direct contact. For example, you may go to church every Sunday with your family because that is what your family does. You may, therefore, identify closely with the culture of your family (i.e., this is the way our family does things) but not identify closely with the culture of the religion.

Each group with which we identify has its own way of doing things, and it is not always the case that what one group expects is harmonious with what another group expects. You may have grown up in a family or a region of the United States that takes a laid back or relaxed perspective on most things. You may also be a member of another group that very much expects things to get done in a particular way, and quickly. In these instances, you

Types of Identity

have a choice to make that may result in conflict with or removal from a particular group. For example, many first-generation college students find that when they return home on breaks or between semesters, they experience an emotional distance from family, friends, and neighbors who now view the student as being different from or "better than" they are (or they think the returning college student sees things this way). In such situations, the individual may feel tremendous pressure to choose which group they will align themselves with and thus risk no longer being part of the other group.

Another concept related to cultural identity is *acculturation*. This term is often used when discussing how immigrants manage living in a new country, particularly when the new country is very different from their country of origin. However, this process is not exclusive to immigration. Acculturation refers to taking on the ideas and values of another culture, usually the majority culture. Whenever you become part of a new group or community, you will likely go through the process of acculturation. Historically, low levels of acculturation have resulted in a lower quality of life because the individual will likely feel isolated, remain unfamiliar with how to effectively navigate the new culture, and is likely to receive much less social support compared to those who are more highly acculturated or are trying to become so. More recently, the notion of global acculturation has been identified and examined in the context of *globalization* (see chapter 11 for more information). Global acculturation refers to how effectively we accept and interact with a highly culturally diverse population.

There are several models of acculturation, the earliest of which espouse the notion that the goal of acculturation is assimilation into the new or dominant culture. The expectation is that the person who is now living in a new culture should assimilate and internalize the values, customs, beliefs, language, and so on of the dominant culture, leaving their previous culture behind. More contemporary theories, however, have suggested that is possible and likely beneficial for individuals to remain connected to their personal culture while simultaneously accepting the expectations of the new culture so that they can interact effectively with those native to that culture.

Disability Identity

Note: The current term used for those with a physical disability is "differently abled"; however, disability identity remains, as of the writing of this book, the term used in the context of understanding one's identity, and the term "disability" will be used for the sake of consistency.

Disability identity refers to the extent to which someone with a disability incorporates their disability into their sense of who they are. The person incorporates not only the fact that they have a disability but also how that disability makes them different from those without that particular disability. Whether the disability itself or the differences associated with the disability are viewed positively or negatively will also affect one's disability identity. However, the assumption does seem to be that if someone has a disability identity, they also align themselves with others who are disabled either similarly or in some other way.

It is important to note that the extent to which someone accepts their disability is not the same thing as their disability identity. For example, someone with a disability may include their disability as part of their personal identity and also view their disability as an asset or positive experience. Alternatively, another person with a disability may acknowledge the fact that they have a disability but fight against including it as part of who they are. They may wish they did not have the disability and may even try to live their lives as though they are not disabled. Researchers have found that those who accept their disability also tend to have a stronger disability identity.

Additionally, some researchers have distinguished between having a healthy or unhealthy disability identity. Those with a healthy disability identity are likely to view their disability as not only a source of personal growth but also as a source of growth for others. They may take on roles that involve educating others about the nature of their disability and the ways in which their disability makes them different but also the same as others. They may also take on roles that involve fighting ableism (i.e., prejudice against those without a fully functioning body or mind) and creating environments in which people of all abilities can thrive.

Not much is known about how disability identity develops and what specific factors may affect the degree to which someone identifies with their disability in a healthy or unhealthy way. However, researchers in this area have identified some general constructs that may be involved in disability identity development. There are several assumptions believed to underlie the development of one's disability identity. The first one is the notion that those with a disability consider their disability as a major part of their personal identity. Second, to be psychologically healthy both as an individual and in one's interpersonal relationships, someone with a disability must also accept the disability as being part of who they are rather than reject it. A third assumption is that aligning one's self with one's disability means the person also becomes more aware of prejudicial and discriminatory behaviors toward those who have a disability. Finally, having a strong disability identity may allow the person to more effectively fight against disability-related stigma, prejudice, and discrimination.

Some researchers have observed that many who are disabled often form disability communities that provide a sense of belonging and that are also mobilized to take action, including political action, with respect to disability rights. One framework for understanding this form of identity was developed to better understand what has been called "political disability identity." Six domains have been identified in the context of understanding political disability identity. The first domain, self-worth, involves the belief that those with disabilities have has much worth as those without disabilities and that those who are disabled are typically undervalued when it comes to overall contributions to society. The second domain, pride, points to the belief that disability is common, not inherently negative, and being disabled means that person is part of a "cultural minority group." As the third domain, discrimination indicates that someone who is disabled believes those who are disabled consistently experience prejudice and discrimination that results in less access to public resources. The fourth domain, referred to as common cause, reflects the idea that those who are disabled have similar experiences (positive and negative), some of which may require organized political action to make changes. The fifth domain, policy alternatives, refers to the belief that public policy is instrumental in how people with disabilities are treated and what their lived experiences are like. The final domain is engagement in political action. This domain refers to the belief that those who are disabled belong to a "political constituency group," which is also a minority group, and that being politically active can have a positive effect on those with disabilities.

Ethnic or Racial Identity

Note: The terms "minority" and "majority" are used in the discussion of the *minority development model* whereas the more appropriate term, as of the writing of this book, for minority is "disenfranchised" and "privileged" for majority.

One of these most well-known models of racial identity is William Cross's *five-stage model of racial identity development*, which was developed in the 1970s. It was developed to help explain how African Americans (*African American* and *Caucasian* are the terms used in this identity model and its subsequent revision) go through the process of identity development that may be different from Caucasians. The original five stages were identified as pre-encounter, encounter, immersion-emersion, internalization, and internalization-commitment. Nearly two decades later, William Cross revised the stage model and reduced the number of stages to three: pre-encounter, immersion-emersion, and internalization. The pre-encounter stage of racial development is essentially a rejection of, or at least low acceptance of, one's race and corresponding culture (specifically the African American culture). What accompanies this is typically a desire to assimilate into mainstream White culture. The immersion-emersion stage is believed to occur when the individual has more contact and engagement with their racial culture. Individuals in this stage are usually strongly aligned with their culture and may actively reject White culture and other cultures different from their own. When the individual identifies with their culture in the context of a racially diverse society, they are believed to be in the third stage: internalization. In addition to identifying with their racial culture, they are also likely to show an attitude of acceptance of other cultures as well.

Several years after William Cross revised his theory, which was specifically designed to understand how African Americans develop a sense of identity, others developed a model of identity development inclusive of all racial and ethnic minorities. This model, created by Donald Atkinson, George Morten, and Derald Sue, is called the *minority identity development model*, and it involves five stages. The first stage is conformity, which is similar to the pre-encounter stage of William Cross's model. During the conformity stage, individuals usually reject themselves and the minority group to which they belong, along with other minority groups, but they will accept and appreciate the majority group. In stage two, dissonance, the individual experiences internal conflict between rejecting and appreciating one's self in the context of their minority status and rejecting and appreciating the majority group. During the third stage, resistance and immersion, individuals fully appreciate themselves and their minority status while struggling to fully accept and appreciate those of other minority groups; they also denigrate the majority group. Stage four, introspection, is characterized by individuals' developing concern about their full appreciation of themselves, their minority group, how they view other minority groups, and how they view the majority group. Finally, in stage five, synergetic articulation and awareness, individuals settle into appreciating themselves, members of their minority group, and members of other minority groups, and they tentatively appreciate members of the majority group. These stages are similar to those proposed by Sue and Sue in the early 2010s, when they developed their *racial and cultural identity development model*.

More recently, the concept of racial identity has been expanded to include ethnicity and is often identified by the initialism ERI (ethnic/racial identity). ERI is believed to reflect a complex interaction of thoughts and feelings about, and attitudes toward, the ethnic or racial group to which one belongs. Researchers have determined that there are a multitude of forces (e.g., family, peers, the larger community) that affect the development of an individual's ERI; however, despite these influences, one's ERI tends not to change from one situation to the next. Thus, how someone thinks or feels about their membership in a particular ethnic or racial group will remain stable whether they are around other members of the same group or those who are not members of the same group or whether they are at home or at school, and so on. What may change, however, is how important their ERI is from one context to the next. For example, in a situation in which the ethnicity or race with which one identifies is disparaged, the individual's ERI may be more

Types of Identity   25

relevant compared to a situation in which any and every ethnicity or race is fully accepted. In such a situation, the individual's ERI may still be relevant, but perhaps to a lesser degree compared to the first example.

One group of researchers found that ERI is not just important for those of ethnically or racially disenfranchised groups but also for those who are White. Camacho and colleagues examined ERI and how it develops among both ethnically and racially disenfranchised and White middle schoolers. They concluded that those who are members of an ethnically or racially disenfranchised group were more likely to explore and ultimately reconcile their ERI compared to their White counterparts. The researchers noted that this was not a surprising finding because members of the privileged group (i.e., White students) are less likely to be challenged with figuring out how their race affects their interactions with others, how others perceive them, and so on. By contrast, students of color are routinely faced with figuring out how to navigate myriad situations, particularly when prejudice or discrimination may be present. For the exploration of one's ERI to occur, Tissyana Camacho and colleagues indicated that White students must first recognize that having an ethnic or racial identity applies to them, and students of color likely need to feel like it is safe for them to experiment with identifying with their ethnic or racial heritage.

Gender Identity

The terms *gender* and *sex* are often used interchangeably; however, they are two distinct concepts. *Sex* refers to one's physical characteristics that typically identify one as biologically male or female—though contemporary understanding recognizes biological sex is more fluid than this. Gender also represents male or female as anchors of a gender continuum, but not in terms of biological characteristics. *Gender* is defined socially and culturally in terms of what it means to be a male or female. Contemporary understanding of gender, like biological sex, has also evolved to recognize that people do not always fit neatly into one of two categories. Gender identity, therefore, is not socially or culturally prescribed but represents one's personal sense of one's gender.

For many people, their gender identity matches their biological sex—when considered from a binary (i.e., male or female) perspective. Thus, most people who are biologically male identify as being male, and most who are biologically female identify as being female. Such individuals act and look as males or females are expected to act and look based on the society or culture in which they live. For example in the United States, boys are "supposed to" play with cars and trucks and engage in roughhousing, whereas girls are "supposed to" play with dolls and engage in cooperative play. Contemporary society is starting to accept a nonbinary perspective on gender. Some people do not identify as either male or female. They may internally feel like they have attributes of both or neither, or they may simply reject the notion that anyone can or should be categorized in such a limited way.

A term related to gender identity, with which most readers may be familiar, is *transgender*. *Transgender* refers to someone who does not identify with their biological sex. Someone who is biologically male may feel more like a female and may change their name to a traditionally female name and use female instead of male pronouns. They will also dress like a female is expected to dress and may disregard more traditionally male activities in favor of those typically associated with females. By contrast, a *transsexual* is someone who goes through the process of physically transitioning from male to female or from female to male via ingestion of hormones that will either suppress or enhance the desired sex characteristics. Some will have gender reassignment surgery, during which features of the existing biological sex are removed and features of the desired biological sex are added. Additional gender-related concepts that are beyond the scope of this book include pangender, bigender, trigender, agender, nongendered, genderless, and neutrois.

Gender identity is believed to be established early in one's life, and once established, it is generally difficult to change, suggesting that it is likely that a child who feels like a boy or girl or who does not really identify with one or the other will likely remain feeling that way throughout the rest of their lives. When someone's sense of gender matches their biological sex, there is usually little internal or social conflict with regard to gender identity. However, if a child feels like the opposite of their biological sex or does not otherwise subscribe to a binary perspective on gender (i.e., they do not feel male or female), they may struggle to accept this feeling, depending on the degree to which those close to them or the society in which they live accepts their view of themselves.

Narrative Identity

The term *narrative* may conjure the notion of stories and storytelling. Historically, those in the field of psychology did not pay much attention to the life stories of individuals, assuming they were fabricated out of nothing and that they did not represent who the individuals truly were. Currently and in the past few decades, the field has come to understand that narrative identity is an important aspect of understanding identity development in general and in understanding an individual's sense of who they truly are. Indeed, in the context of identity, one's narrative identity is the story of one's self that unifies our experiences and that provides us with a sense of direction or purpose. Psychologist Dan McAdams developed what he called the *life story model of identity*, which reflects this notion of constructing a narrative of our

Types of Identity

lives that provides a sense of cohesive continuity throughout our lives, including the fact that our life story may help us to envision our future, which is ultimately incorporated in our unique narratives.

Given the fact that one's narrative identity spans time (i.e., it includes what we recall of our past, what we experience in the present, and what we imagine in the future), you may be able to recall, for example, talking about who you will be come in the future as a child. You may not have had much of a past to draw from, but you may have been able to describe how you "always" wanted to become a doctor or a teacher or an astronaut. The imagined future astronaut may spend their nights looking at the stars and picturing themselves on the moon. They may talk about how one day they will go to school and learn how to fly a rocket ship. This represents a narrative identity, albeit a burgeoning one, and one that may or may not come to fruition. The story for such an individual connects who they were, who they are now, and who they want to become. It provides at least one possible road map for becoming whatever they imagine they will be. Of course, as we gain more life experiences; learn more about ourselves, including where our true skills and abilities lie; and learn more about what the world is truly like, we may abandon our childhood dreams in favor of something that is more realistic for us.

The study of narrative identity has produced empirical findings from various subfields of psychology (e.g., personality, life span, cognitive, counseling). The myriad angles from which each subfield of psychology examines this form of identity provide multiple perspectives that help to explain how and why one's narrative identity develops. We develop our narrative identities in conversations with others, including parental figures, friends, and dating partners. When we talk about ourselves and share who we are, we are actively in the process of constructing our personal narrative. Researchers reveal that the more willing others are to listen to our unique stories, the more likely we are able to accurately construct our narratives and provide details that more fully round out our narrative identity.

A significant aspect of narrative identity is the degree to which it allows us to create meaning in our lives. Researchers have found that as we age from childhood into adolescence, our narrative identities evolve to include stories about ourselves that reflect a sense of meaning. This occurs during a time when exploring and establishing one's identity is paramount (see "Psychosocial Development: Erik Erikson" in chapter 3 for more information). This type of narrative helps us make sense of our lives and what purpose our lives may serve. In terms of identity statuses (see "Identity Statuses: James Marcia" in chapter 3 for more information), the more one actively explores or has explored one's identity (i.e., identity achievement and moratorium), the more likely they are to have a narrative that reflects meaning for their life.

Despite psychologists' early view of narrative identity as no more than child's play, considerable research has been conducted in this area that has resulted in hundreds of studies devoted to understanding how best to define narrative identity; how narrative identity intersects with other identities, such as racial identity and professional identity; and even how specific mental health diagnoses affect one's narrative.

Professional Identity

Professional identity can be considered in the context of social identity (discussed in a section that follows) because our sense of identity as professionals is understood in terms of how we fit with the expectations of a particular professional group. We compare ourselves to how others already in that professional behave. Additionally, when receiving the requisite education and training to become part of a particular profession, we are socialized into that profession by others who are already members of that profession. Therefore, not unlike a parental figure who socializes their child on what is right and what is wrong as it relates to how to interact with others in general, educators and mentors in a profession socialize trainees on what is right and what is wrong with respect to how to be in that particular profession.

It is important to note that professional identity is not simply about the degree to which one identifies with or aligns oneself with the job that they have. A job is not necessarily affiliated with a profession. A profession is a career in which someone receives extensive formal education and training so that they become qualified to work in a particular professional role, such as a teacher, lawyer, electrician, nurse, journalist, or psychologist. One cannot simply jump into these roles without first learning either on the job/as an apprentice or in an academic setting how to do the work, what expectations are associated with this type of work, and what ethics are associated with the work. Your professional identity, therefore, is the degree to which you identify with the role expectations, responsibilities, and ethics of the profession of which you are a part.

Generally speaking, when one is affiliated with a particular profession, there is usually some measure of prestige and privilege that comes with completing the education and training to become a member of that profession. In addition to formal education, there is often standardized testing that must be passed with a minimum score; otherwise, the person cannot become a member of the profession. There are also often expectations that the professional stay abreast of the current information, techniques, standards, and ethics of the profession. This usually involves a substantial commitment of time and money, without which someone cannot remain a member of the profession. When someone becomes a member of a profession, having endured all that it took to get there, it is likely that they will strongly identify as a member of that profession. They will have a strong professional identity, which means

Types of Identity   29

that who they are as a professional will be a significant part of their personal identity. This means that when they are not in their profession (i.e., they are not at work), they still identify as a member of that profession, regardless of the situation or context.

The benefits of having a professional identity may include the power and prestige bestowed upon the individual as well as that which is bestowed on the group or organization with which the professional is affiliated (e.g., a lawyer's family members may not miss an opportunity to say they have a lawyer in the family). Those within a particular profession will be better able to effectively communicate with one another and are more likely to be willing to work with members of other related professions. The drawbacks of having a strong professional identity may include having difficulty interacting with others outside of their profession. This has been conceptualized as *identity threat*, which includes having difficulty working with others outside of their professional discipline, difficulty accepting the development of new specialty areas, and difficulty accepting advances in technology that affect how members of the profession work.

Research examining the intersection of professional identity and being a member of a disenfranchised group (e.g., non-privileged race/ethnicity or sex/gender) has found that being a member of a disenfranchised group can impact one's professional identity in such a way that an individual may not even consider pursuing a particular profession because they do not think it is available to them. Alternatively, if they do pursue a particular profession, their sense of professional identity may be different from someone in the same profession who is considered a member of a privileged group. One study that examined Black journalists' experiences found that their status as a member of a racially disenfranchised group affected how they viewed their role as a member of the profession and how others viewed them in that role. Some journalists reported feeling like an "outsider" because they did not receive guidance when new to the job. Others grappled with how to report stories involving other Black individuals, worrying that they may have "sold out." They may also feel isolated because their White colleagues and White editors were not aware of or did not understand the unique issues faced by being part of a profession while simultaneously being part of a disenfranchised group.

Sexual Identity

Sexual identity and sexual orientation are often used synonymously. Sometimes sexual identity is distinguished from sexual orientation, wherein sexual identity is used to refer to whether someone's physical characteristics (e.g., primary and secondary sex characteristics) as a male, female, or both (i.e., hermaphrodite) match the person's perception of themselves as male, female, or nonbinary. For the purposes of this book, *sexual identity* refers to one's sexual orientation, which refers to whom you are attracted sexually. This means someone will identify as heterosexual, homosexual (i.e., gay or lesbian), bisexual, or asexual. In recent years, additional terms have been used to describe sexual identity, including *pansexual, demisexual, androsexual, bicurious, gynesexual,* and *skoliosexual.* The focus here will be on those who are heterosexual, homosexual, or bisexual, largely because the vast majority of research, as of the writing of this book, has been conducted on those sexual identities.

Regardless of how someone identifies, a person's sexual identity may or may not be reflected in one's sexual behavior. That is, the person with whom someone engages in sexual activity may or may not truly reflect to whom someone is sexually attracted. Many readers may personally know someone or have heard about others who engage in sexual activity that suggests they are one sexual orientation or another, but in reality, the person is not acting on their true sexual feelings. The most common scenario to date is someone who is homosexual who has either not acknowledged or accepted that about themselves or who fears the repercussions of others finding out and therefore only engages in sexual activity with those of the opposite sex so that they "appear," to themselves and others, to be heterosexual.

A concept related to one's sexual identity is the process of "coming out," which is typically reserved for those who are lesbian, gay, bisexual, or another nonheterosexual identity. As heterosexuality has historically been and continues to be assumed until someone says otherwise, those who are heterosexual do not have to "come out." Coming out is considered a process rather than a distinct event. Someone whose sexual identity is not heterosexual may choose to reveal their sexual identity only to their sexual partner(s) and keep this part of their life hidden and protected from others. Some may choose to reveal their sexual identity to those whom they trust, and others may choose to come out to anyone and everyone willing to listen to them. Regardless of the process by which someone chooses to come out, this process will be unique to them and should only occur at whatever pace and with whomever that person wants.

Much of what is known about the health and well-being of those with one sexual identity or another is predominantly focused on those who are lesbian, gay, or bisexual, primarily because there continues to be social stigma associated with a nonheterosexual identity (to date, not much is known about the lived experiences of other nonheterosexual identities). Recent research has found that those who are bisexual may deal with even more stigma and mental health concerns than those who identify as lesbian or gay. This seems to be due to the fact that both the heterosexual and homosexual communities often reject those who are bisexual because someone with this

Types of Identity 31

sexual identity is viewed as belonging to both groups and therefore does not truly belong to either.

Research in the area of how one's sexual identity develops has also predominantly focused on those who identify as nonheterosexual, typically gay, lesbian, or bisexual. This seems to be because heterosexuality is assumed and therefore not something that needs to be figured out. However, understanding how and why someone may identify as nonheterosexual has been something on which researchers and clinicians have focused. The shift in more recent years has been on not merely understanding the *why* of sexual identity formation but also *how* to help those who identify as a member of a sexually disenfranchised group successfully navigate their sexuality. In the early 1960s, some researchers noted that those who identify with a disenfranchised group (whether sexual or otherwise) likely adopted and internalized the assumptions those in the privileged group had about them: there is something fundamentally wrong with them. Though society at large seems to have moved away from this point of view, there are still many who hold this perspective, and it is precisely this type of stigma that can affect the health and well-being of those who are disenfranchised due to their sexual orientation. Since the 1960s, there have been in the neighborhood of twenty different theories on sexual identity formation.

Researchers who have reviewed many of these theories noted that some of them are too rigid in that those going through their own coming-out process may appear to be "doing it wrong." Thus, these researchers recommended a more flexible approach that can be inclusive of all individual processes. They suggested that future models should include the following themes: differences, confusion, exploration, disclosure, labeling, cultural immersion, distrust of the oppressor, degree of integration, internalized oppression, managing stigma, identity transformation, and authenticity. Knowing that there are a multitude of potential aspects related to sexual identity about which someone will have myriad thoughts and feelings can help each of us understand another's experience.

Social Identity

The concept of social identity theory was developed in the late 1970s by Henri Tajfel and John Turner. They suggested that as we figure out who we are and how we define ourselves, we do so in the context of the social groups with which we identify. This can include groups as nondistinct as a group of friends or in the context of more well-defined groups, such as a specific club, organization, sport team, or family. Identification with various groups is believed to support our developing personal identity and helps to define it.

Tajfel and Turner defined *social identity* as "those aspects of the individual's self-image that derive from the social categories to which he perceives himself as belonging." In short, our social identity comes from the groups with which we identity. For example, this author is from the Midwest and is therefore a Midwesterner. She teaches at a university and therefore is an academic. Each of these groups may conjure up a specific image or set of descriptors that are used to describe members of that particular group. Typically, we publicly identify with groups we either do not mind identifying with or that we know will allow others to perceive us positively. Tajfel and Turner determined that we want to be perceived positively by others and suggested that we are motivated to establish and maintain a social identity that is positive. We do this by comparing our group (i.e., in-group) to other groups (i.e., out-groups), and we look for favorable comparisons. That is, we tend to evaluate the groups to which we belong as well as the other people in those groups in terms of which one is better than the other. If for any reason we determine that the groups to which we belong are not satisfactory or are not perceived as better than other groups, we tend to do one of two things. We either attempt to make our existing group better or we leave our existing group for a more positively perceived group.

For those who are fans of various professional sports—particularly those involving teams—we can see this in action now more than ever. Some professional athletes will publicly express dissatisfaction with their current team and express interest in being traded to another, presumably "better" team, thus illustrating the second option, when we think our current group is not good enough. Sometimes, depending on the influence a particular athlete may have, the athlete may pressure the coaches or owners to acquire other celebrated athletes to become a member of the team, thus reflecting the first option of trying to make the existing group better. In short, we tend to want to be affiliated with the best group(s) possible and to dissociate from those we, or others, perceive to be less desirable.

When we go about deciding with which groups we want to be affiliated and how this affects our sense of identity, it is important to not only be an actual member of the group but also to have identified with the relevant in-group. This means that it is not enough to be associated with a group because you happen to be at the right place at the right time. For group membership to influence our overall sense of identity, we have to essentially decide for ourselves that the group in question is one we want to be a part of and, ultimately, are willing to identify with (i.e., "I belong to this group").

The process of establishing one's social identity is believed to encompass three interrelated parts: social categorization, social identification, and social comparison. *Social categorization* refers to identifying various groups of which one could become a member. This process means that when a delineation is made between one group and another, we automatically create in-groups and out-groups. *Social identification* refers to whether or not we identify with a particular group. When we identify with a group, we are initially aware of

Types of Identity

our membership with that group, we contemplate how meaningful it is to us to be a member of that group (i.e., what value does the group hold for us?), and we consider how we feel being a member of that group. Finally, *social comparison* refers to our tendency to compare ourselves to others in myriad ways. We may do so in terms of things like attractiveness, intelligence, athletic ability, degree of popularity, and so on. Making such comparisons helps us to better understand ourselves and how we are the same or different from others. When this comparison takes place as part of group membership, there tends to be an expectation that members of our group, the in-group, will act similarly and will be perceived more favorably compared to members of out-groups.

Recent researchers have suggested that while most of us acknowledge membership in one or more groups, we still understand who we are as an individual separate from those groups. For example, someone may be a member of the cross-country team, the school choir, and, of course, their family, but they also know that they are not the same as those in these various groups. William Swann and colleagues suggested that some people who become strongly identified with a particular group are essentially "fused" with the group, and the distinction between who that person is and who the group is becomes murky. The individual's personal and social identities become one and the same. This can occur among those who have extremely close emotional ties to one another (e.g., family) or groups with which someone identifies but may not know many or all members of the group itself (e.g., a political party, a professional athletic team). These researchers found that those whose personal identities were fused with a group's identity were willing to fight, perhaps violently, for the group itself. This indicates that their personal and social identities are one and the same. The demise or success of the group is unequivocally linked, at least in the mind of such a person, to the demise or success of themselves.

Multiple Identities

Multiple identities refers to the notion that we have multiple ways of identifying who we are, and the degree to which one aspect of our identity may be more salient than another is likely dependent on the situation or context we are in. For example, someone may be female, Black, an author, a lawyer, a mother, a spouse, and a cat owner. Of course, there is more to such a person than all that, but one can see how different many of these facets of such a person's identity are from one another. One may be able to infer from this brief list under what circumstances one or more of these identifiers would be more important than the others. When such a person is at home, they may think of themselves in terms of being a spouse, mother, and cat owner. More specifically, depending on who or what such a person is interacting with, one or two of these facets of their identity may be more important. For example, when their cat is curled up on their lap, it may not matter who else is in the room; that person is in the mode of being a cat owner. When such a person is arguing a case in a court of law, they are likely aware of their identity as a lawyer, which will guide their interactions and thoughts; however, a public role like this is also likely to make being Black, and more specifically a Black female, salient, which will further influence their thoughts, feelings, and behaviors.

Many of our multiple identities can effectively coexist. However, what happens when the values and beliefs you hold as a member of one group interferes or conflicts with the values and beliefs of another? Much of the research in this area has examined one's racial or ethnic identity with another identity, such as one's professional identity or sexual identity. Another way of thinking about this is which identity takes precedence over another—with which group do you more strongly align in a particular situation? For example, one study entitled *Is Gender More Important and Meaningful Than Race? An Analysis of Racial and Gender Identity among Black, White, and Mixed-Race Children* found that most children reported gender as being more important to them than race. Researchers concluded that whether gender or race was more or less important to a particular child was determined in large part by the degree to which a child acknowledged differences between groups (e.g., boy or girl, White or Black).

Multiple identities is one way to identify the various roles we play within our daily lives and across our life span. It is another way of denoting the fact that our personal identities include myriad facets that vary in the degree to which they overlap or are interconnected.

This chapter explored various specific types of identity. As noted at the start, there are many other types of identity not discussed herein. The types of identity included are merely a small representation of how we can define ourselves and ultimately reflect how complex our individual identities can be.

CHAPTER THREE

Theories of Identity Development

Many theories have been developed to explain how and why we develop into distinct the human beings we are. Of course, not all of the theories can be described in this book. The focus for this book will be on Erik Erikson's *theory of psychosocial development formally known as post-Freudian theory*, which explicitly focuses on identity development throughout the life span; James Marcia's *identity statuses*, which are an extension of Erikson's adolescent stage of development; Carl Rogers's *person-centered theory*, which suggests that when others provide an ideal environment to express ourselves we are more likely to the best version of who we truly are; and Richard Ryan and Edward Deci's *self-determination theory*, which outlines what we need to live satisfying lives that are internally directed or self-determined.

Post-Freudian: Erik Erikson

Erik Erikson was a psychoanalyst in the mid to late 1900s who adhered to many of the traditions and ideas of Sigmund Freud. Whereas Sigmund Freud emphasized the impact of our instinctual desires (represented by the pleasure seeking "Id" part of our personality) and the importance of getting those desires under control, Erikson placed greater emphasis on the "ego" portion of our personality that is guided by the reality principle and functions as a reasonable and rational guide to our thoughts, feelings, and behaviors.

Erikson proposed that we encounter eight stages throughout the course of our lives that provide the framework for what he called our "psychosocial development." As we develop psychologically as individuals, we do so in the context of our interactions with others, particularly our parental figures and then, later, our childhood peers and dating partners. The eight stages Erikson proposed span one's entire life. He stated that these stages operate on a construct called the *epigenetic principle* (borrowed from the field of biology), which means development occurs at a fixed rate and a fixed sequence. Thus, the eight stages he proposed occur in a predictable sequence and at predictable times in a person's life. He also indicated that elements of all stages exist within a child in a primitive form and do not emerge until the "right time." For example, he noted that infants have some measure of autonomy when they express displeasure for something by crying or abruptly pulling away from someone; however, he also noted that it is not until the second psychosocial stage that the issue of autonomy is truly explored. With respect to identity development, Erikson specifically stated that the first stage during which we deal concretely with identity is during the fifth stage: adolescence. Each stage thereafter is characterized by an "identity crisis" that will be resolved in either a more or less psychologically healthy way.

Each of Erikson's eight stages is characterized by an interaction of opposites; one side helps to facilitate one's growth and development, and the other disrupts this growth and development. For example, during the first stage of development, infancy, the opposites are basic trust and basic mistrust. Basic trust is the facilitative or *syntonic* element, and basic mistrust is the disruptive or *dystonic* element. Although the facilitative element can be viewed as the most beneficial to development, the reality is that Erikson believed we must experience both sides of this dichotomy to develop in the psychologically healthiest way. The interaction of the opposites at each stage creates what he called a *basic strength* or ego strength. One way to think about this is that each stage produces a skill that one's ego can use throughout one's life to help one effectively navigate one's life. However, if too little of the basic strength is produced, the individual will develop what he called a *core pathology*, which can interfere with one's development through life.

Issues related to identity development take center stage during the adolescence stage of development, but as just noted, each stage produces an ego strength. Although the term *ego* can be used in a variety of ways in the context of Erikson's theory, it refers to our sense of who we are. Therefore, each of Erikson's stages may facilitate or disrupt the development of one's identity.

Stage One: Infancy

Stage one, infancy, occurs during the first year of one's life and is characterized by the interaction between basic trust and basic mistrust. Both of these elements are experienced in terms of the degree to which one's basic needs are met by one's parental figures in a timely manner. Erikson noted

Theories of Identity Development 37

that all infants experience both trust and mistrust. They are fed, changed, and comforted, but they also experience times when they are hungry, frustrated, or uncomfortable. The crisis here has to do with how much trust compared to how much mistrust is experienced. Both are necessary for sufficient development; however, more trust should be experienced to develop the ego strength of hope, which is the belief that things will get better. Without developing enough hope during this time, the child will resolve the stage with the core pathology of withdrawal, which reflects a detachment from the outside world.

Stage Two: Early Childhood

Stage two, which occurs during the second and third years of life, is the early childhood stage. During this time, the child struggles between autonomy and shame and doubt. Children during this time period can be viewed as stubborn and willful. They are, therefore, often met with correction, criticism, and punishment to get the child to act "properly" by parental or societal standards. As a child unabashedly expresses themselves, they experience autonomy. When, however, their behaviors are critically corrected (e.g., making the child feel bad for having an "accident" while potty training or being told critically that they are not meeting parental figures' expectations), the child will experience shame and doubt. To some degree, both are necessary for the basic strength of will to develop; however, if a child has too little of this ego strength, they will develop the core pathology of compulsion. Thus, instead of doing things they want to do (will), the child will do things because they feel like they have to or are supposed to (compulsion).

Stage Three: Play Age

The third stage, play age, takes place between the ages of three to five years and involves the crisis of initiative and guilt. Initiative represents the child's desire to pursue particular personal interests or goals. Some of these goals must be delayed (e.g., wanting to leave home) or are deemed inappropriate or taboo (e.g., wanting to marry your parent—a common, albeit naïve, desire for the very young child). Not being able to pursue a desired goal, a child experiences guilt. When a child experiences more initiative than guilt, they will resolve this stage with the ego strength of purpose. Having purpose allows the child to engage in activities with a goal or purpose in mind (e.g., they want to win the game or to make a new friend). Without enough purpose, the child will resolve the stage with inhibition, the core pathology of this stage, which is characterized by compulsively following the rules laid out by others, which inhibits their own wants or needs.

Stage Four: School Age

From around age 6 to age 12 or 13, we experience stage four: school age. During this stage, we struggle with the conflict between industry and inferiority. Erikson noted that during this stage, we experience a great deal of social growth, as this is the time formal schooling usually begins in the United States; therefore, we are around peers and other authority figures more regularly. Having a sense of industry or being industrious means that we are able to begin and finish tasks—an important skill for school-related work—and we learn through experience how to effectively cooperate with others. As we learn what we are good at, we develop industry. By contrast, when we realize we are not good at something or our efforts do not lead to reaching some goal we had in mind, we experience inferiority. This can come from direct feedback (e.g., a failing grade, not being picked for an athletic team) or from unfavorably comparing ourselves to our peers. Through interactions with our peers, we learn relatively quickly how we measure up.

If we are able to experience enough industry in comparison to feelings of inferiority, we will acquire the basic strength of competence: we are able to effectively use our minds and bodies to manage and solve the challenges we face. By contrast, if we do not develop a strong enough sense of competence, we will resolve this stage with the core pathology of inertia. Erikson described *inertia* as a form of developmental regression in which we end up psychologically stagnant. We do not develop, grow, or flourish; we stay right where we are.

Stage Five: Adolescence

It is during the fifth stage, adolescence, that issues explicitly related to identity are more directly grappled with. During this period, from puberty to age 18, we are faced with the conflict of identity versus identity confusion. Erikson stated that this stage was of paramount importance because the ultimate outcome should be that we have a strong sense of who we are. He also noted that issues related to identity do not start here, nor do they end when we reach the end of this stage. The period of adolescence is a time during which a great deal of exploration occurs to help us figure out what we like and do not like, what we value and do not value, and so on. During this period, we try to figure out who we are and, by comparison, who we are not. As we explore various roles, interests, friends, and belief systems, we unconsciously rely on what we learned about ourselves from earlier stages.

Erikson stated that our sense of who we are is formed by two sources. The first is that we either continue to accept or reject the earlier versions of ourselves from childhood. The second involves the social and cultural forces that affect us and exert pressure on us to conform to societal standards. As one may infer, despite the possible pathological outcomes that reflect rigid

Theories of Identity Development

adherence to others' expectations, adolescence is a time when we can experiment with following along with what others expect or, alternatively, go our own way. We can take stock of who we have been and whether we want to continue as is or change course. Confusion about our identity can be exacerbated as we struggle to figure this out and try to manage the tension between accepting or rejecting the expectations and values of one's parental figures and other important "elders" and accepting or rejecting the values and expectations of one's peer group. Not knowing what to do can leave an adolescent feeling confused and uncertain about who they are. To develop a strong sense of identity, it is important for each of us to experience some identity confusion; however, too much of this can result in leaving this stage without a strong sense of identity. When, however, we are able to experiment in ways that predominantly leave us feeling like we know who we are and who we are not, we acquire the basic strength of *fidelity*.

Fidelity refers to faithfulness, but not in the sense of being faithful to one's dating partner. Rather, fidelity in this context refers to being faithful to one's self. When we have fidelity in this context, we have developed a strong identity that allows us to effectively make decisions. Fidelity also means we have confidence in our personal belief systems and no longer need the guidance of authority figures to tell us what to do or believe. If we do not develop enough of this ego strength, we will leave this stage with the core pathology of role repudiation. *Role repudiation* refers to an inability to develop a coherent sense of who we are. We may have ideas about things we like or do not like or value or do not value, but what we do not have is an understanding of how these facets fit together in a strong, cohesive sense of identity. Erikson stated that those who end adolescence with role repudiation may have a severe lack of confidence in themselves and may consistently look to others to see how they should feel, think, or act. A contrasting consequence of role repudiation is to become defiant, whereby we think, feel, and act oppositionally in the face of authority. Essentially, whatever the powers that be have to say about anything, a defiant individual will do the opposite so that they are not conforming. They are defiant not because it is what they truly believe or because it reflects who they truly are.

As we continue to age, Erikson believed we continue to deal with identity crises during the three remaining stages.

Stage Six: Young Adulthood

The task of the sixth stage, young adulthood, requires us to deal with the conflict between intimacy and isolation. Although finding a lifetime romantic partner is believed to be important during this stage, *intimacy* refers less to physical intimacy and more to psychological intimacy. Erikson believed that true intimacy only occurs when one has first developed a strong, coherent sense of identity—the task of the preceding stage. When someone experiences intimacy with a strong identity, they are able to merge their sense of who they are with another person without the fear of losing their individuality. When we are truly able to be intimate, we know that we still have an identity as someone outside that relationship. Dating and sexual relationships during adolescence tend not to reflect true intimacy. Rather, true intimacy is identified by the ability to trust and be trusted by another, the ability to compromise, and, at times, the ability to sacrifice for the sake of the other, all while maintaining a strong sense of who one is with or without the relationship. Erikson explained that many marriages end because a lot of people get married as part of their identity exploration rather than first having established who they are so that they could find a true partner who shares important ideals and who will work with them toward mutual life goals.

The counterpart to intimacy is isolation. Similar to intimacy, *isolation* does not refer to physical isolation but rather psychological isolation. Readers may be familiar with the notion of being in a room full of people but feeling completely alone. This generally reflects the lived experience of psychological isolation. When someone is psychologically isolated, they are unable or unwilling to share who they are with others; they are unable or unwilling to be intimate. Sharing who you truly are with another person is not an easy thing to do. When we reveal our true interests, beliefs, desires, and feelings, we risk ridicule and rejection. However, taking this type of risk is precisely what is required by intimacy. The inability to do so will leave us feeling disconnected and isolated from others because they do not know who we truly are and what makes us tick. By continuing to take this risk and trying to find out who is a good fit, we give ourselves the opportunity to develop the basic strength of love.

Erikson noted that mature forms of love involve sexual intimacy and passion, commitment to one another, cooperation and competition, and friendship. He also noted that mature love will involve some isolation because we continue to retain a sense of our individuality and aspects of who we are that others may never fully know or understand. If we do not develop a strong enough ability to maturely love someone else, we will develop the core pathology of exclusivity.

Exclusivity is a term often used in the context of romantic relationships that usually refers to not dating or having sexual interactions with another person outside of the relationship; however, that is not what exclusivity means in this context. Here it refers to excluding things and people from our lives. A little bit of this is necessary, as we cannot have everything and all people in our lives; however, too much exclusivity results in an inability to cooperate, compromise, or effectively compete; all of which are necessary for mature love.

Theories of Identity Development

Stage Seven: Adulthood

In the stage of adulthood, which takes place between the ages of 31 and 60, we deal with the identity conflict of generativity and stagnation. *Generativity* has to do with developing a concern for people beyond one's self. It is another term for leaving a lasting legacy or giving back to society. For many people, generativity is expressed through nurturing one's children. For those without children, generativity can be achieved through philanthropy (i.e., charitable works intended to improve the welfare of others), volunteer efforts, the development and nurturing of ideas that may impact others, and so on. The task is to not only leave a mark on the world but also to leave it better than one found it. *Stagnation*, by contrast, refers to self-absorption. When someone experiences stagnation, they are so focused on themselves that they cannot grow, develop, or flourish and therefore cannot give back to the world around them.

As is the case with the other stages in Erikson's theory, it is important for each of us to have the experience of both sides of the conflict to develop the ego strength of the stage. In this case both giving back to the world and being overly focused on one's self are necessary in order to develop the basic strength of care. Care is inferred based on the degree to which we take care of or care for other people or things. Care is not experienced as something we must do; rather, it emerges from all preceding ego qualities as something we naturally want to do. However, if we do not develop enough care, we are predominantly left experiencing the core pathology of rejectivity.

Rejectivity refers to a lack of interest in caring for others or a lack of a willingness to do so. This may look like someone who remains self-absorbed (only focused on their own wants and needs), or it may take the form of someone who believes those who belong to other groups (e.g., another country or religion) are lesser than those who belong to their group. Although one's personal identity is very much involved during this stage, our identities are expressed through caring about the things and people important to us.

Stage Eight: Old Age

The final stage of Erikson's theory is old age, which takes place from approximately age 60 until one's death. Older adults may retain some measure of adulthood's generativity, but they are predominantly dealing with the final remaining identity crisis through the conflict between integrity and despair. Having a sense of *integrity* means that despite any declines one may experience associated with aging (e.g., loss of physical abilities, slower cognitive processing), we are still able to hang on to our sense of identity—a sense of completeness that we ideally first developed during adolescence. The opposing experience one may have during this time period is *despair*, which essentially means that someone is without hope. This lack of hope in old age can look like someone who is fighting the fact that their life is limited and coming to an end. Someone experiencing despair during this time may feel depressed or irritated with life and people in general.

You may recall that hope is the first ego quality to be developed in life. As long as someone can maintain their sense of hope throughout their lives, they will likely enter old age with a sense of integrity—a sense of a life well lived—and will gain the final ego quality of wisdom. *Wisdom*, of course, comes from an extensive constellation of life experiences that can be passed on to those younger than themselves. If wisdom does not prevail and hope is lost, the individual in this final stage of life will be left with the core pathology of *disdain*, which Erikson saw as an extension of the core pathology of adulthood: rejectivity. Another word for disdain is *contempt*. Someone experiencing disdain in their old age years will have a contempt for life and all that is in it. This is seen as a reaction to the realities of the loss of one's own abilities and seeing others lose theirs, along with the understanding that one's life will come to an end, sooner rather than later, and they are helpless to do anything about it.

Erikson believed that from birth to death we have myriad experiences couched in our social interactions with others that help shape who we are. He believed these experiences shape who we become and how we view our life when it draws to a close. Those who are able to develop a strong sense of who they are have a greater chance of finding a lifetime partner who is truly a good fit for them. They will have an interest in giving back to others as they age and share the wisdom they acquired from a life that was lived based on who they truly are and what they truly want and need.

Identity Statuses: James Marcia

James Marcia expanded Erik Erikson's stages of psychosocial development by explicating the struggles faced by those attempting to establish a strong, coherent sense of identity during adolescence. Whereas Erikson essentially saw identity development as a differential engine—you either develop a coherent sense of identity or you do not—in the mid-1960s, Marcia postulated that the development of one's sense of identity can and ought to be considered on a continuum.

Through his theorizing, and ultimately through studying what achieving a coherent identity looks like in adolescents and young adults, Marcia proposed four distinct identity statuses. These include Erikson's poles of identity achievement and identity diffusion along with the foreclosed and moratorium statuses that exist between the two poles. From Marcia's perspective, a hallmark of identity is one's ability to select and commit to an occupation. Of

Theories of Identity Development 43

course, there is more to identity than simply what one does for a living; however, occupational choice has long been identified as a significant reflection of who a person is and, for Marcia, the process by which someone determines their occupational choice reflects one of his four identity statuses.

Identity Achievement

Someone with the status of *identity achievement* has thoroughly explored and experimented with who they are and who they want to become. This includes occupational choice as well as beliefs and ideologies. Such an individual would have experienced an initial identity crisis in the sense of feeling the need to explore so that they can fully understand who they are. The result of this crisis would be a clear understanding of what they believe, what they want to do with their life, who they want in their life, the activities in which they find joy, and so on. Marcia stated that someone who has reached this identity status has "achieved a resolution that leaves him free to act."

Feeling free to act means that when faced with a challenge—whether challenging their beliefs and values or by experiencing unexpected changes to their circumstances—an individual with the status of identity achievement would feel comfortable and likely confident in their ability to remain true to who they are and to cope with what confronts them. It is important to note that while someone with this identity status may have held on to the beliefs, values, and expectations of their parental figures, they have not maintained these positions because their parental figures held them. They have this status because after questioning and exploring what their parental figures taught them or modeled for them, they arrived at their own conclusions as to whether their parental figures' point of view and way of living fits with who they are. Of course, many who go through this process develop parts of themselves that are unique to them regardless of what their parental figures taught them or believed.

Identity Diffusion

The opposite end of the identity status continuum is *identity diffusion*. Marcia indicated that someone who has the status of identity diffusion may not have truly experienced a crisis. The individual in this status has not identified a career path for themselves, and there is not much, if anything, about the person that suggests they are concerned about that or interested in exploring possibilities. Such an individual may express interest in a particular career path or belief system, but they are likely just as enthusiastic about other, seemingly contradictory, possibilities. For example, such a person may decide that they have always wanted to become a physician and then declare their passion for art and a desire to become an artist the following week—neither of which the individual makes any meaningful effort to pursue. If pressed, the person will likely indicate that all things have merit and value. In theory, this is not necessarily a terrible position to have, but when it comes to identity development, not committing to one thing to the exclusion of another (i.e., making a decision and trying it out) will result in someone who will not know what to defend about themselves or others because all things can be defended. Such a position reflects confusion and a lack of a coherent and well-developed identity.

Moratorium

Someone who is in a state of *moratorium* is actively in their identity crisis. They are in the midst of experimenting and exploring without a clear sense of what does and does not work for them. Although, like someone who is in the status of identity diffusion, they do not have a clear sense of who they are, what they believe, and what they want to do. Unlike the person who experiences identity diffusion those in moratorium are actively struggling to figure all of that out. Someone who is identity diffused is disinterested or apathetic when it comes to defining who they are. Someone in moratorium is actively struggling with how to reconcile what their parental figures want for them, what society expects of them, and what they want for themselves. Someone in this identity status is confused and questioning much about themselves and their life but is actively working to figure it out.

Foreclosure

The fourth identity status, *foreclosure*, may look like someone who is identity achieved because they have decided on an occupational path or have declared their deeply held beliefs; however, like someone who is diffused, they have not yet experienced a crisis. Someone who is foreclosed with their identity has, more than likely, taken on the values and wishes of their parental figures without taking the time to determine whether those values are, in fact, a good fit for them. As Marcia put it, "It is difficult to tell where his parents' goals for him leave off and where his begin." Someone with this identity status may talk about plans for the future as though those plans are their own, but when pressed, someone who is foreclosed will likely have a difficult time explaining or defending why they believe one thing over another or why they chose this career path instead of that one. They may say things like, "That's just who I am" or "Who wouldn't want to do that?" Of course, someone in another identity status may say similar things, but what distinguishes the foreclosed individual is a lack of prior confusion and exploration and an inability to truly explain why something is right for them based on who they are.

Theories of Identity Development

Effects of Each Status and Paths to Identity Achievement

When initially studying these statuses, Marcia found that those with the identity achievement status essentially functioned more effectively than those of other statuses. They were more effective in their ability to continue working on challenging tasks and they were able to more realistically discern what their abilities actually were and what they could achieve. Additionally, their self-esteem was found to be quite solid and not likely to yield in the face of negative feedback. Those in the moratorium status were the most similar to those in the identity achievement status. They showed similar abilities, but those in moratorium were more likely to give up easily on a difficult task and were less likely to accurately predict what they are capable of. Those who were foreclosed were more likely to align with authoritarian characteristics. They reported valuing things like obedience and a strong respect for authority. They were also quite different from those who were identity achieved in that they struggled to complete a difficult task and were unable or unwilling to change unrealistic goals. Additionally, the degree of self-esteem for those in the foreclosed status was highly malleable in the face of feedback. If they received negative feedback, their self-esteem would drop, and if they received positive feedback, it would rise. Finally, those identified as identity-diffused scored the lowest in all areas assessed. They struggled to set realistic goals, to know when to persist and when to let go, and to have a stable sense of self-esteem.

Research examining what has been learned from 2000 to 2010 about how identity is formed using Marcia's framework suggests that there may be two pathways to identity achievement: (1) diffusion to foreclosure culminating in achievement and (2) diffusion, moratorium, closure, and achievement. The term *closure* is used to refer to a subtype of what other researchers have called "early closure," which is essentially interchangeable with foreclosure. However, closure is believed to look the same as early closure/foreclosure in that such individuals are moderately to highly committed to their occupational choices and belief systems but have engaged in little exploration. Additionally, they are unlikely to reconsider their decisions or commitments. The difference seems to be that those characterized as early closure/foreclosure started with closure/foreclosure, whereas those ultimately characterized as closure may have gotten there via other statuses. As such, they may have engaged in some exploration but not enough so that their commitments can be viewed as reflecting who they truly are. Whatever they have committed to, they are not likely to explore or question. Finally, this research revealed an additional status called *searching moratorium*. This fifth status is believed to reflect someone who is highly committed and highly engaged in exploration. They also have the well-developed ability to reconsider that to which they have already committed.

Marcia's postulation that the period of adolescence may have a broader range of outcomes than previously suggested by Erikson seems to have been supported both through his own research and by that of others. These efforts help to provide much greater detail about the experiences of burgeoning identity development during adolescence and early adulthood.

Person-Centered Theory: Carl Rogers

Person-centered theory was developed by psychologist Carl Rogers under its original name: *client-centered theory.* The name change reflected Rogers's realization that his ideas did not exclusively apply to the therapist-client relationship within psychotherapy but could also apply to various relationships among people in general. What he believed was beneficial about how a therapist could effectively help their clients could also be used in relationships between all people, particularly between parental figures and their children.

Rogers's theory is categorized as a humanistic approach, which means he believed, like all humanists, human beings are inherently good and that we simply need the "right" or optimal environment in which we can develop, thrive, and ultimately become the best possible versions of ourselves. For Rogers, the best version of ourselves that will lead to the greatest degree of overall life satisfaction reflects what he called *congruence.* Congruence occurs when the version of the person we want to be is who we actually are. This may sound simple enough; however, many of us strive to become someone that does not truly reflect who we are. As such, we fall short of that ideal and are likely to feel that we are not good enough and that we need to be a better person. Before going further, it is important to more clearly explain some of Rogers's fundamental beliefs about human beings in general and what he believes about how we become who we are.

Foundational Concepts of Person-Centered Theory

As previously noted, Rogers believed that we are fundamentally good and that we will naturally strive to become who we are meant to be. He formally referred to this as the *actualizing tendency.* The actualizing tendency is one of two basic assumptions Rogers made about human development. The first, the formative tendency, reflects the idea that we all begin as relatively simple creatures psychologically. As each day passes and we experience more of our lives, we become more and more complex. Biologically, we, like other living creatures, develop from single cells, and like other examples in the natural world, our experiences are initially unorganized and disparate but eventually become more organized as we begin to understand ourselves and the world around us.

Rogers's second basic assumption, the actualizing tendency, is the idea that all living things (e.g., animals and plant life) strive to become the best

Theories of Identity Development

version of themselves by achieving their fullest potential. Those who observe nature have undoubtedly noticed that not all flowers of the same species look identical. They all have the genetics to become whatever they were meant to become (e.g., a rose, a dandelion, a tulip), but they ultimately do not all look the same. This can be a function of the interplay between the inherited genetics and the environment in which they grow. Nonetheless, given their circumstances, these flowers strive to fulfil their floral potential. Rogers believed the same about human beings in terms of our psychological development.

Subsumed within the actualizing tendency are the ideas that we have needs for maintenance and enhancement. We are simultaneously drawn to make sure we maintain our basic needs for things like food and water and to otherwise keep things just as they are (i.e., maintenance), and we are drawn to enhance ourselves and our lives by seeking change and opportunities for growth (i.e., enhancement). Thus, we are paradoxically resistant to change while also moved to try to improve ourselves.

Three Necessary Conditions for Psychological Growth

Like the flower that requires adequate soil, water, and sunlight to reach its fullest potential, human beings, too, have ideal conditions that when in place provide us the opportunity to reach our fullest potential. Rogers initially discussed these conditions in the context of the relationship between therapist and client and then expanded this to include the importance of these conditions in the context of any meaningful relationship. The three conditions he suggested that allow us to thrive are genuineness, acceptance (i.e., unconditional positive regard), and empathy. Originally, these three conditions were within the purview of the therapist or counselor. Subsequently, these conditions were thought to be important for parental figures to embody as they raised their children and for adults to embody as they entered into and maintained meaningful relationships.

Genuineness

Genuineness is a synonym for Rogers's term *congruence* in the context of these necessary conditions; however, as *congruence* is also used in the context of the overlap between self-concept and ideal self (discussed in a section that follows), *genuineness* will be used here. *Genuineness* refers to when someone is fully aware of what is going on within themselves and freely expresses those experiences. Internal experiences (i.e., that which is going on within us) are referred to as one's *organismic self*. What occurs within our body physically and what occurs within us psychologically are considered to be part of our organismic self—essentially our entire existence, mind and body, unfiltered and raw. Of course, the reality is that most of us do tend to filter our experiences. We tend not to freely express all that is going on within us. Some of that may be borne out of conscious choice, whereas much of our censoring is likely done at a more unconscious level.

Regardless of how much or why we censor ourselves, someone who is truly genuine will not lie to themselves or others about what is really going on within them. When they feel sad, they will express that. When they feel physically ill, they will acknowledge that as well. And when they feel happy, others will be able to see that experience through the person's expressed emotions and behaviors. When we interact with someone who is genuine or authentic, we know that what they say or do is not an act nor something contrived for our or someone else's benefit. Those interacting with such a person do not have to guess at what is really going on with them or try to interpret what they really meant by what they said or did.

Acceptance

Another condition that can aid in our ability to be who we truly are is *acceptance*, or what Rogers formally referred to as *unconditional positive regard*. This simply means that when we interact with someone who is accepting, they have the capacity to acknowledge who we truly are and accept us as is. They do not judge or in any way make us feel like there is something fundamentally wrong with us. This does not mean that such a person will like or even condone harmful behavior (e.g., physically or psychologically hurting someone, including one's self); however, an accepting individual will not reject us or ridicule us for our behavior; rather, they will seek to understand our behavior from the perspective of a human being trying to do the best they can.

Using an extreme example to make the point, someone who says they have abused their child will be met by the accepting individual with something like, "Your child did something and you became angry, so you hit your child. What reactions do you have to that?" Of course, to be clear—and Rogers would agree—abuse in any form is unacceptable, and depending on to whom this is revealed (e.g., a counselor), they will likely have to report the abuse to the proper authorities. However, if the intent of the interaction is to help the individual or to understand them, then rendering judgment or saying something like, "That is terrible. What kind of person are you!" will result in the person becoming defensive, fighting back, or shutting down and not sharing anything further, which ultimately hinders their growth.

Empathy

The third and final condition is empathy. Most readers likely know that *empathy* and *sympathy* are not the same thing, but the two terms are often confused with one another. Sympathy is typically experienced when we feel bad for someone because of what that person is going through. We have

Theories of Identity Development 49

sympathy for those who have lost a loved one or experienced some misfortune. In these contexts, we are likely to say something like, "I'm so sorry to hear that. Is there any way I can help?" By contrast, the experience of empathy is a deeper understanding of what the person is going through. The phrase often used to describe empathy is the ability to "put yourself in someone else's shoes." This means that you have the ability to understand someone else's experience at an emotional level that perhaps the person themselves may not have realized or directly communicated. When someone shares that they have experienced a terrible loss, they may do so by visibly crying and simply saying, "My grandmother died." An empathic statement might be something like, "Her death is devastating for you." Or if they have shared a bit more about the impact of such a loss, an empathic response might be, "The loss of your grandmother has left you feeling like life has lost meaning for you."

These three conditions, as previously mentioned, are paramount for creating a fertile environment for growth and the development of one's fullest potential. Of course, we, as human beings—including counselors—will not be perfect in all three of these conditions. However, the more we strive to embody genuineness, acceptance, and empathy, the greater the likelihood that those around us will show who they truly are and will have an opportunity to flourish. One way to think about this and to more fully understand why these things are so important would be to consider something about yourself that you know but have either never shared with anyone or have only shared with one or two people. Why have you never shared it? If you have, why did you share it with that particular person? If you have never shared it, there is a good chance you are afraid of what others will think of you if they knew and, perhaps more importantly, whether you can trust what their reaction is if you did share your secret. If you knew someone would always be honest with you (genuineness/congruence), would not judge you, would accept you no matter what you shared (acceptance/unconditional positive regard), and would do their best to fully understand what you shared (empathy), you are more likely to share your secret with them, thereby allowing you to share and more fully understand your own organismic experience. Even if we do this, how well do we really know ourselves? And if we do fully understand who we are, do we accept and love ourselves, including our flaws, or are we judgmental and critical of ourselves?

Overlap between the Self-Concept and the Ideal Self

Rogers used the term *congruence* to refer to two separate concepts of his theory; however, in this section, *congruence* will refer to the degree to which who you think you are and who you want to be overlap. The more these two views of yourself overlap, the greater the degree of congruence. Who we think we are is encapsulated by the term *self-concept*, and who we want to be is reflected in Rogers's notion of the *ideal self*.

Self-Concept

Self-concept refers to our conscious awareness of who we think we are. When someone asks you to describe yourself, the things that come to mind are part of your self-concept. However, your self-concept likely does not reflect all of who you are, and in many cases, it may not accurately reflect who you are. Rogers talked about how the experiences we have on a daily basis either fit with our self-concept or they do not. Depending on what our experiences are and the degree to which we believe they reflect who we think we are, we will then (1) allow this experience fully, as is, into our self-concept; (2) distort the experience to make it fit with who we think we are; or (3) deny the experience altogether because it does not fit with our self-concept at all. For example, if part of your-self-concept is that you are a nice person but you do or say something that is not nice (e.g., you tell someone their outfit looks terrible), you may distort the experience so that such a comment can still reflect you as a nice person (e.g., "I said her outfit looked terrible so that she wouldn't embarrass herself. I was trying to help her!") or deny it altogether (e.g., "I would never say that.").

The reality is that a person with *niceness* as part of their self-concept will still do or say things that are not nice. Someone who fully accepts themselves as they are will be able to acknowledge that. They may know, for example, that they are generally a nice person who sometimes makes mistakes or that sometimes says or does mean things. Thus, our self-concept is only as accurate as the degree to which we either freely allow in all experiences, no matter what, or we distort or deny our experiences.

Ideal Self

Whereas the self-concept is who we believe we are, the *ideal self* is who we want to be. Usually, the ideal self is how we imagine our "perfect" self would be, and it predominantly contains positive attributes. We rarely want to be anxious or absentminded or mean. Rather, our ideal self will contain attributes such as relaxed, happy, organized, thoughtful, smart, and successful. Most of us are likely not perfectly satisfied with who we think we are. We may even be really dissatisfied. The idea of wanting to be different, better, or someone else entirely is probably not a foreign concept to most readers.

Becoming the best version of ourselves is a foundational construct of Rogers's theory. However, he was clear in that the greater the gap (i.e., lower congruence) between who you think you are (self-concept) and who you want to become (ideal self) is a recipe for psychological suffering and

Theories of Identity Development 51

decreased well-being. Paradoxically, the task for the person whose ideal self is very different from their self-concept is to accept themselves as they are right now—flaws and all. That may seem counterintuitive, particularly if you can identify all kinds of flaws within yourself and argue that divesting yourself of those flaws would make you a better and happier person. Remember, however, for many of us, who we think we are, as reflected in our self-concept, is not entirely accurate. Moreover, the disparagement of flaws of any kind suggests that the only way to be totally fulfilled is to never make mistakes or to not have any flaws, which is impossible.

In his book *On Becoming a Person*, Rogers states, "The curious paradox is that when I accept myself just as I am, then I can change." The idea here is that you cannot change what you do not know or do not understand. If we cannot accept the fact that there are things about ourselves that are not that great, we will deny or distort those things as if they have not occurred, thus rendering them unchangeable. If, however, we can allow all our experiences into our awareness and accept ourselves as we are right now, we have the chance to try to do things differently.

Effects of Conditions of Worth

Self-acceptance is not easily gained, particularly if one has not first been shown love and acceptance by others. In fact, Rogers was adamant that one cannot love and accept themselves until they have first received love and acceptance from others. Take a minute to let that sink in. If you have not first been shown genuine love and acceptance of who you are, just as you are, then you cannot do that for yourself. You will be unable to acknowledge that your less than ideal attributes are no more than aspects of a flawed person who is fundamentally good and doing the best they can. Self-judgment and self-ridicule are usually the products of having been judged and ridiculed by others. Rogers called this "conditions of worth."

Conditions of worth constitute standards you have to meet to receive love and acceptance from someone else. If you meet those expectations, you are rewarded with approval and affection. If, however, you do not meet those expectations, you are essentially punished with disapproval, disappointment, ridicule, or rejection. Not surprisingly, conditions such as these not only leave us feeling bad about ourselves but also contribute to our moving further and further away from who we truly are as we try to do what others expect or want from us.

When someone in our lives embodies the three conditions of genuineness, acceptance, and empathy, they help to create an environment in which we are more likely to admit our mistakes and apologize for them without feeling like we are a terrible person. Imagine something like this: A parent tells their child, "Be a good girl/good boy and do what you're told." What if you don't? Does that mean you are a bad person? Rogers would not think so; however, you may be explicitly told that you are bad if you do not do what you are told, or you may not be explicitly shown that you are still loved and accepted even if you did not do something correctly. Without a separation between bad behavior and who we are as a person, we are at risk for equating "bad" behavior with being a "bad" person and "good" behavior with being a "good" person.

Remember, one of Rogers's basic assumptions is that we are fundamentally good and trying to become the best possible versions of ourselves. If we are told early in our lives that we are not good, then who we genuinely are will be equated with being bad, and we will want to be as far removed from that version of ourselves as possible. We will then try to mimic other "good people" or try to figure out what our parental figures or important others mean when they talk about being a "good girl" or a "good boy," and we will contort ourselves into knots trying to become that person rather than becoming the person we truly are.

When we are shown genuineness, acceptance, and empathy by others, we will have a greater capacity for allowing into conscious awareness all aspects of ourselves, both good and bad. We will be able to express those things without fear of judgment or loss of love and affection. We then have the opportunity to take stock of the parts of ourselves that we would like to make some changes to, but we are unlikely to be left feeling like we have to fundamentally change who we are—because that would mean we would have to become someone we are not.

Self-Determination Theory

At its most basic level, *self-determination* refers to the concept of autonomous choice. Each of us chooses what we want to do or what we do not want to do, and the control for making such a choice lies within us. That may seem like a no-brainer; however, it is often the case that the choices we make are not truly of our own determination. We may have been pressured in one direction or another for so long that we do not think we have any other choice; therefore, the choice seems "natural" or "obvious," as though we are making that choice on our own. There are myriad important aspects of self-determination theory, and we will merely skim the surface of some of these elements in the remainder of this chapter.

Intrinsic Motivation

In an early publication on motivation and self-determination, Edward Deci and Richard Ryan, the codevelopers of self-determination theory, emphasized the importance of being "free from pressures, such as rewards or contingencies." They were specifically addressing the notion of intrinsic

Theories of Identity Development 53

motivation, which refers to the type of motivation that involves only engaging in those activities that are internally satisfying; we are intrinsically motivated to do certain things because they are naturally rewarding to us. We do not need anyone to encourage us, to reward us, or to punish us to do things that are intrinsically rewarding; we simply want to do them. Thus, for any behavior to be truly intrinsically motivated, we cannot feel pressure one way or another from any outside/external source.

Research in this area has found that when something we are already intrinsically motivated to do becomes associated with a reward, such as money or getting privileges, our intrinsic motivation for continuing to engage in that behavior drops. For example, if you love to play soccer and will play it every chance you get, you are likely intrinsically motivated to engage in this sport. If, however, someone (e.g., a coach, a parental figure) rewards you in some way for practicing more hours or you get a reward for every goal you score, there is a good chance that your internal drive to play soccer will diminish. You may either only play to get the rewards, or you may stop playing altogether because it is no longer enjoyable for you.

Another concept Deci and Ryan noted as important in the experience of intrinsic motivation is the feeling of competence, which refers to our ability to successfully complete a task. However, whereas other researchers have indicated competence alone is an important factor when it comes to intrinsic motivation, Deci and Ryan noted that it is not merely competence but "self-determined competence" that is key. That is, we have to find the tasks that we are good at (competence) as well as those that we elect to engage in on our own (self-determination/autonomy).

Some readers may have had the experience of someone (e.g., a teacher, a coach, a parental figure) telling them that they should do X career or X sport because they would be good at it. And perhaps you are or would be good at it; however, if you feel compelled to select that activity or career path because others have suggested it for you, you are not self-determined and are less likely to find that task intrinsically rewarding. According to Deci and Ryan, the importance of self-determination cannot be overstated, and they noted that we can only achieve self-determination when we have specific psychological needs met. These needs are outlined in one of several "mini-theories" under the umbrella of self-determination theory.

The Mini-Theories of Self-Determination

In their first book on self-determination, published in 1985, Deci and Ryan noted that self-determination theory was composed of three "mini-theories": cognitive evaluation theory, organismic integration theory, and causality orientations theory. Currently, self-determination theory has expanded to encompass six mini-theories, the aforementioned three mini-theories with the addition of the basic needs theory, goals contents theory, and relational motivation theory, all of which are explored in Ryan and Deci's extensive and authoritative 2017 publication on the theory. These mini-theories are briefly described in the sections that follow.

Cognitive Evaluation Theory

The first mini-theory developed, cognitive evaluation theory, often denoted by its acronym CET, is focused on the nature of intrinsic motivation. Early in the development of self-determination theory, researchers uncovered the paradoxical effect of reward on behaviors that were originally intrinsically motivated (as discussed briefly at the start of this section). One researcher concluded that for some people, intrinsically motivated behaviors were punished by external rewards. Whatever they previously enjoyed doing lost its appeal once an external control was implemented. These controls could take various forms, including rewards (a way of controlling behavior by encouraging it to continue), deadlines (a way of controlling behavior by limiting the amount of time that can be spent on it before a certain outcome should occur), or surveillance (a way of controlling behavior by monitoring what the person is doing). The key to whether or not these types of controls would undermine the intrinsic value of a person's behavior is contingent on an individual's perception of why these external controls were implemented. If someone believes they are being controlled rather than supported by these external factors, intrinsic motivation will likely be undermined, and the behavior that was once inherently enjoyable may become something the individual leaves behind for a very long time, if not for good. Thus, CET reflects the experience of cognitively evaluating the meaning of the rewards and punishments received from our environment and their respective impact on what we are motivated to do.

Organismic Integration Theory

The second of the mini-theories, organismic integration theory, directs its attention to intrinsic motivation's counterpart: extrinsic motivation. Given the fact that life cannot realistically be lived exclusively from an intrinsically motivated point of view, Deci and Ryan explored how, why, and under what circumstances human behavior is extrinsically motivated. For example, they sought to determine what accounts for a behavior we might willingly engage in but is not necessarily something that we find enjoyable or rewarding. Such behaviors might include doing chores, going to work, or even stopping ourselves from doing something we know we would find enjoyable (e.g., stopping ourselves from overeating, going home early from an enjoyable party).

Theories of Identity Development

A significant construct involved in this mini-theory is *internalization*, which Deci and Ryan characterize as an active rather than passive process. Internalization involves adopting as one's own the rules, expectations, beliefs, and so on that others (e.g., parental figures) have indicated are important. Internalization is thought to have occurred when the individual enacts these things without having been told to do so or out of concern that someone may be watching them. For example, if one's parental figures have raised their child in a particular religious tradition, they likely expect that child to adhere to the tenets of that faith and regularly engage in related practices. Internalization will have occurred when the child thinks and acts in a way that reflects this religion even when "no one is looking." That is, their parental figures (or anyone else) do not have to remind or cajole them to say their prayers or go to church/temple/synagogue; they simply do so on their own.

Ryan and Deci suggested that the psychological needs for competence and relatedness (discussed in more detail in the section on basic psychological needs theory) are paramount for explaining why extrinsically rewarded behavior and ideals are internalized. Rather than the conventional understanding of motivation that we are either intrinsically or extrinsically motivated, they suggested a continuum with six points that ranged from what they called "impersonal" control, which involves a lack of any motivation and no regulation, to "internal" control, which involves full intrinsic motivation and intrinsic regulation. The four points in between represent various degrees of external or internal control: external regulation, introjected regulation, identified regulation, and integrated regulation, all of which involve some measure of extrinsic motivation.

Causality Orientations Theory

The third mini-theory, causality orientations theory, is essentially a way of describing what type of person someone may be with respect to how they interact with their environment and how they understand why they do what they do. Deci and Ryan identified three styles under this mini-theory: autonomy orientation, controlled orientation, and impersonal orientation.

Autonomy orientation suggests that when an individual with this orientation interacts with their environment, they do so with curiosity. They see whatever exists in their environment as a source of information while also paying attention to what their inner experiences are as they interact with their environment. While such individuals tend to have a high degree of intrinsic motivation, they are also extrinsically motivated. However, when influenced by external forces, they still act based on their own values and the degree to which what they are doing is congruent with who they are. They are, therefore, not likely to be unduly influenced by others to do things that do not fit with their own values and beliefs. Ryan and Deci noted that this orientation is associated with greater overall well-being compared to the other two orientations.

Someone with the *controlled orientation* style processes their environment in terms of consequences and interpersonal pressure, rather than viewing their environment as a source of information they can analyze and digest based on who they truly are. That is, they determine what to do or even how they should think or feel based on what their environment is telling them they should do. Someone with this style often leaves behind their own interests and values in favor of what they are "supposed" to do according to others. It is common for someone with this orientation style to be overly concerned with what other people think.

The third style, *impersonal orientation*, is characterized by a lack of motivation or intention behind their behavior, and the person does not see that what they do has any impact on their environment. When their behavior seems like it may have had an impact or resulted in change to their environment, they attribute this to other factors beyond their control (e.g., luck, a higher power, someone else's decisions). Given this perceived complete lack of influence, individuals with the impersonal orientation style tend to be highly anxious, see themselves as incompetent, and are prone to "give up" because they perceive whatever they do does not matter. Whatever behaviors such an individual engages in will be done without passion, urgency, or even an understanding of why they are engaging in them in the first place. This orientation is believed to be the least healthy of the three orientations.

Basic Psychological Needs Theory

Developed somewhat later than the first three mini-theories, the basic psychological needs theory encompasses the three basic psychological needs for autonomy (self-governance), competence (the ability to make desired changes to one's self and one's environment), and relatedness (meaningful connections with others), each of which are theorized to lay the groundwork for intrinsic motivation. Ryan and Deci contend, via their summary of the research on these components, that these three needs help facilitate intrinsic motivation, and when these three needs are met, they are also consistently associated with overall well-being. It is in the context of these three psychological needs that Ryan and Deci identified the concept of autonomy support.

Autonomy support refers to an environment that supports the autonomy of the individual. This usually means the important people within an individual's life help to facilitate this type of environment. When this occurs, Ryan and Deci state that those in an autonomy supporting role "are responsive to the perspective and important issues faced by the individuals. . . . this will in turn facilitate satisfaction of multiple needs." In essence, those who support

Theories of Identity Development

someone else's autonomy are able to see things from that person's perspective rather than merely their own.

What Ryan and Deci contend, unique to this mini-theory in comparison to other needs-based theories, is that someone does not have to explicitly value autonomy, competence and relatedness for them to experience the ill effects of having those needs unmet or, by contrast, the wellness-facilitating effects when those needs are met. In short, we must have these three basic needs met for optimal well-being whether we personally think they are important or not. Additionally, Ryan and Deci assert that although all three needs must be met for people to have a sense of vitality and overall life satisfaction, the three needs are interdependent. That is, if your need for autonomy is met, it is also highly likely that your needs for relatedness and competence are also met.

Goal Contents Theory

Goal contents theory, the fifth of the six mini-theories that underlie self-determination theory, focuses on what people choose to pursue in their lives. Ryan and Deci state that the organismic integration theory (described previously) answers the question, Why do we do what we do?, whereas goal contents theory answers the questions, To what end is our behavior directed? "What goal are we trying to achieve?" Generally, goals, like motivation, can be categorized extrinsically or intrinsically. However, like motivation, it is not quite that simple. Extrinsic goals have historically been associated with a lower level of well-being compared to intrinsic goals. That is, extrinsic goals, which are designed to pursue some kind of extrinsic reward, such as money or notoriety, do not leave us feeling completely satisfied. However, intrinsic goals, which are fueled from within, such as the pursuit of growth, service, and meaningful relationships, are linked to overall well-being and greater life satisfaction.

Self-determination theory suggests that the explanation for these consistent findings has to do with the degree to which goals contribute to our basic psychological needs for autonomy, competence, and relatedness. When one pursues an extrinsically oriented goal, such as making as much money as possible, one must do what is expected of them by society and others to make that kind of money (lower autonomy). They may have to ignore or relinquish important relationships to pursue this goal (lower relatedness), and they may, for any number of reasons, not attain the type of wealth desired (lower competence). By contrast, if one chooses to purse an intrinsically rewarding goal, such as learning a new language, not because one has to but because one wants to, they would be pursuing this on their own terms and at their own pace (higher autonomy), they will be inclined to seek out others pursuing a similar goal (higher relatedness), and they will likely keep at the task and develop a new level of proficiency as a result of their efforts (higher competence).

Relationships Motivation Theory

The final mini-theory underlying self-determination theory is the relationships motivation theory, which was the most recently developed of the six mini-theories. As already noted, Ryan and Deci identified relatedness as one of three basic psychological needs of human beings. The relationships motivation theory suggests that the need for connection to others is intrinsic, and thus we are inherently motivated to try to connect with others in a meaningful way. Though the need for autonomy and the need for relatedness may seem to be diametrically opposed, Ryan and Deci contend that the fulfillment of one need is inextricably linked to the fulfillment of the other. That is, one cannot have one's need for meaningful interpersonal relationships met until and unless they also experience "autonomous motivation" in those relationships. This means that the person genuinely wants to be in the relationship; they do not feel in anyway obligated or coerced to do so (high autonomy).

Moreover, relationships that can be considered high quality and highly satisfying occur when all three of one's basic psychological needs are met within the relationship itself. We are not left feeling helpless and hopeless within the relationship, nor are we left feeling coerced or otherwise manipulated. Rather, relationships that meet the relatedness need allow us to feel a sense of efficacy and competence, and we are able to maintain our sense of individuality and autonomy despite being committed to being in a relationship with another person.

Self-determination theory is a comprehensive theory that was in its infancy in the mid-1980s. By 2017, this theory had been expanded to include six mini-theories that help to explain the importance of self-determination and what self-determination truly looks like. This theory has garnered significant attention from numerous researchers who have helped to elucidate and support various aspect of the theory. Moreover, these findings help to explain the importance of being self-determined as we seek to craft highly satisfying and psychologically healthy lives that reflect our true needs and desires, thereby reflecting who we truly are.

The theories included in this chapter represent a subset of the myriad theories about how and why we develop into and become the people we are. Each theory offers a unique perspective, and taken altogether, they provide a more complete understanding of what factors and experiences influence us, for better or for worse, as we navigate our lives and determine which choices and paths are the best fit for who we are.

PART 2

For Better or for Worse: The Factors That Affect Identity

Part 2 of this book examines some of the major factors that affect our identity. We initially take a look at the factors that affect our identity throughout our lives. While some things are important regardless of the stage of one's life (e.g., relationships), other factors are more likely to affect us during specific stages of our lives (e.g., increase or decline in physical abilities). We then explore the degree to which we may desire or feel pressured to fit in or to express our individuality, regardless of what others think. This will be examined at the individual as well as cultural levels. The remaining two chapters in part 2 examine, respectively, what a well-developed identity looks like along with how that may benefit you and what a poorly developed identity looks like and how that might negatively impact you.

CHAPTER FOUR

Biopsychosocial Factors across the Life Span

Although adolescence is the prime time during which a great deal of exploration and commitment to one's identity takes place, the reality is that the childhood years lay important pieces of the foundation for later identity development. Moreover, we do not stop developing our identity once we leave adolescence. Erik Erikson (see chapter 3) suggested that we encounter a significant identity crisis during adolescence and continue to experience identity-related crises throughout adulthood. What this means, of course, is that our identities are not fixed at birth, nor do we have the finalized version of who we are by the time we reach adulthood. Biopsychosocial changes in our lives include changes to our bodies as we age, to our occupations as we advance in our careers and retire, to our relationships as our children leave home or important loved ones move away or die, to our perceptions of these experiences, and to our ability to accept reaching the end of our lives. All of these changes continue to shape who we are and what is important to us.

The biopsychosocial perspective is an approach that states we cannot fully understand someone or their experiences unless we look at the whole person, which means we attempt to understand who they are biologically, psychologically, and socioculturally. Biological understanding involves respecting the fact that how our bodies function matters and ultimately impacts our experiences of ourselves and the world around us. Biology, in this context, also includes one's genetics, which, of course, we inherit from our biological relatives. Psychological understanding represents how well we understand the inner world of the individual. Do we understand what they are thinking, how they are feeling, and what memories they have? Finally, having a sociocultural understanding of an individual involves understanding the impact one's relationships as well as one's culture and the larger society have on an individual. The following sections will highlight some of the important biopsychosocial issues we face at various stages in our lives that influence identity development.

Identity Formation in Childhood

Childhood begins in infancy, of course, and ends prior to entering puberty. As previously noted in this and other chapters, a great deal of identity formation occurs during adolescence. However, it is a mistake to think that our childhood experiences have no impact on our perception of ourselves and the decisions we make later in life that ultimately affect what comprises our identity and how we feel about who we have become.

Changes to Our Bodies that Can Impact Identity

Although most of us do not have memories of learning to grasp things with our hands, learning to crawl, learning to walk and then run, or learning how to control our bodies during toilet training, we go through rapid physical development when we are very young. Our brain (the physical organ contained within one's skull, not to be confused with the mind) begins its development while still in utero and undergoes rapid development following birth as we are exposed to an enormous amount of stimuli, all of which the brain has to organize and interpret. As we begin to develop self-awareness (see the following section for more information), we become more acutely aware of what our bodies are capable of. In addition, as we develop a greater understanding of those in our lives (e.g., family, friends), we become more aware of how our bodies are the same as or different from other people. All of this impacts how we see ourselves and how we construct our identity.

Being born male or female is beyond one's control, as is the experience of whether or not the physical body we have matches with how our brain organizes our thoughts and feelings about ourselves and the world around us. This has a direct impact on gender identity and, for some, their sexual identity (see chapter 2 for more information on these and other types of identity). Someone who is born able-bodied will not think twice about their normal physical functioning, but they may develop an awareness of the ways in which their able body out- or underperforms those who are similar to them. By contrast, someone who is born with a physical, cognitive, or emotional disability may not be aware that they are different until they are told that they are or until they notice that their body or brain does not work the same as someone who is able-bodied or differently abled. This experience may contribute to their disability identity.

Biopsychosocial Factors across the Life Span

Suffice it to say, who we are physically, both in obvious and less than obvious ways, contributes to how we see ourselves individually, how we see ourselves in comparison to others, and how we view our ability to navigate the world around us. Thus, our biology and our genetics interact with both the psychological (how we perceive and feel about ourselves) and the social (the impact of our relationships, including the impact of the culture and society at large) aspects of who we are—all of which influence our identity.

How We See Ourselves and Others during Childhood

One of the first tasks of identity development in our lives is recognizing that each human being is distinct and separate from one another. Although it may seem strange to think it is possible to not have known that you were separate and distinct from your parental figures, some theorists in psychology have indicated that as an infant, you did not know there was a boundary between you and your primary parental figure. That person fed you, bathed you, dressed you, and comforted you. As infants, our bodies and minds are only focused on getting our needs met. Most parental figures do this well (though not perfectly) and thus respond to our needs as quickly as possible, which contributes to the notion that you and that person are one and the same. It is not until our brains begin to develop more fully and we have more and more experiences with our surroundings, including how those experiences affect us, that we begin to recognize the separation that exists between us both physically and psychologically. We also begin to develop a greater awareness of how the objects in our world exist.

Some readers may be familiar with the concept of *object permanence*, associated with Jean Piaget's theory of cognitive development, which is a developmental task of infancy. In this case, an object is anything or anyone that you relate to in some way. We usually think of objects as things rather than people, but in the field of psychology, the term *object* refers to whatever or whomever we have contact with. Object permanence is something that young children develop over time. Before mastering object permanence, very young children believe that if they cannot see an object (i.e., a thing or a person), that object does not exist. This is why a young child will cry when a parental figure leaves the room, sometimes inconsolably, until the parental figure returns. To the child's very young mind, the fact that the child can no longer see their parental figure means that they no longer exist. Because infants and very young children are completely dependent on their primary caretakers for everything, the vanishing of their parental figure is catastrophic.

As a child approaches the age of two, the brain has undergone significant development, and the child can understand more of themselves, those around them, and their environment in general. Because of these changes in the brain, which are facilitated by the child's experiences, the child will begin to look for an object that was previously visible but that they now cannot see. Around this age, children who have not yet fully developed object permanence love the game of peekaboo. This is because you, the object, appear and reappear seemingly by magic. They are not distressed by this when they enjoy the game. They have not yet developed object permanence, but at a primitive level, they understand, tentatively, that you will reappear. When the child looks for you, even if they do not find you right away, the fact that they are looking for you means their brain finally understands that just because an object is no longer visible does not mean that it no longer exists; therefore, the child has graduated to understanding object permanence.

Developing object permanence is a critical developmental milestone. Knowing that something you can no longer see still exists allows children to eventually develop abstract reasoning, but it is also an indicator that the child is developing object representations that simply refer to how, in our minds, we represent or think of an object. Very early on, our representations of ourselves and our parental figures are merged. That is, when we think of ourselves and we think of our primary parental figure (i.e., usually the mother figure), the representations of self and other are the same. So, if we recognize that our mother figure is sad, we also feel sad. If they are happy, we are also happy. It is around age six or seven months that we are able to recognize that we are separate from our primary parental figure. This is good for overall development and the development of one's identity, but this usually means we will struggle with separation anxiety when our parental figures leave us. It takes time for us to trust that when they leave, they will, in fact, return. This occurs around age two, when object permanence should be fully or nearly fully developed.

Concurrent with this type of development, infants begin to recognize that the things they do have consequences. We can cry, and that results in someone coming to try to "fix it." We can reach for things, grasp them, and pull them toward us. We can pull the cat's tail, and it will hiss or swipe at us with its paw. All of these things are important parts of our developmental process and help us learn that there is cause and effect between what we do and what happens next. This means we are beginning to recognize that *I* did that rather than some external force. Recognizing that there is *me* and *not me* is an important step toward establishing a unique identity.

It is also around age two that children can recognize themselves in a mirror. If you hold a much younger child and stand in front of a mirror, there is a good chance the child will look at the mirror and then look behind them to see where the other child is, not having yet developed the ability to recognize their own reflection. This is not unlike when a cat or dog sees themselves in a mirror and then hisses or growls at the "other" cat or dog that is in the room with them. Thus, when a child is able to recognize that a reflection in a mirror is actually an image of themselves, they take another step toward laying a foundation for identity development. They now can see what they look

Biopsychosocial Factors across the Life Span 65

like and will learn that each of us looks different from one another; we are all different and unique.

Learning, Play, and Language Development

According to Jean Piaget, the first stage of cognitive development is the *sensorimotor stage of development*. This stage lasts from birth until approximately age two. Because the brain and body are underdeveloped, there are only very basic things we can do when we are a few weeks or months old. Brand-new babies eat, cry, and coo, and their bodies engage in automatic functions. They cannot do much else. They can, of course, move their limbs, but much of this early movement is not intentional movement. By around age two months, infants begin to hold their heads up, but they still need support. They may also begin to push themselves up when they are laying on their stomachs. It is not until four months of age that babies can hold their head up without support, roll from their stomach to their back, push up on all fours, and so on. From there, they start sitting up, standing while hanging onto something, rocking back and forth on all fours, and eventually crawling, walking, and then running.

Similarly, babies' language development starts slow and then explodes once they master some basics. Prior to the age of about three months, any noises an infant makes are likely random spontaneous noises that are not made on purpose. As they approach age three months, they may start making a variety of sounds or facial expressions, such as smiling, that they associate with specific people or things (e.g., cooing when a parental figure talks to them). At this time, babies also develop distinct cries for what they want or need. By six months of age, babies begin babbling and may accidentally stumble on something that sounds like a word, such as "da." Initially, infants are simply vocalizing and experimenting and do not realize the significance of the sounds until parental figures make a big deal out of a particular vocalization, such as "da." By the end of their first year, most children can say a few words (e.g., mama, dada, no, uh-oh) and may understand more basic instructions (e.g., come here) or recognize the names for objects (both things and people). By eighteen months a child's vocabulary has expanded to approximately ten words, and by the end of their second year, they know five times that many words and can ask simple questions and follow basic instructions.

During the process of language development, children initially struggle to differentiate between *mama* and *dada*. A child is likely to say "dada" first because that is an easier sound to make, but the child may call everyone and everything dada until they learn that dada only applies to one person. As they are learning this, they are also learning words such as "I" or "me" and "you." When they are able to use these pronouns reasonably accurately, they are further developing their sense of self. When a child declares that something is "mine," they are communicating (without fully realizing it) that they understand this thing is *mine*, which also means it is *not yours*, further reinforcing the difference between *me* and *not me*.

Similarly, by around age three, children may start to display complex emotions such as shame, guilt, or pride. For example, a child may exclaim, "I did it!" when they throw or catch a ball, thereby displaying pride, or they show shame by hiding in their room after they knocked something over and broke it. A child much younger than this will not likely display these types of emotions. The display of more complex emotions is a further indicator of self-development, as showing these kinds of emotions suggests they are developing awareness of who they are and what they do; they are displaying self-consciousness, which is another way of saying that the child is becoming self-aware.

Another important self-related milestone actually involves a greater recognition of and appreciation for other people and their experiences. During the toddler years (until approximately age three) and into early childhood (prior to age six or seven), we struggle to understand other people's experiences. Jean Piaget referred to this as being "egocentric." We usually think of egocentrism in terms of an adolescent or adult thinking that the only things that matter are themselves and their own experiences. Although the definition of *childhood egocentrism* is technically quite similar, the difference is that a child has not yet developed the capacity to understand things from another person's perspective, whereas an adolescent or adult should be able to do this. In many ways, egocentrism is about a lack of empathy or the inability to understand at a deep emotional level what someone else is experiencing. A young child literally cannot do this. Their brain has to be sufficiently developed to process this type of complex interpersonal understanding. Until that time, the child assumes that whatever they are thinking or feeling is exactly the same as what other people are thinking and feeling. This is why a young child will not be able to comprehend that another child is not having fun when they change the rules of a game so they always win.

At around the age of six, we should have developed the capacity to notice and understand that someone else has a different experience than we do. We simultaneously realize that what that other person is experiencing may or may not be the same thing we are experiencing. This continues to lay a foundation for further understanding of who we are, as we start to realize that *I* may have a very different reaction to something than *you*, which means in yet another way that *I* am different than *you*.

Memories and the Self-Reference Effect

One of the reasons most of us do not have many memories of childhood prior to the age of three or four has to do with what is called the *self-reference effect*. This effect refers to our capacity to remember things that we have

Biopsychosocial Factors across the Life Span   67

connected to ourselves. That is, if we do not understand how an experience relates to us, we are less likely to remember it (this holds true for adolescents and adults). We cannot do this, of course, until we recognize that there is a _me_ to which we can relate our experiences. When you share a memory, it is nearly a guarantee that you will say something like, "I remember when I did ____" or "I did not like it when ____ happened." Your memories are encoded in terms of the impact those things had on you. You may, for example, remember the death of an important family member when you were four or five years old. This is because the loss of that person was meaningful to you. He was "my grandfather" rather than some random person, and your brain had the language capacity to label what the event was and the effect it had on you.

The Impact Family Relationships Have on Identity

Peer and family relationships are critically important to myriad aspects of our lives, including identity development. These relationships can be good or bad or, more likely, a complex mixture of the two. Our family gives us an early sense of belonging because we learn that we are a part of this particular family, and it takes something extraordinary, such as marriage or the birth of a child, for others to become part of this special group. Our peers, by contrast, may or may not leave us with a sense of belonging. We may feel alienated from our peers or like we fit in no matter whom we are around. Some friendships feel more like family than our family of origin. What is more common, of course, is that we learn to develop friendships with select people from our peer group, which makes up a small subset of our peers to whom we feel connected. There may be others we mark as acquaintances and still others we do not know at all, or we may know them well enough to know whether we fit with them or whether we like them (or whether they like us). Both family relationships and friendships essentially provide feedback to us about who we are and whether or not we are likeable. In the following section, we focus on the role that family, with an emphasis on parental figures, plays in our identity development. The impact of peer relationships, though important in childhood, is explored in the section on adolescence.

Our family dynamics play a role in our identity development. _Dynamics_ refers to the ways in which members of a system (in this case the family) interact with one another. The nature of the interactions among family members affects individual growth and development as well as the growth and development of the family itself. Moreover, the nature of the dynamics between family members affects how the system or the individual may change. A divorce, for example, will have a significant impact on all involved, which, of course, results in significant change within the family. Each individual will be impacted by such an event, which may further affect how growth and development occur.

With respect to parental figures, specifically, most children want to please their parental figures and make them feel proud. This usually means we will try to do things that they expect us to do or that we think they will approve of. Although we may value their approval or perception of our choices less and less as we age from childhood into adolescence and then adulthood, our early desire to please our parental figures will continue to shape the decisions we make later on in life. One of the most important aspects of the parental figure–child relationship has to do with the nature of the psychological and emotional bond (i.e., attachment) that exists between them.

Attachment

Attachment is typically discussed in the context of the bond between a child and their primary caretaker, but we can be attached to others. The attachment literature has extensively explored the various kinds of attachment and how the nature of those attachments impacts a child and their development, including their social and emotional development. John Bowlby was among the first to identify the importance of attachment for survival. He determined that without being sufficiently attached to a primary caretaker, an infant would literally not survive.

Subsequent to Bowlby's work, developmental psychologist Mary Ainsworth developed a way to identify different types of attachment. She developed an experience she called the "strange situation," which involved a parent and child who were brought to a room with toys in it. The parent was instructed to allow the child to explore the room and its contents on their own with the parent present. After a brief period of time, a "stranger" (i.e., researcher) enters the room and talks with the parent. At some point, the parent is instructed to leave the room, without making it known to the child, and then later returns. What Ainsworth and her colleagues were interested in observing was how the child reacted when they realized the parent was gone and how they responded when the parent returned. The researchers initially identified three forms of attachment and later added a fourth: secure, anxious-avoidant, anxious-ambivalent, and disorganized. Ainsworth and her colleagues found marked differences between the attachment styles.

When the parent of a securely attached child leaves the room, the child is likely to be upset and cry and will show happiness when the parent returns. In essence, the securely attached child is not thrilled about their parent not being around, but when they are, the child trusts that their parent creates a point of safety from which the child can explore and return to as needed. The parent is able to soothe and reassure the child, allowing the child to feel comfortable exploring the room again.

The anxious-avoidant style of attachment is displayed when the child shows little emotion when the parent leaves as well as when the parent

Biopsychosocial Factors across the Life Span

returns. Ainsworth and her colleagues believed that the child's seeming indifference to the parent is a defense of sorts that hides the fact that they are quite distressed. Later studies revealed that these seemingly unflappable infants showed elevated heart rates, indicating that their bodies were processing the situation as something to be alarmed about—they just did not show it emotionally or behaviorally.

The anxious-ambivalent attachment style is demonstrated by a child who could be characterized as "clingy." These children appear distressed even before the parent leaves the room and are not easily soothed when the parent returns. Moreover, they may display overt signs of anger or resentment toward the parent or may appear to be helpless.

The final attachment style, disorganized, was added later because it became clear that not all infants appropriately fit in the first three categories. It was found that some children showed behavioral signs of stress and tension, indicating these children were not comfortable in the strange situation, even with the parent in the room, and the behavioral indicators of stress (e.g., appearing afraid, having jerky movements, behaviorally freezing) are believed to be attempts at controlling their fear, particularly when the parent leaves the room. When around the caregiver, disorganized children may run away from the parent, and not in a playful way; their behavior suggests that the child does not want to be near the parent.

How we are attached to our parental figures in our early years impacts the nature and quality of our relationships later in life and can also affect our identity development and overall well-being. Generally speaking, the more securely attached we are to our parental figures, the more likely it is we will feel comfortable exploring when we feel safe. As exploration is a critical component of adequate identity development, this is an important early skill to develop.

The experiences we have throughout childhood, biologically, psychologically, and socially, help to lay the foundation for later identity development. In the next section, the focus is on the pivotal teenage years, during which we contemplate our childhood interests in people and activities and determine what from those early experiences we wish to keep as part of who we are, what we desire to let go of, and what things we would like to keep but make some changes to. Similar to our childhood experiences, there are a multitude of biopsychosocial factors heavily weighted to our interpersonal relationships that influence this process during adolescence.

Identity Formation during Adolescence

The adolescent years are commonly characterized as "stormy" partly due to changes during puberty but also due to our development with respect to identity development and decision-making. Adolescents are often accused of having no idea about what they are doing in large part because the decisions they make are often contrary to the decisions their parental figures might make for them. As such, adolescents' decision-making abilities are often perceived as being ineffective at best and broken at worst. Recent studies examining what is going on in the brains of adolescents suggest that how adolescents behave is normal and to be expected—thus, not broken.

The Adolescent Brain

Researchers Jennifer Pfeifer and Elliot Berkman, from the University of Oregon, examined magnetic resonance imaging (MRI) scans of adolescent brains to specifically look at the activity in portions of the prefrontal cortex (the part of your brain immediately behind your forehead). The prefrontal cortex (PFC) is implicated in processing complex behaviors such as planning and decision-making, controlling emotions, and anticipating consequences, and it is instrumental in the development of individual personalities. It is among the last regions of the brain to fully develop and is often not completely developed until one's midtwenties. Knowing this, it can be tempting to assume that adolescents, far from their midtwenties, are impaired when it comes to the functions associated with this part of the brain.

Pfeifer and Berkman, however, concluded that there is more going on in the PFC than previously believed. They suggested that the activity in this region of an adolescent's brain indicates they are able to understand the value of the decisions they make in their current context as well as subsequent choices, which is an important and pivotal process in identity development during the adolescent years. Their findings suggest that adolescents are more thoughtful than typically acknowledged, and these researchers characterized what they saw in terms of adolescent brain activity as a "value-based decision-making process" that focuses on the value of things, people, and experiences. In the sections that follow, we will examine how these value-based decisions are made in terms of an adolescent's exploration and experimentation as well as important relationships that can influence how we explore options related to identity formation.

Exploration and Commitment in Adolescence

According to Erik Erikson and others, the adolescent years are the prime time for exploring who we are and who we are not. In our teenage years, we experiment with what clothes we wear, what music we listen to, how to style our hair, and what kind of person we want as a friend or as a dating partner, and we begin to more seriously think about who we want to be when we fully "grow up." Erikson believed that it is important for us to have a

Biopsychosocial Factors across the Life Span

reasonably good idea of who we are by the end of our adolescent years and moving into our adulthood years (see chapter 3 for more information). However, he also noted that understanding one's identity was something that we continue to grapple with throughout adulthood, but it is our understanding of our identity by the end of adolescence that creates the foundation for continuing to develop and understand ourselves for years to come.

When we establish our identity, we incorporate what we already know about ourselves through our experiences during childhood into what we learn about ourselves as we begin a new developmental chapter in our lives (i.e., adolescence), not only socially but also cognitively and physically. A great deal of activity in the brain occurs during adolescence. New neural connections (i.e., connections between neurons that form neural pathways en masse) are formed, and some established connections disintegrate. These changes help to explain the confusion, lack of empathy, and awkwardness that is often seen among teenagers. Moreover, a milestone that demarcates the change from childhood to adolescence is puberty, during which our bodies are flooded with hormones at levels not previously experienced. This, of course, is part of what produces the physical changes that evolve a child's body into that of an adult. This unseen activity within the body and brain can make things quite confusing for someone trying to find their place in the world. While we are weathering this particular developmental storm, we are also continuing to form our identity.

When sifting through the experiences we have had prior to adolescence, we may reject some things we found important in childhood simply because we have outgrown them or are no longer interested in them. We can also carry with us preferences and interests that are still important to us. As children, we also learn a good deal about what skills we have and what deficits we may have. As adolescents, those skills continue to be tested, and what may have been a challenge for us as children may come easy as an adolescent, or vice versa. Regardless of what is kept and what is pruned, ideally, we emerge from adolescence with a coherent sense of identity that involves incorporating myriad disparate facets of our identity into a coherent sense of who we are. Despite potentially radical shifts in our physique, preferences, and skills and abilities, we are able to recognize ourselves and understand how we got to where we currently are. In short, when we look back on our childhood years, we do not tend to *not* recognize ourselves. We may believe we are very different now compared to our eight-year-old self, but we still recognize that younger person as an early version of who we are now. An analogy used by James Masterson to help explain this is the kaleidoscope.

A good description of a *kaleidoscope* comes from Merriam-Webster's online dictionary, which states that a kaleidoscope is "an instrument containing loose bits of colored material (such as glass or plastic) between two flat plates and two plane mirrors so placed that changes of position of the bits of material are reflected in an endless variety of patterns." If you have never looked through a kaleidoscope, there are YouTube videos that show what one looks like. The colored pieces, if viewed outside of the kaleidoscope, do not look like much and may not appear as if they go together in any meaningful way. But when viewed through the kaleidoscope, they yield a complex, coherent image that can change depending on how one looks at it.

The kaleidoscope analogy as it applies to identity is that the myriad bits of colored plastic of the kaleidoscope are like the myriad facets of who we are. If you do not view them in the context of who someone is as a whole, the pieces do not make much sense. But when understood in the context of an ever-changing, evolving identity, these apparently disparate pieces of ourselves come together to form a complex but coherent whole. Thus, as you turn a kaleidoscope, the image changes. However, there is always order to the image, and it is always the same bits and pieces forming the intricate image you see. It is the same for a coherent identity.

As you consider various points in your life (each point representing a turn of the kaleidoscope), you can see how it all fits together and makes sense in terms of who you are. You can essentially imagine a much different time in your life (several turns of the kaleidoscope) that also reveals an ordered pattern, but it is one that looks different compared to where you are right now. The same pieces are arranged or collected differently, but you still recognize them as being pieces of you rather than random images or memories that you cannot explain or make sense of. This is what it means to have a coherent sense of identity.

Someone without a coherent sense of identity or who is in a state of identity confusion, to use Erik Erikson's terminology, does not have this sense of integration and coherence. They are likely to look at various points in their life and not see order or patterns, or they may not recognize themselves in their memories. This is not to suggest that such a person literally does not recognize themselves, rather that they do not know how that point in their life connects to or fits with where they are now. They are essentially looking at all the bits and pieces of themselves outside of their kaleidoscope, which means there is no discernable pattern or order to the pieces.

To expand on Erikson's understanding of how a coherent sense of identity is formed (or not), James Marcia suggested that we need to also consider the degree of exploration someone has gone through and the degree of commitment they have to various aspects of their identity (see chapter 3 for further information). Those who have a well-developed identity have reasonably explored their options; they have experimented with the types of things adolescents experiment with to figure out what works for them and what fits with who they believe themselves to be. Without this type of exploration, we are inclined to simply adopt the interests, values, and beliefs of our parental figures or our friends without considering whether those things truly work

Biopsychosocial Factors across the Life Span 73

for us. Exploration requires actively questioning and contemplating what facets we might want to include in our identity and which ones we want to leave behind.

In addition to exploration, Marcia noted that we also need to commit to various aspects of who we are or who we are becoming. We make decisions or choices about the facets we want to include in our identity and then take action to implement them. For example, we may question the religious teachings with which we were raised (which also usually means these are our parental figures' beliefs) and conclude that we believe most of what we were taught but not all of it. To demonstrate commitment to this part of our identity, we might find a congregation or other type of group that shares similar beliefs as our own.

At the end of adolescence, those who emerge with a well-developed sense of identity have also developed a sense of fidelity (see chapter 3, "Psychosocial Development: Erick Erikson," for more information), which refers to being faithful to one's identity. That is, we display fidelity when we defend whatever it is we profess to value and believe in. If questioned, we know what our beliefs or opinions are about most things, and we are able to express them without apology or equivocation. By contrast, without a sense of fidelity, we are left with what Erikson called "role repudiation," which refers to a person's inability to integrate the various and disparate aspects of their identity into a coherent whole (the kaleidoscope represents the coherent whole). We are left with a fragmented identity without a clear path behind us and cannot see clearly where we are headed.

Subsequent theorists and researchers noted that Marcia's additions of exploration and commitment to Erikson's theory are important because these concepts allowed for the recognition that there are more options in identity development than just the dichotomy of identity or identity confusion. However, it has also been noted that the constructs of exploration and commitment in and of themselves do not fully capture the degree to which or the intensity with which people might engage in exploration and commitment. One group of researchers led by Elisabetta Crocetti proposed what they referred to as a *three-factor identity model.* They noted that their model helped to further explain how our identities might change overtime (not unlike turning a kaleidoscope). The three components of their model are commitment, in-depth exploration, and reconsideration of commitment.

Elisabetta Crocetti and colleagues suggested that when we reach adolescence, we have some ideas about what is important to us and at least a tentative commitment to those things, but we are also able to evaluate the degree to which our childhood-based commitments remain relevant to us. They further noted that there are two cycles to the identity process. Cycle one represents identity formation through vacillation between commitment and reconsideration of commitment. Cycle two represents identity maintenance involving the interaction between commitment and in-depth exploration. In-depth exploration can, of course, cause us to question some aspects of our identity we thought were a good fit for us. We may realize that some aspects of our identity do not fit well with our actual skills, abilities, and preferences. This process can redirect us to cycle one, the identity formation cycle, in which we reconsider our degree of commitment to various aspects of ourselves. It is, of course, possible for us to move back and forth between identity formation and identity maintenance as we continue to have life experiences that challenge our current understanding of who we are. This points to Erikson's acknowledgment that while a great deal of identity formation ought to take place during the adolescent years, it is, in fact, a lifelong process.

Important Relationships in Adolescence

Some of the most important relationships we will have in our lives involve those with close family members and friends. Close family relationships typically refers to our relationships with our parental figures and siblings. Of course, not all of us have siblings, and not all of us have a two-parent household. Nonetheless, relationships like these are known to impact how our identities develop and evolve. With respect to our friendships, we are usually talking about relationships with our peers. While we have influential interactions with peers well before adolescence, it is typically not until this time in our lives that peer relationships have a significant influence on identity development.

As children, we often adopt the values and customs of our parental figures. We may even elect to participate in one activity or another (e.g., sport, club, hobby) because we are encouraged to do so by our parental figures, or we may see our sibling participate in something and want to be involved too. This is not necessarily a bad thing, though we may not be selecting these activities based on our true interests and abilities. Moreover, children tend to have a fairly underdeveloped understanding of occupational choice. Nevertheless, most children declare what they want to be when they "grow up," which usually reflects the jobs or professions most salient to them: teacher, firefighter, police officer, what their parental figures do for a living, and so on. During adolescence, we have an opportunity to reflect on these childhood allegiances and make changes based on our evolving understanding of who we are, what we are truly interested in, and what we genuinely have the skills and abilities to succeed in. During adolescence, it is possible for a teen to seem to have their identity figured out only to have that same teen, sometime later, believe they really do not know who they are or what they believe in. Recent research by Wim Meeus and colleagues determined that throughout adolescence, teens may move in and out of the various identity statuses

Biopsychosocial Factors across the Life Span

proposed by Marica (see chapter 3 for more information), reflecting movement between not knowing who we are with varying degrees of concern about that to being committed to a particular identity with varying degrees of exploration.

Parental Figures

Note: The term "parental figures" is used here and throughout the book to reflect the fact that not all of us have biological or adoptive parents, but we do have important adults that serve a similar function (e.g., foster parents, grandparents).

Numerous theorists and researchers over the years have examined how parental figure–child relationships affect identity development of the child. They have also examined the type of parental figure–child dynamics that may facilitate optimal identity development. Some historically relevant theories have focused on how adolescents separate from their parental figures and develop their own sense of identity. Separation and individuation from one's parental figures is believed to be critical in becoming a fully functioning and autonomous adult and was the focus of Peter Blos in the late 1960s, who specifically explored what separation and individuation look like during one's adolescent years.

Separation and individuation refer to the process of psychologically separating from one's parental figures and developing a sense of who someone is independent of those relationships. This process, which first occurs in childhood, was initially discussed by Margaret Mahler, who suggested that children go through a series of three stages during the infant years, ending with stage 3, the separation-individuation stage, which takes place from five to twenty-four months old. Mahler conceptualized this stage as comprising two distinct tasks: the process of separation and the process of individuation. *Separation* refers to a child's growing recognition that the mother (historically viewed as the primary caretaker for children) is separate from the infant/child and therefore their own person. *Individuation* involves the child's growing awareness of their sense of self—that which makes them unique in comparison to others. Blos believed that adolescents go through a second separation-individual process, whereby adolescents often "act out" or rebel in developmentally appropriate and expected ways.

Adolescents may push back against curfews, experiment with drugs and alcohol, or go out of their way to do things their parental figures explicitly say they do not want them to do. Although these may seem like problematic behaviors, Blos suggested these behaviors are necessary for the second separation-individuation process, whereby adolescents establish more firm boundaries between themselves and their parental figures, further establishing a distinct identity. He stated that without this process, adolescents would struggle to form their own unique identity. Other theorists have examined identity development in adolescents from the perspective of attachment (discussed earlier in this chapter), and have suggested that for adolescents to successfully define their identity and become autonomous, they first need to have a secure attachment with their parental figures.

Both the separation-individuation and attachment approaches suggest a pathway to adolescent identity development as it relates to one's interactions with one's parental figures. Blos's approach suggests that the adolescent must psychologically and behaviorally push away from their parental figures to adequately establish and define their identity, whereas from Bowlby's perspective, children must have a strong emotional connection with their parental figures if they have any hope of determining who they are as autonomous human beings with values and interests of their own. Recent research has shown that identity development is facilitated by caring relationships between parental figures and the child. Moreover, the exploration and commitment to various aspects of one's identity have been linked to trust in the parental figure–child relationship. Therefore, for an adolescent to essentially detach from their parental figures so they can establish their own identity, they first have to be adequately bonded with them.

What may help establish the bond we have with our parental figures are the beliefs and values that they hold that are often reflected in our own value and belief systems. Interesting questions in this regard are, To what extent do we accurately perceive what our parental figures believe, and to what degree do we accept those beliefs? Ariel Knafo and Shalom Schwartz studied these issues by examining the various identity statuses as identified by James Marcia (see chapter 3 for more information) and determining which statuses are better at accurately perceiving what their parental figures value and which statuses are more likely to accept what their parental figures believe. They found what they expected, which was that those who are in statuses that emphasize exploration (i.e., identity achievement and moratorium) more accurately perceived their parental figures' values and beliefs. Statuses that emphasize commitment (identity achievement and foreclosure) were more likely to accept their parental figures' values and beliefs. They suggested that those who are actively exploring their own identity would more accurately identify what their parental figures' beliefs are because they are more open to the experience and are curious not only about themselves but also others' experiences. Thus, they are more apt to listen carefully to what others are doing, how they act, what they say, and so on. Those who accept their parental figures' values and beliefs may not have engaged in exploration of them; they may have simply accepted them as is without question.

An additional factor that can affect identity development is parenting style. Parenting styles are typically categorized as authoritarian, authoritative, and permissive. The authoritarian parenting style is characterized by

Biopsychosocial Factors across the Life Span

strict rules that are expected to be followed without question. There tends to be little warmth or emotional support, and parental figures using this style tend not to be responsive to what the child may need emotionally. The authoritative parenting style, by contrast, involves rules that are expected to be followed; however, there is room for discussion, and children are usually provided an age-appropriate rationale for the rules. Parental figures using this style tend to be warm and responsive to a child's emotional needs. In addition, authoritative parental figures will listen to the opinions of their children and will consider taking that into account when establishing or following through on rules. Finally, the permissive parenting style is characterized by supportive and encouraging parental figures who do not expect their children to follow particular rules (they may not have any rules), and they tend to allow, without consequence, their child's inappropriate behavior. Given the explanations for these styles, it is not hard to imagine that children are affected differently based on the style of parenting with which they are raised.

Some researchers have examined the interaction between parenting style, identity, and differentiation of self in adolescents. *Differentiation* refers to figuring out how one is different and distinct from one's family of origin (i.e., the family you grew up with). Those with a high degree of differentiation of the self are able to accept the differences that exist between people and share their own thoughts and opinions regardless of what others may think or feel. Self-differentiated individuals tend to function autonomously and take responsibility for their behavior. Although differentiation of the self can impact one's identity, they are two distinct concepts. *Identity* has to do with how we think and feel about who we are and where we belong in life. *Differentiation of self*, on the other hand, is most obvious in interpersonal relationships in which someone with a high degree of differentiation of self is able to psychologically and emotionally remain separate, rather than fused or enmeshed, with others. Murray Bowen believed that differentiation of self was intergenerationally transmitted, which means that if the parental figures have low differentiation of self, they are more likely to raise children with the same degree of differentiation. Therefore, differentiation of self is believed to be highly impacted by one's family of origin, and this may help to explain the relationship between parenting style and an adolescent's identity development.

Tija Rageliene and Viktoras Justickis suggested that an adolescent's degree of differentiation of self may help determine whether the parenting style used by their parental figures is adaptive and therefore facilitative of identity development. They found that male and female adolescents whose parental figures utilized the authoritarian parenting style were found to have lower differentiation of self, which further predicted a higher degree of identity diffusion. That is, if a teenager is raised by authoritarian parental figures, they are less like to have a differentiated self and are therefore more likely to have a diffused or incoherent identity. The authors concluded that this makes sense because parental figures who have their own low level of differentiation of self are more likely to use the authoritarian parenting style.

Because the authoritarian parenting style provides little emotional support with the expectation that all rules will be obeyed, it follows that an adolescent parented in this way does not have room to think for themselves, express how they feel, and make decisions for themselves; therefore, they will not have a high degree of differentiation. This, in turn, can make it exceptionally difficult for a teenager to freely explore aspects of their burgeoning identity, which can result in confusion about their identity as a whole. In addition, parental figures who are low in differentiation will have a diminished capacity for clearly articulating their own thoughts and feelings to others (which can account for a preference for an authoritarian parenting style: "Just do as I say."). This can subsequently make things confusing for the child during adolescence, when they are "supposed to" figure out who they are and what they believe in.

By contrast, the authoritative parenting style is believed to be ideal for facilitating adequate identity development as evidenced by the findings of Carolyn Sartor and James Youniss. These researchers found that higher degrees of parental support (indicative of the authoritative and permissive parenting styles) and higher degrees of monitoring how teens were doing in their school and social activities (indicative of the authoritarian and authoritative parenting styles), in combination, were found to be robust predictors of identity development (rather than identity confusion), thus providing evidence that the authoritative parenting style is the ideal parenting style for supporting optimal identity development.

The ability to separate and differentiate from one's family—one's parental figures in particular—is important for adequate identity development. How one's parental figures parent (i.e., their parenting style) impacts their child's ability to adequately explore who they are and what preferences they have that may or may not be the same as their parental figures. Parenting style interacts with exploration and commitment to identity, which may help to facilitate adequate identity development during childhood and into adolescence, or it may interfere with this important process.

Siblings

When it comes to the impact of family relationships on identity development, the focus has been nearly exclusively on the parental figure–child relationship, with very few researchers examining the impact of intragenerational, or sibling, relationships. One study that examined the impact of sibling

Biopsychosocial Factors across the Life Span

relationships on identity development found that both the genders of the siblings and the order in which they were born affected identity development.

Thessa Wong and colleagues noted that siblings have been found to be affected by two general processes: sibling identification and sibling differentiation. *Sibling identification* refers to the idea that we can vicariously learn from our siblings by watching and imitating what they do. Thus, what our siblings do and do not do may affect what we end up choosing to do or not do. This in turn influences our identity development. In this regard, our siblings serve as role models for what our identities can look like. *Sibling differentiation*, by contrast, refers to the efforts we exert to signal that we are different from our siblings. While we may develop and retain some things about ourselves that are the same or similar to our siblings, sibling differentiation suggests we will find ways to highlight what makes us distinctive. For example, my sibling and I may both be athletic, and I may have chosen to pursue sports in general because of my sibling (sibling identification); however, I may emphasize my interest and abilities in the specific sports in which I participate that are different from my sibling (sibling differentiation). Interestingly, birth order effects may determine whether a sibling is more likely to identify with or differentiate themselves from their sibling(s).

Research on birth order and identity development has shown that older siblings are more likely to engage in sibling differentiation, whereas younger siblings are more likely to engage in sibling identification. In short, younger siblings want to be like their older siblings, and older siblings want to be sure they can be seen as unique in comparison to their younger siblings. This differentiation effect seems to get stronger as the older sibling ages. Moreover, siblings closer in age (i.e., less than two years apart) tend to be more interested in differentiation compared to those who have more years between them in age. The implication is that siblings too closely linked by age may feel compelled to ensure others understand that they are, in fact, different from one another.

Given these findings, Wong and her colleagues expected to find in subsequent studies that the processes of sibling identification and sibling differentiation more profoundly affect the exploration part of identity development compared to the commitment part of identity formation. They suggested that both the identification and differentiation processes are primarily affected by the things we can "see" in our siblings. This means we can see what activities they participate in, whether they use drugs, and so on, which further suggests that what we observe of our siblings' behaviors will affect our own exploration, which is also visible to others. Commitment to one's identity, on the other hand, tends to be a more internal and private process. Of course, we can infer someone's degree of commitment to something based on how much time and energy they spend on a task or interest area, but the degree to which someone is committed to keeping or eliminating something from their life, specifically related to their identity, remains less obvious. Therefore, identity-related commitment would be less affected by what our siblings do and do not do.

Ultimately, the results of the study by Wong and colleagues confirmed the findings conducted by other researchers. They found that birth order affected siblings' degree of commitment and exploration such that the elder siblings (i.e., those born prior to other siblings) had greater degrees of identity commitment and identity exploration along with having developed a more mature identity. In terms of the direct impact one sibling might have on another, these researchers found that siblings do impact one another's identity development, but only in terms of sibling identification. They suggested that since much of what occurs with respect to identity development is private, it may take some time before one sibling notices the ways in which another sibling explores and commits to various aspects of their own identity. For example, from one moment to the next, changes with respect to a sibling's identity may be subtle and therefore not noticeable; however, after months or years, a sibling may be able to see the differences that have taken place over time that were not obvious from one day to the next because the changes occurred too gradually.

Wong and colleagues also found that if the siblings are the same sex, their exploration of and commitment to aspects of their own identities were more similar compared to siblings of the opposite sex. As the nature and quality of the relationships between same- and opposite-sex siblings can be quite different, it is not surprising that this would impact how each sibling's identity is influenced. Overall, these researchers concluded that siblings have a greater impact on identification processes compared to differentiation processes, and while both exploration and commitment are affected by sibling relationships, the effects are greatest for exploration.

Another study by Meike Watzlawik and Sandrine Clodius discussed the impact of sibling relationships on identity development in terms of how siblings essentially jockey for position within the family. They suggested that when siblings try to find their place within the family, not only in terms of how they fit in and are similar to their family but also in terms of how they are different from one another, they engaged in the exploration process by "trying on" various aspects of their identity. These researchers examined not only sibling relationships but also friendships and dating relationships. In terms of sibling relationships, they differentiated between different types of siblings to included monozygotic twins (i.e., identical twins), dizygotic twins (i.e., fraternal twins), and nontwin siblings. Differences between types of siblings were found in the degree of dedication each has to one another. Monozygotic twins were found to have the highest degree of dedication to one another compared to opposite-sex non-twin siblings. Thus, the more

Biopsychosocial Factors across the Life Span   81

biologically similar siblings are to one another (the most similar being identical twins and the least similar being opposite-sex non-twins), the more likely they are to have similar identities, and they will also have a greater degree of commitment to that particular relationship. However, Watzlawik and Clodius found that as all siblings aged, regardless of what type of siblings they were, their nonfamily peer relationships (i.e., friendships and dating relationships) took on a greater level of importance compared to their sibling relationships. This is believed to be due to the fact that as we age and experience more things in life, including more types of relationships, we are apt to engage in greater exploration of what types of people and relationships we want to have outside of our families.

Peers

As we grow from infancy, we become more and more aware of our environment, including the people in it. When we are younger, our parental figures tend to take a central role in our identity development compared to our peers. As we age, however, our peers supplant our parental figures and take on a more central role in influencing identity exploration and commitment to an identity.

Friendships are believed to be important for one's overall well-being and sense of belonging. Researchers have examined to what extent peer relationships, including friendships and dating relationships, influence identity development. Much of this research has involved adolescents and young or emerging adults (i.e., those between the ages of eighteen and twenty-five), as it is this time in one's life when identities are more fully explored and, ideally, established. Friends have been described by some researchers as providing the "scaffolding" for our identity exploration. A scaffold, outside of the context of the construction of a building, is a psychological structure that provides temporary support as we learn new skills, try out new abilities, and explore our preferences. Friends, who by definition are those we know, like, and feel emotionally connected to, provide us with the safety and security we need to practice and experiment with the preferences, opinions, and values we may incorporate into our identity. We may, for example, share with our friends what we truly think about an issue or what we truly value in other people. We are, in effect, trying out various forms of our identity or revealing certain parts of our identity with friends to see if these aspects of our identity are acceptable or are rejected in some way. The expression of one's self in the context of our peer relationships has been found to affect specific aspects of our identity, such as our ethnic or racial identity.

Our peers have been found to impact the degree to which our ethnic or racial identity (ERI) is central to our overall identity. Researchers out of Arizona State University led by Sara Douglass found the nature of one's same-ethnic/racial peer relationships affected how central one's own ERI was to their overall identity. When adolescents had a greater proportion of same-ethnic/racial friends, this contributed to the centrality of their own ERI. However, they determined that when adolescents had a greater proportion of same-ethnic/racial peers in general while in school, the centrality of their own ERI diminished. They noted that the intimate nature of same-ethnic/racial friendships and the more detached nature of generic same-ethnic/racial peer relationships differentially affected how important one's ERI is to their overall understanding of themselves.

Additional research in this area examined peer influence on ERI over time. Carlos Santos and colleagues concluded, as did the group led by Douglass, that school-aged peers affect an adolescent's ERI over time. For example, they found that an adolescent with an ERI that was not as central to their overall identity when compared to their friends who had an ERI that was more central to their overall identity, the adolescents with the less centralized ERI gradually established a more central ERI. They also found variations in how adolescents perceived the degree to which their ERI was viewed positively by others and how they privately viewed their own ERI based on the strength of the ERI in their peer relationships. Overall, Santos and his colleagues concluded that peers can have a significant impact on one another with respect to the degree to which one's ethnic or racial identity is of paramount importance to one's overall identity, the degree to which we view this aspect of our identity positively, and the degree to which we think others feel similarly.

Beyond our regular peer relationships and friendships, we also enter into romantic relationships with members of our peer group. Some researchers have examined the ways in which both our dating relationships and our friendships influence our identity formation. Results indicate that both friendships and dating relationships are interconnected with respect to identity. We may, for example, talk with our friends about our interactions with a romantic partner and what we personally think about those interactions. By having these discussions with friends, some of the things we value about our romantic partners may be validated. At other times, these beliefs or values may be confronted by our friends, causing us to question our dating choices. Essentially, our friends give us advice, provide feedback, make jokes with us, and may relate to our experiences, all of which influence how we construct our identity. Both our close friendships and our dating relationships provide us with a source of intimacy we may not get elsewhere.

Intimacy is often associated with sexual activity in our everyday language; however, in the context of psychology and relationships in general, *intimacy* refers to psychological and emotional intimacy. Erik Erikson defined *intimacy* as the ability to fuse one's own identity with another person's without fear of losing one's individuality that remains independent of the other

Biopsychosocial Factors across the Life Span

person. In this regard, intimacy is typically found among strong romantic relationships, but it can also be found among family members and close friendships. Interestingly, there appear to be differences between males and females in terms of how intimacy in friendships may be impacted by the identity status one is in (e.g., foreclosed, achieved; see chapter 2 for more information).

Researchers and theorists have indicated that identity and intimacy are highly linked. For example, Erikson noted that establishing one's identity is necessary to be intimate with someone else. The emotional process of attachment (the emotional bond typically formed with parental figures) has also been linked to identity development. The consensus seems to be that when one is able to establish a well-developed identity, one is more likely to be truly intimate with others and is therefore better able to enter into healthy, satisfying relationships of any kind. And, as previously discussed, being able to establish a clear sense of individuality is facilitated by the strength of one's attachment to parental figures. What seems to matter most in terms of intimacy in friendships among adolescents or emerging adults is how long the friendship has existed and an individual's identity status. When the friendship relationship was relatively short, there was less intimacy in friendships among males who were foreclosed in their identity status and for females who were identity achieved. When the friendship had existed for a long time, the highest levels of intimacy in friendships were found among males who were in the moratorium identity status and among females who were identity achieved. This has suggested to some researchers that males and females use their friendships differently in exploration and service of establishing their own identity.

The impact our peers have on our identity in general and to specific aspects of our identity, such as our ethnic or racial identity, is clear. The interactions we have within our peer relationships has led some to characterize how we go about establishing our identity during our adolescent and emerging adulthood years in terms of a "co-constructing" process. Within our various relationships, the nature of our interactions with others, our perception of these interactions, and our subsequent seeking of feedback about our interactions with others mean that these are reciprocal relationships in which both people provide feedback to one another in domains related to identity. Thus, in the context of our friendships and other important peer relationships, we help one another explore and establish our unique identities, thereby co-constructing them.

When examining all the existing literature on how peer relationships affect identity development during adolescence, one researcher, Tija Ragelienė, out of the Mykolas Romeris University in Lithuania, concluded that "good relationships" with one's peers is associated with identity development. She noted that when we feel like we have a peer group to which we belong and when the friendships we have established within our peer group are built on a foundation of mutual respect for and acceptance of the other person, identity development will be facilitated. We will feel safe and secure enough to share our true thoughts and feelings with our friends, who will provide us with genuine feedback on what we have shared. These types of relationships, she concluded, help us to feel less lonely, less competitive with our peers, more satisfied in our dating relationships, and less controlling in our relationships. These things help us to explore and eventually establish an identity that reflects our true needs and desires. This serves us well as we seek to establish satisfying relationships, careers, and our overall plans for our lives throughout adulthood.

Identity Changes in Adulthood

As has been discussed in earlier sections of this chapter and in previous chapters, our identity development does not stop after adolescence. We continue to refine and reshape our identities in the decades following adolescence and into old age. A number of biopsychosocial factors can potentially impact our view of ourselves overall and our sense of identity in particular. Those things include changes to one's body (e.g., it does not look or work like it used to), changes in one's career (e.g., laid off, promotion, retirement), and changes in relationships (e.g., death of family and friends, narrowing of connections). Some of these things can have a negative impact, while others may be beneficial for us as we age.

Things Do Not Work the Same: Physical Changes

We endure identity-related crises throughout our lives beginning in adolescence, according to Erik Erikson, and changes to our bodies as we age both in terms of how they look (e.g., gray hair, sagging skin) and how they function (e.g., decrease in stamina, problems with major systems of the body) become center stage as we grow older. This part of the normal aging process pulls our attention away from other aspects of life on which we may want to spend more time, energy, and finances. Our bodies start to age (as opposed to grow and develop) in our mid to late twenties or early thirties. It is generally not until much later that we begin to notice these changes (e.g., in middle adulthood). When we enter old age, there may be no denying that changes to our bodies interfere with what we have been used to doing, or they may keep us from being able to do these things altogether.

As we enter late adulthood, physical changes that are part of the normal aging process can include changes that are clearly visible. For example, many visible changes to the body are cosmetic and include the development of

Biopsychosocial Factors across the Life Span

wrinkles, sagging skin, the elongation of the nose and ears, and thinning and graying hair. More significant changes to the skin involve skin that has a more difficult time healing. This can lead to bruises that take a long time to dissipate or cuts and scrapes that remain as open sores due to the skin's difficulty in healing itself. We also experience decay in the sensitivity of our sensory organs, with the most common being declines in vision and hearing. Such losses can be annoying at best and potentially dangerous at worst. For example, if an aging driver does not see or hear something that will allow them to maneuver their vehicle safely, they may end up in a minor fender bender or a serious car crash.

Internal changes that may become visible include changes to one's bone density, which can affect our height, making us shorter than we once were. When loss of bone density is more severe (i.e., osteoporosis), older adults can be prone to breaking bones, and they may have difficulty standing up straight and will therefore be stooped over. When we lose bone density as we age, we also lose muscle mass, and together this can result in weight loss. However, we tend not to lose fat deposits but muscle mass. Therefore, whatever fat one may have accumulated during one's earlier adult years may be retained (e.g., around the midsection), while one's arms and legs become more thin.

With regard to internal systems, declines in cardiovascular and respiratory function can affect anyone's quality of life, but they more commonly occur the older we get. In addition, our ability to move with ease both in a coordinated and efficient manner declines with age. This may affect our quality of life as well as our safety. Muscles may ache more frequently, and pain in the joints caused by arthritis is a common consequence of an aging body. For women, the loss of reproductive capabilities in middle age signals that they can no longer bear children, and the accompanying declines in the hormone estrogen may make older adult women more susceptible to cardiovascular events such as stroke and coronary artery disease. The loss of estrogen is also important for bone remodeling (the skeleton's process of absorbing and rebuilding bone tissue); as estrogen levels decline, bone density also declines, making women more likely to develop osteoporosis compared to their male counterparts.

All the biological changes we experience as we age undoubtedly affect our overall sense of identity and in many cases may require us to jettison specific parts of our identity because they are no longer possible. For example, one type of identity that is emerging in terms of our understanding of one's overall identity is our *reproductive identity*. Aurélie Athan defined *reproductive identity* as a process in which each of us considers our potential to reproduce (e.g., are there any problems with our reproductive system, do we have someone with whom we want to procreate) and then comes to an understanding about whether we want to reproduce. Depending on the degree to which someone identifies with this particular type of identity, aging can be more or less devastating. Of course, as we age, both men and women (women earlier and more dramatically) lose their reproductive capacity, which may impact their overall identity. For some women, entering perimenopause and then menopause itself clearly signal the end of their reproductive capacity. Even women who have had biological children may experience distress related to the loss of this facet of who they are.

Biological aging impacts nearly all facets of our individual identities. If we were athletic, we will become aware, with age, that we are no longer able to be athletic in the ways we were as an adolescent or young adult. In some cases, we may have to discontinue participating in athletics altogether. In addition, we may realize we cannot process information as quickly or as efficiently as we once did, which may impact our work-related abilities. The older we get the more likely we are to lose important relationships (i.e., parents, spouse, siblings, friends) due to death or incapacity. This directly impacts various facets of our identity because it is within and from our important relationships that much of our identity is formed. Losing these relationships may contribute to someone not only feeling alone but also, in the context of identity, like they do not know who they are any longer. Of course, these and other aspects of our respective identities can be challenged or lost for nearly any reason at any point in our lives, but biological aging and all that comes with it seems to stand alone with respect to the depth and breadth of the impact it has on our sense of who we are.

Occupational Changes and Their Impact on Identity

Working in the twenty-first century has its challenges, not the least of which has to do with the number of times people may change jobs or even careers. This has led some social scientists to abandon more traditional stage-based models about career and occupational development. Daniel Levison's model, developed in the 1970s, stated that career development occurs in stages based on where one is with respect to adulthood (i.e., pre-adulthood, early adulthood, middle adult stage, late adulthood stage, late, late adult stage). In the 1950s, Donald Super's career development stages (i.e., growth, exploration, establishment, maintenance, decline) reflected what was happening in one's career. Contemporary career-based theories are more flexible and reflect the different realities of people's careers across their lifetimes. One such theory is the *kaleidoscope career model* (not to be confused with the kaleidoscope analogy offered by James Masterson discussed earlier in this chapter).

The kaleidoscope career model (KCM) was developed by Lisa Mainiero and Sherry Sullivan to help explain why so many highly educated and occupationally successful women have chosen not to pursue what men in the workforce have traditionally pursued: climbing the corporate ladder into

Biopsychosocial Factors across the Life Span

high-powered careers. This trend has been labeled the "opt-out revolution," and Mainiero and Sullivan used the analogy of the kaleidoscope to better account for how women manage their relationships at work and outside of work. They suggested that as women navigate these relationships in the context of work and family, they rearrange the pattern of their careers (like the colored pieces of glass in a kaleidoscope that shift and rearrange with each turn), which can mean traditional models of employment success do not fit for career women. There are three elements of the KCM that represent the colored glass within the toy. These facets are arranged differently in women compared to men, and therefore the patterns revealed are also different. The three aspects, or parameters, of the KCM are authenticity, balance, and challenge.

The authenticity element is the person's need to act in accordance with their true self, but acting in line with who they truly are may not align with how they have to act in their work setting. The balance element reflects the desire for having good, meaningful experiences in both work and with one's family. To attain and sustain this balance, some career paths may be abandoned in favor of others that allow individuals to strike their desired balance. Finally, the challenge element reflects an individual's need to partake in work that is personally meaningful, to develop and use one's skills and abilities, and to make progress in one's career.

The research conducted by Mainiero and Sullivan revealed two patterns that differentiated men and women: alpha kaleidoscope and beta kaleidoscope. The alpha kaleidoscope pattern is most commonly found among men and shows that in the beginning of a man's career, there is a need for a high degree of challenge, which gives way to a need for authenticity at midcareer and a strong need for balance late in one's career. The beta kaleidoscope pattern is most likely found among women and some younger men. This pattern reflects a primary need for balance, particularly in the middle of one's career. The needs for challenge and authenticity tend to vary throughout one's career path with this pattern.

Mainiero and her colleague Donald Gibson examined the various patterns that emerge among these three elements of the KCM between men and women in midlife who were unemployed or formerly employed. They found support for the general theory of the KCM in that at the start of one's career, both men and women are interested in being challenged, but as women become settled midcareer, they are more likely to prioritize balance in comparison to men. The need for authenticity was shown to markedly increase in late career for women as compared to men, whose need for authenticity seems to decline at the start of the midcareer stage. Overall, Mainiero and Gibson concluded that it is during midlife when men and women tend to diverge, and women tend to display a stronger preference for the beta kaleidoscope career pattern over the alpha kaleidoscope pattern, which sacrifices balance for challenge and authenticity. Their findings, they suggest, ought to compel human resource professionals and career counselors to ensure that advice and opportunities reflect the various career trajectories and how these trajectories may diverge based on the differing expressed needs of males and females.

Although these researchers did not look at how one's career trajectory and preferences with respect to the three facets of the KCM interact with one's identity, applying the notion of self-complexity or possible selves in this context can reveal how identity intersects here. Researchers in the 1990s (e.g., Hazel Markus, Paula Nurius, Patricia Linville) suggested that the more facets of ourselves that we have the greater the likelihood that we can handle stress and disruptions (e.g., retirement, divorce) to our identity. We can have different versions of ourselves based on which aspects of ourselves are more or less important. It is clear that men and women differ in important ways when it comes to the elements of the KCM depending on where they are on their career path. Women appear to more strongly identify with their role as parent or spouse compared to men, which is reflected in women's preference for balance. This, of course, does not mean that men do not care about nor identify with their family-related roles, but they appear to be of secondary importance compared to wanting to be challenged and authentic in their careers.

A critical and sometimes highly disruptive career change that occurs as we advance in age is retirement. Many people look forward to retirement. They say they "can't wait," and they talk about what they plan to do (or not do) when they retire. Of course, not everyone can retire when they would like to, and some cannot retire at all. This is often due to financial reasons. Regardless, retirement is a significant life event that may or may not go well for the retiree. While many look forward to their newfound freedom from having to work, the reality of what it means to be retired may not hit the retiree until they are into retirement itself. Some retirees find that their health declines too rapidly or in ways that prevent them from doing what they had postponed until retirement (e.g., travel, moving to a better climate). Some run out of money faster than they thought they would, and others may feel a profound loss of identity because they no longer work.

For those who strongly identified with their career, job, or place of employment, the loss of their employment status can be disorienting at best. Those who might not look forward to retirement likely have foreseen the difficulty they may have adjusting to a nonworking role. Therefore, they may stay working longer than the typical retiree, or if they have to retire (e.g., their employer "encourages" retirement or a decline in health forces retirement), they may take up part-time employment elsewhere or fill their time volunteering in ways that become like going to work each day. Regardless of how one thinks they might handle retirement, the reality is often different from what was anticipated—sometimes better, sometimes worse. One group of

Biopsychosocial Factors across the Life Span

researchers applied *the social identity model of identity change* to explain how retirees can come closer to guaranteeing a relatively smooth transition into retirement.

The social identity model of identity change (SIMIC), developed and refined throughout the late 2000s, suggests that having a relatively large number of social groups helps to protect individuals from the difficulty that can come from a major life transition. This model has been applied to, among other things, those who have had a stroke, those who have received a life-changing or terminal diagnosis, and those who are entering retirement. The idea behind the model, which has been supported through the research, is that the more social groups someone belongs to the more likely it is that they will have a better time adjusting to the major life change they have endured. Having a larger number of social groups provides broader social support and a secure foundation from which the individual can establish a new or shifting identity. Researchers Jolanda Jetten and Nancy Pachana noted that an identity reconstructed in the context of already established social groups following a significant change in identity (e.g., retirement) means that the newly constructed identity will not be entirely different from who the person was prior to the identity-changing event. Thus, the individual does not have to completely reinvent themselves. They simply need to make alterations.

Having a larger number of social groups prior to a life-changing event that impacts one's identity provides needed psychological and emotional support. This also provides an opportunity to expand one's social groups while the individual reconstructs their understanding of themselves. Jetten and colleagues used the analogy of standing on the shore of a large body of water to illustrate this. They stated that the shore is familiar and is literally the ground under our feet that provides stability. Leaving that which is familiar and solid underneath us can be disorienting and can give rise to significant fear. Thus, the shore, the ground we stand upon, represents one's already established social groups from the perspective of SIMIC. Leaving such groups can leave us feeling alone and afraid because we are now in unfamiliar territory. The notion, however, is that if we have multiple groups to which we belong, the loss of any one group, though not necessarily ideal, does not have quite as large an impact if one maintains membership in the other groups. In the context of retirement, the loss of one's social group of fellow employees can be very disruptive for the retiree, especially if one's work group is composed of the retiree's friends and acquaintances.

Catherine Haslam and her colleagues also examined retirement from the perspective of SIMIC and identified several lessons learned from those who effectively transitioned into retirement. Consistent with the underlying tenets of the model, those whose retirement was relatively smooth—leading to a more psychologically and emotionally satisfying process—had multiple social groups to which they belonged. This allowed them to benefit from the psychological and emotional support each group could provide while they underwent the retirement process. Staying connected with these already established groups provided the retiree with a sense of continuity. That is, while they may no longer work at all or in the way they once had, their life is not completely turned upside down. They still have many of the social connections they had prior to retirement. An additional lesson these researchers identified was that the retiree stayed connected with the groups that benefited them while also establishing new connections with other meaningful groups. Thus, the retiree was able to expand their social network to fill in the social "blanks" left open by the lost social group(s) associated with work.

Finally, the establishment of connections with new groups is beneficial when the new groups are compatible with the group memberships the retiree had before retirement. Essentially, if the new group memberships pull the retiree away from their existing group—the ones that provided support throughout the transition—then establishing new group memberships will not benefit the retiree. They may find themselves in a position of having to choose between their "old" groups, which may not completely fill their social needs given their work-related social losses, and their new groups, which are still unfamiliar and may not be as supportive as the retiree needs.

Relationship Changes Accompanying Aging

As we age, we go through myriad relationship changes. We may marry, have or adopt children, divorce and remarry, have stepchildren, and so on. Moreover, as we get closer to and enter into old age, we will lose relationships due to death. We will lose friends and may even get to the point that we do not have any friends left. We will also lose family members and may eventually have no family left. Regardless of how this plays out for each of us, the changing relationships due to changing life circumstances and death mean that our identity is affected. When our parents die, for example, we know that we are no longer the child of someone who is living. If our siblings die, we are no longer a sibling to anyone alive. Outside of the context of death events, divorce and remarriage can also radically change how we see ourselves (e.g., you become a stepparent). Thus, as we age, our connections with others change and eventually shrink. Although this may seem like a painful part of the aging process, some have suggested this is not necessarily a bad thing.

An interesting theory developed in the early 1990s by Laura Carstensen, a psychologist out of Stanford University, is called *socioemotional selectivity theory*. This theory recognizes that changes occurring during the aging process happen in large part due to an increasing awareness that the time one has left to live continues to dwindle; we becoming increasingly aware of the fact that the number of years we have remaining in our lives are far fewer than those

Biopsychosocial Factors across the Life Span

we have been alive. As our time remaining shrinks, so do our relationship connections. This, of course, can be emotionally difficult; however, Carstensen suggests that not only is this a normal part of the aging process, but it is also beneficial because we come to focus our time and energy on only those relationships that truly matter to us.

Carstensen designed a study in which she followed a couple dozen adult males and females over the course of nearly thirty-five years to track how often these men and women interacted with others, how satisfied they were with those interactions, and how emotionally close they felt in various types of relationships (e.g., family, coworkers, friendships). She found that over the years, these adults' interactions with both acquaintances and close friends diminished beginning in early adulthood. That is, these relationships did not necessarily go away, but the frequency with which these adults interacted with acquaintances and close friends became less and less over time. At the same time, she observed an increase in the frequency of interaction with one's spouse and siblings. Moreover, as these adults shifted how often they interacted with those in these various types of relationships, they also experienced an increase in emotional closeness with relatives and close friends.

As previously implied, the narrowing of interpersonal connections and how often we interact with others can be seen as a red flag or something that may signal a problem, such as social withdrawal due to depression or some other concern. However, Carstensen pointed out that this type of interpersonal pattern may signal a shift in how and with whom aging adults spend their time. She noted that we focus on things and people that are most important to us, thereby developing closer bonds with a smaller group of people, and we are also likely to view past experiences more positively than we did in our earlier years. This is referred to as the *positivity bias*.

Positivity bias is a concept that essentially refers to putting a positive spin on, or reframing, one's experiences. This means, for example, that someone may look back on a particular event or time in their life that was not enjoyable or was objectively bad for them (e.g., struggled in school, dealt with an abusive relationship, was unemployed for a while), and with emotional and temporal distance, they may reframe or reconstruct their view of the experience in a more positive way. For example, someone may look back at their poor grades in school through the lens of, "My grades helped me realize that seeking a job that required more school was not for me, and since then I've had a career in a field I really enjoy." Similarly, we may reflect more positively on bad past relationships by thinking to ourselves, "That person I dated years ago that emotionally abused me was struggling with their own significant issues, and I was able to get out of the relationship a stronger person and more clear about what I want and need in a partner."

This may sound like a way to make excuses for ourselves or another person; however, positivity bias in the context of aging suggests that as there continues to be less and less time remaining for us as we age, we may decide that it does not help us at all to remain focused on the negative; instead, we shift to focusing on the positive aspects of our lives, including what is positive about previously negatively viewed experiences. This shift in bias toward the positive may reflect changes in the brain associated with aging (i.e., aging-related declines in the brain), or it may be associated with a clear, coherent desire to view things more positively on purpose rather than because our brain will no longer allow us to view things negatively.

A study conducted by Sandrine Kalenzaga and colleagues examined brain activity in the context of the positivity bias to determine whether this shift away from the negative and toward the positive was reflective of an intentional shift in thinking or whether it was indicative of changes in the brain that reflect age-related deterioration. Their study included dozens of cognitively healthy adults who were either young adults (ages twenty to thirty-three years old), old adults (ages sixty-five to seventy-eight years old), or very old adults (ages seventy-nine to ninety-four years old). They also included over three dozen old and very old adults (ages sixty-eight to ninety-four years old) with Alzheimer's dementia. Their results essentially provided partial support for both the *motivation* and the *degradation* theories of positivity bias. This means it is possible that the positivity bias is due to an intentional process by which some adults decide they no longer want to view their life experiences through a negative lens and shift to a more positive one (motivation theory). By contrast, for other adults, the shift to a more positive view of their life experiences may be an artifact of abnormal aging processes in the brain, which essentially means their brain may no longer allow them to see things as negatively as they previously had (degradation theory).

The biopsychosocial factors examined in this chapter highlight some of the primary relationships that impact our identity, including the important roles that parental figures and, to a lesser extent, siblings play early in our lives and the importance of peer relationships as we experience adolescence and enter into adulthood. We are also differentially affected by how our brain and body develop and age, from the beginnings of cognitive development that allow us to comprehend that there is a *me* and a *you* to the normal declines associated with adulthood that change how we see ourselves and how we interact with the world around us. While it is not possible to accurately predict for any one person precisely what their aging process will look like or how their lives will subsequently be changed, recent research shows that aging does not have to be filled with negative experiences. How we manage our connections with others, how we view past events in our lives, and perhaps, more importantly, how well we know ourselves allow us to have a sense of integrity in our later years that is associated with a greater degree of acceptance of aging and overall well-being.

CHAPTER FIVE

Fitting In versus Individualism

There are benefits and drawbacks to fitting in and, alternatively, to being unique. When we fit in, we are more likely to be accepted by others. When we behave in unique ways, we may be expressing aspects of ourselves that are not "mainstream" but authentic expressions of who we truly are. Standing out too far from the crowd may be comfortable for some people, but for many, it can make us feel alienated and ostracized from others. We may be actively rejected or ignored for being *too* different. However, fitting in can also have its drawbacks. When we fit in at the cost of being true to who we are, we risk becoming alienated from ourselves and lose sight of what is most meaningful and important to us. Fitting in for the purpose of being liked or so that we do not stand out is a form of conformity that also has its drawbacks and benefits.

Fitting In

There are myriad reasons we might desire to "fit in." When we fit in, we are motivated to behave like others in a group that we are already part of or that we may want to join. Sometimes we simply want to be part of a group because it reflects an interest area (e.g., a club) we have or a skill set we would like to try out (e.g., a sports team). Sometimes we want to fit in with a group purely so we can feel liked and included. We may not care what the group itself is about; however, we know who is in the group, and we want to associate ourselves with those people. Fitting in can certainly benefit us by giving us a sense of belonging, which is a strong human motivator; however, the act of fitting in depends on why we are doing so, and how we go about fitting in can also be psychologically harmful. The construct of conformity helps to explain why we might go along with the group which may feel good to us;

however, there is a strong downside to conforming particularly when one changes their strongly held beliefs to fit in.

Conformity: Fitting In with the Group

According to a popular introductory textbook in psychology written by David Myers and Nathan Dewall, *conformity* is defined as "adjusting our behavior or thinking to coincide with a group standard." Most of us conform in one way or another. We conform to our family's traditions and expectations. We conform to the established group norms and expectations of our athletic team, musical group, or club. Of course, one moniker used to identify conformist behavior is "peer pressure," which refers to our tendency to go along with whatever our peers do, think, and feel. Regardless of whether the pressure to conform comes from our peers, family, or within ourselves, conforming can lead us to question ourselves and what we know to be true about the world around us.

One of the most well-known experiments in the field of psychology that illustrates the powerful influence of others, and thereby illustrates the power of conformity, was conducted in the 1950s by psychologist Solomon Asch. In this relatively simple experiment, Asch showed a small group of men a "standard line" and three "comparison lines." That is exactly what it sounds like. One vertical line was shown to the group, and each person was asked which of the three vertical comparison lines was the same length as the standard line. The answer, by experimental design, was obvious. One by one, each man took turns stating their answer. Each participant gave the same accurate response. There were several rounds of this; the group was shown a different standard line and a different group of comparison lines with the same question, "Which comparison line is the same as the standard line?" The answer was always obvious, and for the first two rounds, everyone in the group agreed on the answer.

In the third round, something changed. Unbeknownst to the actual subject in the experiment, who was always one of the last in the group to give an answer, everyone else in the group was in on the experiment (i.e., confederates). The confederates were told ahead of time what answer to give in each round. In the third round, one by one, each confederate in the group gave the same obviously incorrect answer. When the actual subject of the experiment was asked for their answer, after the others had given the incorrect answer, they had to decide whether to go along with the group or to draw attention to themselves by giving a different, but correct, answer, going against the group's consensus. Although Asch's results indicated that most participants gave the correct answer anyway, he was apparently alarmed by the fact that one-third of the subjects gave an obviously wrong answer simply to go along with the group.

Fitting In versus Individualism 95

In postexperiment interviews with the subjects who appeared to go along with the majority by conforming and giving the wrong answer, Asch noted that these participants initially experienced confusion as to what was going on because they could tell the answer given by others was clearly incorrect. Some participants attempted to justify or explain to themselves what was going on. One subject reportedly stated, "Thought there was some trick to it—optical illusion." Another subject stated, "I thought [the other group members] were measuring width after a while." Solomon Asch found, when digging deeper during the postexperiment interviews, that these subjects started to doubt themselves, noting things such as believing they must be wrong because everyone else had a different answer. One subject stated, "At first I thought I had the wrong instructions, then that something was wrong with my eyes and my head." Another said, "Maybe something's the matter with me, either mentally or physically." At some point, these subjects thought that they must be wrong or that they did not fully understand what was being asked of them. They also began to assume that they must, personally, have some kind of defect that impeded their ability to process the task accurately.

Despite the fact that most of the subjects provided the correct answer in the face of a majority providing a different and incorrect answer, Asch still found that most subjects experienced some concern that they were providing a different response than the rest of the group. Thus, a group of strangers seemingly showing unanimity in their wrong responses strongly impacted the experiences of another stranger who had no idea what was going on. What would you do in a situation like this? How do you think you might respond? Now imagine that the group is made up of people you know and like. Does that matter? Does that change what you think you might do?

Over the years, researchers examining the psychology of conformity have determined that there are certain conditions in which we are more likely to conform. We tend to conform when we feel unsure of ourselves and our abilities, when the group we are a part of has at least three people in it, when everyone else in the group has the same perspective (e.g., no one disagrees), when we like the group due to its status and overall attractiveness, when we have not previously committed to a particular response or course of action (suggesting we still have an "open mind"), when we know that the others in the group will know how we respond (i.e., our behavior is not anonymous), and when we exist in a culture that values the respect of social standards. When all these conditions are met, we are more likely to conform. When fewer of these conditions are met, we are less likely to conform. Interestingly, one of the more powerful conditions for conformity, everyone else in the groups agrees, falls apart when just one other in the group disagrees, no matter the group's size. The power of conformity significantly weakens, and we are less likely to simply go along with everyone else. Similarly, if our responses are anonymous, we are also less likely to conform because we feel protected by the fact that no one will know we were the one to disagree with the group.

Two related concepts to conformity are *normative social influence* and *informational social influence*. When we want to avoid being rejected by others and want others to approve of us, we experience normative social influence. In short, we want and need to feel like we belong. Most of us do not like being the odd person out or the one that stands out from a crowed because that can draw unwanted attention and has the potential for criticism. By contrast, when we want to be correct about something, we are more likely to be swayed by informational social influence, which suggests we are strongly impacted by others' views of reality. For example, some people will only go to movies that others have highly rated on some forum or will only eat at certain restaurants if others have consistently rated that restaurant highly. My guess is that most readers have selected an experience like this based on others' opinions only to find that their own experience was much different.

Informational social influence can explain certain behaviors that we may characterize by saying the people are acting like lemmings, which are rodents that are not too bright and that have been known to throw themselves off a cliff by the hundreds when there is overcrowding. Human beings are described as lemmings when they go along with others without thinking at all or critically examining what is happening and why. Indeed, some of the subjects in Asch's experiment stated that they assumed the others in the group must have seen something they had not, so they went along with the group.

Social Norms: Doing What Is Expected

The term *social norms* refers to rules that let us know how we should behave. These rules are often unspoken, and thus we have to figure out what these rules are by observing others or through our own experiences. When someone engages in a particular behavior, there will be some type of consequence. The environment around us, which, of course, includes people, will respond positively, negatively, or in a neutral way. When we observe how the environment responds to others' behavior, we learn what behavior is acceptable, what is unacceptable, and what behavior no one seems to care about one way or another (i.e., neutral). Of course, we also learn about how a particular environment responds to behavior by engaging in a behavior ourselves and observing the response. As many readers already know, social norms are not universal. That is, knowing the social norms of one group does not mean you can seamlessly enter another group knowing what is expected by that group. In fact, we may learn the hard way that what one group accepts another may clearly reject. Undoubtedly, readers have

Fitting In versus Individualism

experienced this in the context of how we behave with our friends or how we behave with family members. For example, a joke you tell may be seen as hilarious by your friends but offensive or merely not funny by one's family. A major theory in the field of psychology that helps to explain how we learn about things like social norms by watching others is the *observational learning theory* proposed by psychologist Albert Bandura.

Research with both human beings and other mammals has demonstrated that tasks are learned more quickly when we observe others engaged in the task. Similarly, when we see others engage in kind, helpful behaviors, we are more likely to engage in those behaviors ourselves. Helping others is also referred to as *prosocial behavior.* Prosocial behavior has been demonstrated to result in others doing good for others. Findings in this area of research have shown that one of the ways we learn to engage in "good" behavior is through observing others, which is the crux of the observational learning theory. Although there is quite a bit to this theory in terms of whom we imitate, when we engage in mimicking others' behavior, and why we mimic others, observational learning simply states that we are more likely to imitate someone else's behavior when the person engaged in the behavior is important to us in some way (e.g., parental figure, friend, celebrity). So when we see others engaging in helpful or prosocial behaviors and we behave in kind (i.e., we do what they are doing), is that good for our own well-being? A group of researchers out of Germany examined just that. They wanted to know whether there were conditions in which helping others was not good for the individual person.

Cristina Oarga and her colleagues from the University of Cologne in Germany used self-determination theory (see chapter 3 for more information) and what we know from previous research on social norms to figure out the effect of how offering help to others impacts our well-being. They used data collected in twenty-three countries and examined factors such as the degree to which an individual believes in the importance of reciprocity (giving back, in kind, based on what you receive from others) and the degree to which helping others is highly valued in a person's culture. Overall, these researchers found that helping others is likely to result in an increase in well-being and life satisfaction, but they did find some exceptions to this. These exceptions illuminated conditions in which helping others is, in fact, not good for the individual.

Those who helped others who did not expect to receive anything in return (i.e., low importance of reciprocity) had higher life satisfaction compared to those with higher expectations of reciprocity (i.e., if I do something nice for you, you should do something nice for me in return). Helping behaviors were also found to be beneficial to the individual when they lived in a culture that places a high value on helping others. Therefore, those with the highest well-being and life satisfaction were found among those who did not expect to receive anything in return for their helping behavior (i.e., low reciprocity) and who live within a culture in which helping others is a highly valued social norm (i.e., the culture prizes prosocial behavior). In terms of conformity, what this means is that those who conform to their culture's social norm of helping others are likely to have a higher degree of life satisfaction because they will receive social approval. Thus, even though such an individual did not expect to receive anything in return, the fact that others within their culture praise them for their behavior reinforces the prosocial behavior, so the individual is more likely to engage in that behavior again. By contrast, however, if the individual expects reciprocity (i.e., they engage in prosocial behavior with the expectation that members of their culture will praise them), they are not likely to be as satisfied.

With respect to the United States, prosocial behavior appears to be declining. One study compared prosocial behavior in the United States to Canada and found that despite similar changes within each country over time, the United States showed a 10 percent decline in helping behavior that was not found in Canada. The researcher, Keith Hampton, from Michigan State University, reported that an increase in new technology and growing racial and ethnic diversity seemed to be contributing factors. He specifically found that in neighborhoods within the United States where there was an influx of noncitizens, there was an accompanying decline in prosocial behavior, whereas the opposite was found in Canada; as neighborhoods increased in diversity, there was also an increase in prosocial behavior. He pointed to differences in public policy between the two countries as a possible explanation. Canada's policies reportedly more clearly favor social inclusion and acceptance of diversity, including a variety of cultures, compared to the United States.

In another study, a group of researchers out of Israel examined the impact of acculturation on immigrants. Sonia Roccas, Gabriel Horenczyk, and Shalom Schwartz found that immigrants believed those in their new country expected them to "relinquish their distinctive identity" and to take on their new culture (i.e., assimilate) more so than the immigrant wanted to. This pressure to become more like those in the new culture was found to negatively impact well-being. They concluded that even immigrants who want to become more like those in their new country/culture felt pressure to divest themselves of their cultural identity, noting that these individuals likely feel connected to multiple groups at the same time (e.g., their culture of origin and the new culture they intend to a part of). However, the pressure to leave their previous culture behind gave rise to a decrease in well-being (see also "Ethnic or Racial Identity" in chapter 2). These researchers further concluded that immigrants who highly valued conformity were more likely to be less satisfied. This may seem counterintuitive; however, as previously noted, these immigrants are likely struggling to manage conforming to their original culture while simultaneously trying to also conform to their new culture,

Fitting In versus Individualism

which in many ways may be at odds with one another. The greater the perceived difference between how strongly they value acculturation or conforming with the new culture and the expectations of those native to the new culture resulted in higher degrees of dissatisfaction and lower well-being.

Carlos Torelli, of the University of Illinois, examined the impact of the independent self-concept and the interdependent self-concept on behavior. The *independent self-concept* refers to our thoughts and feelings related to our own traits, abilities, attitudes, and preferences. The independent self-concept is responsive to resisting intense social pressure and functions autonomously. The *interdependent self-concept* is our internal representation of social norms and expectations, group memberships, and other peoples' opinions. This version of the self-concept is responsive to adjusting one's self to the expectations and demands of others in the service of preserving harmony.

These two types of self-concept are not mutually exclusive, meaning that one can have both an independent self-concept and an interdependent self-concept. What Torelli was interested in was whether the concept of priming can influence which self-concept is activated and therefore predict how someone may respond in various social situations. *Priming* refers to activating mental associations we have that can predict how we might feel, what we might remember, or how we might behave, all of which often occur at an unconscious level.

An example of priming is seen in research that attempts to determine whether one's emotions can be manipulated. In this experiment, two groups of participants are put into separate rooms in front of apparently blank screens. Their mood is measured before going into the room and immediately after being in the room. Both groups are instructed to stare at the screen for several minutes. Participants universally stated that they did not see anything on the screen except for maybe some flashes of light. What they did not know, however, was that one group was shown flashes of positive images, such as flowers and puppies, and the other group was shown flashes of negative images, such as death and destruction. These images were presented so quickly that the conscious mind could not process the images, which is why all participants stated they did not see any images. The results yielded that those who were subliminally (i.e., below conscious awareness) shown the positive images were primed to have an increase in positive mood, and those shown the negative images were primed to have an increase in negative mood. This was confirmed, therefore demonstrating that the two groups' emotions were primed by the type of images to which they were exposed.

In Torelli's experiment, participants were given a story to read that either primed their independent or interdependent self-concept. After reading the story, they were then asked to complete a seemingly unrelated task by evaluating a product. They were told that they would either have to explain their judgments about the product to others or that their judgments would remain anonymous. Torelli found that when the interdependent self-concept was primed, these participants were more likely to exhibit conforming behaviors. By contrast, when a participant's independent self-concept was primed, they were more oriented to rely on their own personal beliefs, regardless of whether their evaluations would remain anonymous or have to be explained to others. Interestingly, those in the primed interdependent self-concept group who were told that their evaluations would remain anonymous behaved in ways more similar to those in the primed independent self-concept group, indicating they relied more on their own personal beliefs. Thus, the condition of anonymity seems to have a powerful effect on whether we remain true to who we are and what we truly think and believe, which suggests that we may be able to resist the pressure to conform under such circumstances.

When we experience the pressure to conform, we experience the pressure to change our attitudes and behaviors to align with whomever expects our allegiance. A group of researchers out of Oakland University examined how approval-based contingent self-esteem may be linked to conformity and whether someone's sex and the difficulty of a task might affect this. *Approval-based contingent self-esteem* refers to self-esteem that hinges on the approval of others. Those with this type of self-esteem will only have high levels of self-esteem when they perceive that others approve of who they are. Absent that approval, they will have low self-esteem. In this study, participants completed a variation of Solomon Asch's conformity study, which was described in detail at the beginning of this section. Although the findings were not as clear-cut as the authors would have liked, they concluded that self-esteem alone may not provide the best explanation for why people conform.

These researchers found that approval-based contingent self-esteem, being male or female (nonbinary options were not available), and the difficulty of the task all impact the degree to which people may conform. For example, the highest levels of conformity in men were found among those completing a moderately difficult task when the men had a high level of self-esteem stemming from approval-based contingent self-esteem. For women completing a moderately difficult task, those with the highest conformity behaviors were found among those with low self-esteem stemming from a non-approval-based contingent self-esteem. The researchers concluded that predicting conformity is a highly complex process involving myriad factors. Adding to the constellation of factors that may influence whether someone conforms, some types of mental health concerns may predispose people to be highly sensitive to the perceived opinions or attention of others. This can lead to some forms of maladaptive, and therefore potentially harmful, ways of coping.

Social anxiety, previously known as *social phobia*, a common anxiety disorder, has at its core fear of being judged by others, fear of being publicly

Fitting In versus Individualism   101

embarrassed or humiliated, fear of offending someone by accident, and fear of being the center of attention. Essentially, what drives this disorder in someone is the possibility of what others may think about them and the fear that the perception will not be favorable. This directly intersects with our social and personal identities (see chapter 2 for more information on these types of identities). Social anxiety often leads people with this disorder to avoid situations in which they may be evaluated by others or may be publicly embarrassed. If, however, they are unable to avoid such a setting, it is highly likely that they may use a substance (prescribed or otherwise) that helps them feel more relaxed and able to endure a particular social situation. Researchers from Louisiana State University examined how conformity may impact whether someone relies on consuming alcohol to cope with their social anxiety. They found that those with high levels of social anxiety were more likely to engage in drinking motivated by conformity. That is, if someone is highly socially anxious and engages in drinking, a likely explanation for that is that they want to fit in, or conform. This dovetails with the core of social anxiety, which is that they do not want to stand out in any way.

Following along with others can have benefits and drawbacks to individuals and to society at large. For example, understanding social norms and conforming to them can help members of society get along with one another more harmoniously. Individuals who conform can feel as though they have a place where they fit in and feel a sense of belonging. With respect to one's identity, conformity can have a devastating impact when one compromises one's own beliefs and values or discounts what they know to be true to go along with the group. In the next section of this chapter, we examine the constructs of individualism and collectivism, which are often described in terms of the culture a particular country or large groups of people.

Individualism and Collectivism

The concepts of individualism and collectivism are believed to be opposites. *Individualism* refers to being independent, relying on one's self, and therefore prioritizing one's self, whereas *collectivism* is defined as prioritizing the group as a whole (e.g., family, larger culture) rather than the individuals who comprise the group. With respect to these two concepts, in the context of culture, we often think of individualist cultures as being more *Western* and collectivist cultures as more *Eastern*. This usually means that when considering individual behavior, we tend to think that those from a more Western culture are engaging in specific behaviors because they want to and because it is what that particular individual thinks is best for them. In collectivist cultures, individual behaviors are understood in terms of serving the larger group or culture; therefore, an individual's behavior is solely for the benefit of the group and not the individual themselves. While this may be the case for many people within these respective cultures, it is certainly also the case that those who live in Western cultures may seek a more collectivist lifestyle and those in an Eastern culture may seek a more individualistic lifestyle.

Generally, when individualism and collectivism are studied, individuals are sampled from countries believed to represent either construct. For example, individuals from countries such as the United States, Great Britain, or France are studied as representatives of an individualist culture, and individuals from countries such as China, Japan, or Thailand are studied as representatives of a collectivist culture. When research is carried out this way, there are what can be considered predictable findings. One study comparing citizens from the United States and Great Britain (i.e., individualist countries) and citizens from China and Japan (i.e., collectivist countries) found that participants from the individualist countries were more satisfied with their lives in general and were more optimistic, more financially satisfied, and more likely to travel compared to their collectivist counterparts. Another study comparing Dutch citizens (individualist) and Surinamese and Turkish citizens (collectivist) found measurable differences in how emotions are experienced.

Participants who were classified as collectivist had emotional experiences connected to their perception of their social worth such that changes in how they perceive their social worth relative to others resulted in a predictable change in emotions. In addition, emotions experienced by those identified as collectivist were believed to reflect what was transpiring in the world external to them as opposed to emotions being tied to their inner world. For example, an expression of sadness from someone in a collectivist culture would reflect something sad that occurred in their culture or their world, and sadness expressed by someone in an individualist culture would reflect something sad that occurred to that particular individual. Another study by researchers from Australia and the United Kingdom found that an individual's preference for individualism or collectivism can be influenced by the group itself. They found that behaviors generally reflecting a collectivist position, thereby signaling that the individual values the group as a whole over the individual, were perceived more favorably by others. They further found that if the group valued diversity and uniqueness, those in the group that valued collectivism over individualism would reduce that preference in favor of the more individualist approach favored by the group. Yet another research group examined individualism and collectivism by comparing these approaches with respect to how strongly any given individual identified with their country's dominant culture.

Researchers from the Netherlands, Australia, and the United Kingdom conducted a series of studies that demonstrated that those who highly identified with their individualist culture were more individualistic themselves, whereas those who highly identified with their collectivist culture were less

Fitting In versus Individualism

individualistic. When the researchers manipulated what was considered "normal" within each type of culture, those who highly identified with their respective culture were more likely to internalize prominent group norms into their self-concept if the group itself was threatened. This means that if sharing one's wealth is highly valued, then someone who strongly identifies with the culture or group in question will state that sharing their own wealth is important to them as well. In another aspect of their study, these researchers found that conformity to a group's norms was more likely found among those who strongly identified with and therefore internalized the importance of the group. They concluded by stating that when the group values individualist behavior, those who strongly identify with the group will, ironically, show more individualist behavior as an effort to adhere to the expectations of the group.

The question of which approach is best, individualism or collectivism, can be answered in part by the research summarized in the preceding paragraphs. However, one multinational group of researchers found that how we ask questions related to overall well-being affects the results of the study. Researchers from twelve different countries noted that, historically, well-being is usually associated with individualism. They also noted that measures of well-being used in studies attempting to determine whether individualists or collectivists tend to be better off align more closely with individualism because they inquire about happiness at the level of the individual (e.g., my life is the way that I want it to be) rather than the group (e.g., happiness found within interdependent family relationships). This research group found support for the notion that when people are asked about the importance of the well-being of a group (e.g., family), there was a reduction in individualism being associated with the overall well-being of the individual. This means that how we ask questions about well-being matters. Another perspective on whether an individualist or collectivist way of living is better than the other is viewed through the lens of self-determination theory (see chapter 3 for more information).

In their 2007 publication, Marilynn Brewer and Ya-Ru Chen noted that the terms *individualism* and *collectivism* are not adequately defined, so they sought to identify a more robust and precise description. Moreover, recent research has challenged the notion that considering one's self and one's personal motives for behavior is only an individualist cultural perspective. Researchers applying the self-determination theory have come to what may be seen as a counterintuitive conclusion. Researchers from Canada and the United States sought to determine whether functioning autonomously regardless of one's culture (i.e., Eastern/collectivist or Western/individualist) affects overall well-being. The founders of self-determination theory contend that we have several fundamental needs, including the need for competence, the need for relatedness, and the need for autonomy, and when all three needs are met, individual well-being increases. If any of these needs are thwarted for any reason, overall well-being will decrease. Valery Chirkov and colleagues, which includes one of the founders of self-determination theory, Richard Ryan, noted that among these basic needs, the most controversial is the need for autonomy—the need to self-govern—in terms of whether or not this need is universal. They cite evidence showing that the need for relatedness (i.e., feeling connected to others) is universal, as is the need for competence (i.e., feeling like you can use your skills effectively).

With regard to the need for autonomy, these researchers discussed other evidence that disputes the universal nature of autonomy, contending that the need for autonomy is not evident across all cultures and can interfere with well-being within some cultures. One study concluded that those identified as autonomous were essentially equal in regard to life satisfaction compared to those who were less autonomous. Another study concluded that satisfaction is dependent on the culture in which one exists; in some cultures, yielding to external pressures produces more satisfaction compared to being more individualistic. Chirkov and her colleagues stated that all the researchers who had concluded that autonomy is not universally satisfying had not used descriptions of autonomy that align with how the term is understood in the context of self-determination theory. They noted that these researchers incorrectly asserted that autonomy occurs when there are no external factors influencing the individual, which does not accurately represent this theory's definition of autonomy.

Richard Ryan and Edward Deci, the cofounders of self-determination theory, noted that *autonomy* means that the self is what regulates behavior, and to be *fully autonomous* means one is able to make decisions for one's self free from undue influence and then stands by their actions (e.g., similar to Erik Erikson's concept of fidelity; see chapter 3). Chirkov and her colleagues explained that autonomy is seen in an individual when "behavior is experienced as willingly enacted and when [the individual] fully endorses the actions in which [the individual] is engaged and/or the values expressed by [the behaviors]." They contended that the constructs of autonomy and independence are often conflated. They stated that the opposite of autonomy is not being dependent on others but that the true opposite of autonomy is referred to as *heteronomy*, which means that one is governed or regulated by forces that exist outside of one's self. They further distinguished these terms by stating that whereas *independence* connotes not relying on others for support, *dependence* means the individual is reliant on others for support. With these definitions in place, it can be easier to wrap one's mind around the notion that it is possible for someone to be autonomously dependent. That is, we can rely on others to help us with something (dependence) because we have individually decided that is what we want or need to do (autonomy).

Fitting In versus Individualism

Thus, as we self-govern (autonomy), we can consciously make the decision that we will rely on others for resources that we do not have or need more of (e.g., time, money, emotional support).

The self-determination theory's definition of *autonomy* can also be understood in the context of conformity. As noted earlier in this chapter, *conformity* refers to aligning how we think and how we behave within a particular group's standards. We can autonomously decide to conform (e.g., we value a team or club and decide to adhere to the group's norms and expectations). Proponents of self-determination theory indicate autonomous conformity would align with overall well-being. Conforming in a heteronomous way would mean that someone conforms to a group's norms and expectations due to external pressures (e.g., joining a team or club because it looks good on a résumé or because our parents demand that we do so and we do not want to get punished).

In their efforts to further distinguish between the concepts of autonomy, individualism, and independence, Chirkov and her colleagues incorporated the concept of considering collectivism and individualism on both horizontal and vertical axes. That is, there can be horizontal individualism and vertical individualism as well as horizontal collectivism and vertical collectivism. *Horizontal individualism* refers to having the desire to be different from others while believing that all individuals are equal and should all be equally respected. By contrast, *vertical individualism* refers to being focused on status and achievement reflecting one's personal goals and therefore distinct from others. Someone who is *horizontally collectivistic* means that they see themselves as similar to others; the primary aim is to affiliate and get along with others for the good of the group. *Vertical collectivism* refers to having a preference for members of one's own group (i.e., in-group) over others not in the group (i.e., out-group) and recognizing the status and hierarchy inherent within the in-group.

Overall, Chirkov and her fellow researchers found that regardless of the culture in which someone lives and whatever cultural practices the individual values, that individual will be happiest and feel the most fulfilled when they engage in cultural practices autonomously; the individual may autonomously value and engage in behaviors that serve the good of the group, or the individual may autonomously value and engage in behaviors that serve the good of the individual. They also found that it did not matter whether a person's individualist or collectivist behaviors were horizontal or vertical in nature. What mattered was whether the individual behaved autonomously. Greater well-being was associated with all types of behavior as long as the behavior was enacted autonomously. This further means that being from a collectivist or individualist culture is not predictive of well-being. What matters is whether someone freely (i.e., autonomously) adheres to and follows their culture at large or chooses a more personal path.

This chapter examined various aspects of what happens when others are around. Do we go along with the group in order to fit in? Do we "stick to our guns" and therefore our own perspectives in the face of disagreement by others? Do we value ourselves more than others in the group or vice versa? These are complex questions that have complex answers. What seems clear, however, is that there is no single right way to live. Sometimes it is beneficial for us to conform and fit in, and other times it is not to our benefit. For some of us, living individualistically is a better fit; for others, it is living more collectivistically. However, a preference for either way of living can be influenced by others around us. At least one group of theorists and researchers concluded that as long as you feel as though you can freely make such decisions for yourself, whatever you decide will be a good fit and lead to overall satisfaction.

CHAPTER SIX

Signs and Impacts of a Well-Developed Identity

Having a well-developed identity may seem simple and straightforward enough; however, hopefully after reading some of the preceding chapters (and those that come later) in this book, you have come to understand that identity is a complex construct that is complex in its development. There are myriad factors affecting how and how well your identity develops. This process does not always go smoothly. When it does, at least relatively so, we can say one's identity is well developed and that certain consequences of having a well-developed identity can be expected. Chapter 7 will explore what can happen when one's identity is not well developed.

Self-Discrepancy and Identity

Work in the area of identity development, particularly that of Erik Erikson and James Marcia (see chapter 3 for more information), has suggested that a solid foundation to one's identity truly takes shape during one's adolescent years. Our childhood years influence the future development of our identity, and our adulthood years serve to further shape our identity. But it is our teenage years that are believed to be among the most critical.

Erikson outlined what needs to happen throughout development to have a well-developed identity and to experience overall well-being and life satisfaction. Marcia expanded on Erikson's ideas to describe more possible outcomes related to identity than Erikson originally identified. Carl Rogers (see chapter 3 for more information) discussed the importance of one's self-concept and that ensuring that who one wants to be (ideal self) is precisely who one is (self-concept) will lead to greater overall psychological well-being. The discrepancy, or incongruence, between one's ideal self and one's self-concept is what Rogers believed would lead to psychopathology—the greater the discrepancy, the greater the psychopathology. Related to this notion is E. Tory Higgins's theory on another type of discrepancy, which he called *self-discrepancy*.

Higgins presented his self-discrepancy theory in the late 1980s. He related this concept to others' examinations of the psychology of holding conflicting or incompatible beliefs (students of psychology may know the term associated with this type of incompatibility identified by Leon Festinger is *cognitive dissonance*). Self-discrepancy occurs when we have conflicting or incompatible beliefs about ourselves that subsequently leads to experiencing unpleasant emotions. Although Higgins and others had pointed to the fact that these conflicting or incompatible experiences about one's self lead to negative emotional experiences, no one had previously provided a framework or mechanism through which one can determine more precisely what types of emotions will be experienced. Higgins stated in his theory that holding conflicting and incompatible beliefs can lead to feelings such as guilt, sadness, gloominess, fear, or alarm. Moreover, he noted that while each of these emotional experiences can be considered "negative," they do not reflect the same type of emotional experience, and they can be categorized based on whether the emotion reflects something like dejection or agitation. "Dejection-related emotions" include sadness or gloominess, and "agitation-related emotions" include emotions such as guilt, fear, or alarm. Thus, one important aspect of his examination of self-discrepancy was to identify more precisely what emotional experiences this construct is linked to. However, before delving into the particulars related to these emotional states, it is first important to describe how and why self-discrepancy can occur.

Higgins theorized that self-discrepancy was not a singular idea but represented various self-states. He identified various "domains of the self" and various "standpoints on the self" and that one domain of the self accompanied by one standpoint of the self represented one self state. In terms of the standpoint of the self, Higgins theorized that there are two standpoints from which one's self can be considered: you or someone else (usually someone important to you). These standpoints combine with the three domains of the self he proposed: the actual self, the ideal self, and the ought self. The *actual self* is believed to represent the traits and attributes you or another person believe you have. The *ideal self* represents traits and attributes that you or another person would ideally like you to have. And the *ought self* represents the traits and attributes that you or another person think you ought to or should have. The distinction between the last two domains of the self (i.e., ideal self and ought self) is small, but it can be understood in terms of the difference between who *I wish I was* (ideal self) and who *I think I should be*

Signs and Impacts of a Well-Developed Identity

(ought self). The ideal self may show up in daydreams when we think about whom we would rather be, whereas the ought self can be thought of in terms of having a sense of duty or obligation to be a particular type of person whom you may or may not want to be, suggesting that your desire one way or another does not matter. You feel compelled to be that version of yourself.

The combination of the self domains and the self standpoints means, for example, that your own description of your actual self (the traits and attributes you believe you have) may be the same as or different from another's description of your actual self (the traits and attributes another believes you have). When combining the three domains and two standpoints, Higgins theorized that there are six different self-states: actual/own, actual/other, ideal/own, ideal/other, ought/own, and ought/other. Higgins further stated that the actual/own and actual/other self-states are two representations of someone's *self-concept* (see chapter 1 for more on the self-concept), and the remaining four self-states (ideal/own, ideal/other, ought/own, and ought/other) he referred to as "self-guides." He added that we do not necessarily utilize all four versions of the self-guides, and on an individual basis, we may be more motivated to seek guidance from what we should ideally have as part of our self-related traits and attributes, or what we ought to have as part of our traits and attributes. Therefore, any of these self-guides can provide a road map of sorts between where you are now with yourself (actual self) and where you are headed with yourself (who you ideally want to be or who you ought to be). Regardless of which of the different guides any one person might use, it is the discrepancy between these self-guides and one's self-concept or actual self that leads to negative emotional experiences.

When our actual self is not the same as our ideal self or our ideal self is not the same as our ought self, we experience self-discrepancy. This self-discrepancy leads to the negative emotion states such as those characterized earlier as agitation-related emotions or dejection-related emotions. Regardless of the type of emotion experienced, self-discrepancy causes a great deal of psychological discomfort, which we usually seek to resolve. Higgins stated that the two types of emotion-related clusters can be understood in the context of the type of discrepancy (i.e., which two self domains do not align) and from whose standpoint (ideal self) (i.e., you or someone else important to you). Moreover, it does not matter whether the discrepancy is actually true or imagined; what matters is that there is the perception of a discrepancy by you or someone close to you.

Research has revealed that the type of emotions experienced (i.e., agitation related or dejection related) are somewhat predictable. When one's actual self as seen from one's own perspective is different from one's ideal self as seen from one's own perspective (i.e., how you see yourself now does not match up with who you want to be), this discrepancy has been linked to dejection-related emotions such as disappointment, dissatisfaction, and frustration. When your actual self as seen from your perspective is different from your ideal self as seen from another person's perspective (i.e., how you see yourself does not match up with how someone else wants you to be), you are also more likely to feel dejection-related emotions such as shame, embarrassment, or sadness. When there is a discrepancy between your actual self from your own perspective and your ought self from another person's perspective (i.e., how you see yourself now does not match up with how someone else thinks you should be), you are more likely to experience agitation-related emotions such fear, anxiety, and resentment. Finally, when there is a discrepancy between your actual self from your perspective and your ought self from your own perspective (i.e., how you see yourself now does not match up with who you think you should be), you are also more likely to experience agitation-related emotions such as guilt, self-contempt, and uneasiness.

While it may be a simpler explanation to say that when your actual self from your own perspective does not match up with your ideal self, regardless of the standpoint (i.e., you or someone else), you will feel dejection-related emotions, careful readers will note that while this is true, the specific dejection-related emotions experienced differ depending on from whose standpoint one's ideal self is considered. Similarly, agitation-related emotions are associated with the discrepancy between your actual self and your ought self regardless of standpoint; however, careful readers will note in this context as well that the specific agitation-related emotions differ depending on from whose perspective one's ought self is considered.

When examining the differences between the emotions that depend on one's standpoint, you can see that self-discrepancy based on your own perspective results in feelings that are directed at one's self, and self-discrepancy when another person's perspective is involved results in feelings reflecting the importance of someone else's view of us (e.g., feeling fear or shame because we are not living up to how someone else sees us). For example, researchers point out that the difference between shame and guilt is that shame stems from feeling like you have disappointed others, and therefore they think less of you; guilt stems from feeling like you broke your own rules regarding how you should live your life.

Positive Identity

Positive identity has been defined by Richard Catalano and his colleagues as "the internal organization of a coherent sense of self," which ideally occurs during the period of adolescence. Elements that are believed to contribute to positive identity are self-esteem, exploration, commitment (see chapter 3 for more information James Marcia's explanation of exploration and commitment), and reducing self-discrepancy (discussed in the preceding section).

Signs and Impacts of a Well-Developed Identity 111

Self-esteem is characterized in terms of how we evaluate ourselves. Those with high levels of self-esteem evaluate themselves more positively than those with low self-esteem. Self-esteem directly impacts how our identity is formed. It also impacts how we feel and how we perform related to our identity. Many readers may know that not all self-esteem is authentic. That is, some people can appear to think well of and feel good about themselves; however, in reality, their self-esteem is fragile, and it does not take much for the person to feel badly about themselves. This usually means such a person's self-esteem is not built upon who they truly are (e.g., they believe they are better, more accomplished, have higher status, and so on than they actually do).

Authentic self-esteem, by contrast, refers to self-esteem that is based on how things really are and who the person truly is, and it is believed to have several components: feeling secure and self-assured, feeling a sense of self-worth and that one's identity is accurate (i.e., authentic), feeling like one belongs and is accepted by others, feeling a sense of purpose, and feeling a sense of competency, which can also be experienced as feeling empowered. Someone with authentic self-esteem knows who they are and what they are capable of. They know what and who is important to them, and they know they are important to others.

As described in chapter 3, exploration and commitment are aspects that help define James Marcia's identity statuses. Marcia's identity statuses are intended to provide more detail regarding Erik Erikson's stage of adolescence, during which time the establishment of and commitment to a coherent identity is the ultimate task. Completing this task requires exploration, which means that the adolescent is experimenting with preferences, roles, and ideals. This period of time can appear chaotic for this reason (one day a teenager may vow to never eat meat again and the next cannot wait to eat a slab of BBQ ribs); however, the apparent chaos serves identity development because experimentation and exploration are the only ways to know what one likes and does not like, what one believes in and does not believe in, where one's skills and abilities lie and where they do not, and so on. The depth of exploration involved in identity development ultimately leads to clarity of identity and commitment to one's identity—or, as Erikson called it, *fidelity* (i.e., faithfulness to one's beliefs).

As described earlier in this chapter, *self-discrepancy* refers to discrepancies between who you are and who you want to be or who you think you should be. It also refers to whether who you think you are is discrepant from how others want you to be or how they think you should be. Among adolescents, large self-discrepancies have been linked to both emotional and behavioral problems. The impact of self-discrepancy on how one feels and how one acts is influenced by how recently you were aware of a self-discrepancy, how often you experience self-discrepancy, and how applicable self-discrepancy is to whatever is going on around you. The applicability of self-discrepancy simply means that if you have already experienced self-discrepancy, you will not process this discrepancy in the moment unless what you are experiencing is a reminder of your self-discrepancy. For example, Higgins noted that if you experience what he called an "unambiguously positive event" (i.e., an event that is good and makes you feel good), your already existing self-discrepancy will not be activated, and therefore you will not be reminded by this particular event that you have self-discrepancy.

Being True to Who You Are and Its Benefits

Being true to who you are is a simple notion in theory, but in reality, it is a highly complex idea. Involved in this notion are the questions, What does being true to who you are "look like," and how do you know if you are being true to who you are? While this book will not delve into these more philosophical musings, it is possible to use the construct of authenticity as an indication that someone is being true to who they really are. *Authenticity*, or being authentic, is defined as being genuine and real, not fake or copied. Someone who is authentic is believed to behave in ways that reflect their own true motives, values, and ideas. Descriptions of authenticity have indicated that being authentic means one is behaving autonomously, congruently, and genuinely.

Congruence and *genuineness* are often used interchangeably. They refer to the notion that when we behave genuinely or congruently, our behaviors reflect what is really going on internally. When we are feeling angry, we will show an angry face and use an angry-sounding tone of voice, and thereby we are acting congruently or genuinely. By contrast, when we feel angry but smile and moderate our voice so we do not sound angry, we are behaving incongruently or disingenuously. Acting in this way also reflects inauthenticity, which simply means that in those moments, we are not showing who we truly are and what we are truly experiencing internally.

A study conducted by researchers from Louisiana Tech University sought to connect authenticity and well-being. In an effort to fully understand the nature of the relationship between these two constructs, they also identified two distinct ways we can engage in self-focused behavior: self-rumination and self-reflection. *Self-rumination* is characterized as a type of self-focus that is negative and ongoing. It is believed to be prompted by experiences that indicate a threat to one's self, the loss of the self, or ways that our self has been subjected to injustice (i.e., unfairness). When we self-ruminate, for example, we are more likely to become depressed. *Self-reflection*, which is rarely, if ever, associated with depression, has to do with contemplating one's character, actions, and motives of behavior. Although self-reflection as a form of self-focused behavior is not associated with depression, it is common for self-reflectors to also engage in self-rumination.

Signs and Impacts of a Well-Developed Identity

The researchers from Louisiana Tech University found that self-reflection was associated with higher levels of authenticity. The connection between self-reflection and authenticity mediated the effect of self-reflection on increased life satisfaction and lower levels of distress. This suggests that self-reflection that leads to authenticity further leads to feeling better about one's life and experiencing less distress. By contrast, those who self-ruminate were found to be less authentic, which lowered life satisfaction, and to have an increase in distress. Self-ruminators will excessively think about the "bad" or less desirable aspects of who they are or who others think they are, which will likely activate the desire to reduce such a discrepancy by trying to act like they *should* be or who they or others *want* them to be. They are not acting based on what is truly going on internally, and therefore they are not acting authentically.

Authenticity and its impact on life satisfaction and well-being have been criticized as having only been studied in the context of traditionally individualist cultures such as the United States. Researchers from India and Korea examined the connection between authenticity and overall well-being among those living in traditionally collectivist cultures. They found that even among those living in collectivist cultures, being high in authenticity was associated with higher levels of well-being and life satisfaction. This may be further evidence in support of how an accurate understanding of the construct of autonomy, as understood from the perspective of self-determination theory, can help to explain how it does not matter whether someone lives in an individualist or collectivist culture (for more information see chapter 5) or whether they live according to what is expected based on these types of cultures. What matters is whether someone is able to self-govern or make the personal choice to live their life based on an individualist or collectivist culture. Thus, someone can be autonomously individualistic or autonomously collectivistic. The act of making that choice autonomously means someone is likely acting from a more authentic perspective and is therefore going to benefit by having greater well-being and overall life satisfaction. The alternative to both is being heteronomously governed, which means the individual is not relying on one's internal compass to help make decisions but on forces outside of one's self (e.g., cultural or religious teaching, opinions of important others).

A group of researchers out of Houston, Texas, confirmed what other researchers have found, which is that authenticity is predictably associated with overall well-being such that the greater someone's authenticity the greater their well-being, and the lower their authenticity the lower their well-being. These researchers also sought to determine the extent to which the nature of one's relationships and interpersonal interactions may affect this connection. Thus, they were interested in knowing whether you could be an authentic person, which normally would predict a high level of well-being, but have a large enough number of negative relationships or interpersonal interactions that they ultimately negatively impact your well-being.

In addition to analyzing the authenticity–well-being connection, they also examined the degree to which relationships impacted well being regardless of one's degree of authenticity. They found that the greater the number of positive interpersonal interactions the greater the likelihood that that we will experience well-being. So what happens when someone is authentic (which should mean they have higher well-being), but they also have a lot of negative interpersonal experiences (which on its own should mean the person has lower levels of well-being)? The findings reported by this group showed that being authentic helps us in our interpersonal interactions, particularly as it relates to conflict in these relationships. When we are high in authenticity, negative interpersonal interactions tend to not have as much of a negative impact on well-being compared to those who are less authentic. This means that if there is significant conflict in one's relationships and the person is acting authentically (e.g., they believe, value, and accurately express their point of view regardless of what the other person believes, values, or expresses), the conflict that arises between them and the other person(s) will have less of a deleterious impact on their overall well-being compared to their inauthentic counterparts, who will experience a significant decline in well-being. Thus, despite the fact that having a significant number of negative interpersonal interactions should predict a decline in well-being, being authentic acts as a buffer against this type of negative experience.

As discussed in chapter 3, Erik Erikson noted that the prime time for establishing one's sense of self, or identity, is during adolescence. Students of this developmental time period and, indeed, those who are living through it or can recall being an adolescent know that this can be a confusing time in one's life, as we are simultaneously exploring what our options are (which can make an adolescent appear fickle) and desiring to figure out who we are and to act accordingly (i.e., act authentically). One of the factors that may interfere with this process is the fear of what our peers think; if we do not act the "right" way, we may experience disapproval or rejection.

Researchers found that adolescents who acted authentically were associated with well-being such that the more they were authentic the greater their well-being. They also found that authenticity was connected to self-determination theory's basic psychological needs of relatedness (i.e., feeling connected to others) and competence (i.e., knowing you have and can effectively use your skills and abilities). This means that as relatedness and competence needs are met, the adolescent will be more and more authentic, which further leads to greater overall well-being. Another study examining the importance of authenticity in adolescence attempted to answer the question of how authenticity impacts friendships. It found that adolescents who engaged in more authentic behavior viewed themselves more positively, and

Signs and Impacts of a Well-Developed Identity   115

perhaps more importantly, it stated that they were less lonely than their inauthentic counterparts. In addition, these adolescents reported that their peer relationships were more satisfying. These researchers concluded that authenticity is such an important factor in adolescence that a measure of this construct should be included in all research examining the nature of friendship processes. They further conceptualized authenticity as a "relational construct," meaning that depending on the nature of a particular relationship, that relationship may encourage or discourage authenticity.

We tend to be more likely to show who we really are in our close, more emotionally intimate relationships, though authenticity levels do vary depending on whether the relationship in question is with a parental figure, teacher, or friend or a same- or different-sex relationship. Some research found that the highest level of authenticity displayed in relationships during adolescence is with one's closest friends. Interestingly, however, true authenticity can be compromised when one's innermost thoughts and feelings are disclosed because the person thinks this type of disclosure is expected of them. Thus, they are not disclosing because they necessarily want to (i.e., not autonomously) but because they think they should (i.e., heteronomously). It is possible, then, that in these instances, there is a difference between autonomous authenticity and heteronomous authenticity. Authentic behavior expressed for heteronomous reasons rather than autonomous ones likely leads to a lower satisfaction in an adolescent's close friendships.

Researchers out of China examined power contingent self-esteem in the context of authenticity and well-being. *Power contingent self-esteem* is precisely what it sounds like. Someone's self-esteem hinges or is contingent on the degree to which that person has power. Although the accumulation of power has been associated with higher levels of self-esteem and higher levels of well-being, others have found that once someone's self-esteem is based on power, the impact is that the person's well-being will decrease. This difference can perhaps be understood in terms of seeking power and getting it and needing to keep power to keep feeling good about one's self. Self-determination theory specifically notes that when self-esteem is contingent on anything (e.g., you *have* to have power, you *have* to have a lot of friends, you *have* to have a lot of money), it is likely to be experienced differently than genuine self-esteem (i.e., intrinsically feeling good about who one is without the need for external validation). The implication is that contingency-based self-esteem requires external validation that may or may not come. As such, contingent self-esteem is theorized to be negatively related to authenticity such that the higher the need for external validation of self-esteem the lower one's authenticity, as authenticity reflects an internal process of choice and self-expression.

The researchers out of China confirmed previous research on the connection between authenticity and well-being but extended these findings by adding the concept of power contingent self-esteem. Their results show that when people engage in inauthentic behavior, which already means they will experience lower levels of well-being compared to their authentic counterparts, adding power contingent self-esteem contributes to even lower levels of well-being. Moreover, they noted that once power contingent self-esteem is established, the person is likely to engage in less authentic behavior and will ultimately wind up with a lower level of overall life satisfaction.

Given the importance of authenticity to well-being and overall life satisfaction, it is important to be able to accurately measure it. Measuring an elusive construct such as authenticity can be a challenge; however, an international group of researchers led by Alex Wood, of the University of Manchester in England, developed a twelve-item measure of authenticity that included three subscales, meaning that this measure of authenticity is believed to comprise three separate aspects of one's identity and the degree to which we remain faithful to those aspects of ourselves. They relied on the work of Carl Rogers (see chapter 3 for more information) and other researchers to identify the three elements of authenticity. Thus, their *Authenticity Scale* includes questions that measure self-alienation, authentic living, and accepting external influence.

Self-alienation refers to the extent to which a person is aware of what they are actually experiencing. Actual experience in the context of authenticity refers to what is going on internally for a person physiologically (i.e., related to biology) and emotionally and in terms of their deeply held beliefs about themselves, others, and the world around them. Being aware of these actual experiences means someone is able to consciously process what is going on in their body (e.g., they know when they feel hungry, thirsty, or tired) and how they are feeling emotionally, and they know what they truly think about themselves, others, and the world around them. They know, with a high level of accuracy, what they are experiencing. Those who are self-alienated are not aware of what they are actually experiencing, which in turn means they are less authentic.

The second aspect of authenticity, *authentic living*, refers to an alignment, or congruence, between the person's awareness of what they are experiencing internally and how they actually behave and express their emotions. Therefore, if someone is living authentically, they base their actions and expressions of feelings on what they are truly thinking and feeling. For example, if they are aware of being hungry, they will go get something to eat. If they are feeling sad, their face, tone of voice, word choice, and accompanying behaviors will clearly communicate their feeling of sadness. Readers may already see the importance of the connection between all three elements of authenticity at this point. If living authentically means we are acting in ways that we are consciously aware of, then the only way we can truly live authentically is to be aware of what is truly going on inside of us. If we are not in

Signs and Impacts of a Well-Developed Identity 117

tune with our body's physical signals of such things as pain, discomfort or satisfaction, our emotional experiences, or the beliefs that we have then whatever we are consciously aware of will not represent what we are truly experiencing, and whatever we express outwardly is not likely to reflect what is really going on with us. We, therefore, do not know who we are and cannot be authentic.

The third and final element of authenticity is *accepting external influence.* This piece of authenticity is fairly straightforward. It represents the degree to which we accept the influence of others and the accompanying expectation that we have to behave in ways that reflect others' expectations. In other words, this facet of authenticity represents conformity (see chapter 5 for more information) or its lack thereof. There is consensus among scholars that we do not exist in a vacuum separate from external influences. Thus, we are all impacted by people and the social experiences outside of ourselves. The question is, To what degree are we influenced by these external experiences and influences? Those who are higher in authenticity will be impacted less by others and therefore are much less likely to conform. Such people will report lower levels of accepting external influence.

Wood and his colleagues found that, overall, authenticity is strongly linked to higher levels of well-being and life satisfaction, and each of the three aspects of authenticity have been found to be differentially linked to well-being and life satisfaction as well. High levels of well-being and life satisfaction are found to exist with someone who has a high level of living authentically and low levels of both self-alienation and accepting external influence. Thus, knowing who you are and not being heavily influenced by others lead to living authentically, which further leads to feeling well and enjoying life.

Of the three factors, self-alienation has been touted to be the most important feature of authenticity. Some have referred to the lack of self-alienation as the core of authenticity; the more one is alienated from one's self, the greater the chance of psychopathology. When examining the relationship between the three factors of authenticity and well-being, Wood and his colleagues found that this factor (i.e., self-alienation) was more strongly connected than the other two factors to well-being. This means that in order to experience greater levels of well-being, it is imperative for individuals to *not* be alienated from one's self. It is paramount for us to be consciously aware of what is going on inside of us (i.e., our body's signals, our emotions, our beliefs) and to accept it all as is. When another group of international researchers, led by Selda Koydemir, examined the respective roles of self-alienation, authentic living, and external influence on happiness, they confirmed Wood and colleagues' findings.

Koydemir and her colleagues examined the various facets of authenticity as they relate to one another and to overall happiness. As expected, they found that having a personal sense of uniqueness meant that an individual was also more likely to live authentically and to have lower levels of self-alienation. Self-alienation and happiness were found to be connected as well, such that lower levels of self-alienation were connected with higher levels of happiness and authentic living. Finally, they also determined that the connection between a personal sense of uniqueness and happiness was mediated or changed by self-alienation. This means that to be happy, it is not enough to be unique. If one is unique, it must come from a place of knowing one's self and expressing that uniqueness authentically. This suggests, as Wood and colleagues found, that it is critical to not be self-alienated when finding one's way to happiness.

An interesting inclusion in the research on authenticity conducted by Koydemir and her colleagues was the concept referred to as a "personal sense of uniqueness." They noted that previous descriptions of *uniqueness* suggest that being unique can leave people feeling different and therefore separate from others. They suggested that such a description in the context of authenticity does not accurately capture what being unique feels like. They suggested that having a personal sense of uniqueness simply means that the individual recognizes their unique existence (i.e., one does not necessarily have to stand out in a crowd). They further explained that someone who experiences this type of uniqueness reflects an acceptance of who one is as a distinctive individual and an accompanying feeling of being special for being who they truly are. As such, these researchers' examination of this construct aligned with the elements of authenticity as expected. Feeling unique was moderately connected with authentic living and self-alienation. That is, having a personal sense of uniqueness meant the person was more likely to live authentically and was less likely to be alienated from one's self. There was a small but not meaningful connection with accepting external influence in the expected direction: a higher sense of personal uniqueness and a lower likelihood of accepting external influence. There was a connection between one's personal sense of uniqueness and happiness; however, as noted previously, this connection is explained by self-alienation. This means that although having a strong sense of personal uniqueness is connected to higher levels of happiness, the factor that explains that relationship is having a low level of self-alienation. In short, if you want to be happy, make sure you accurately know who you are and what makes you unique in comparison to others.

Authenticity is typically understood as a personal experience that requires the elimination of the influence of others so that one can tune into what is truly going on inside of one's self. This allows us to behave in ways that reflect our inner workings (i.e., thoughts, feelings, and signals from the body). Some researchers have noted that since human beings are inherently social beings, considering what it means to be authentic outside of the

Signs and Impacts of a Well-Developed Identity

context of relationships does not adequately capture the lived experience of authenticity. Some of these researchers identified three aspects of authenticity specifically as authenticity may be affected by others. Identifying these three aspects of other-related authenticity drills down deeper into the notion of the influence of others. The three other-related elements of authenticity are egocentric authenticity, other-distorted authenticity, and balanced authenticity.

Egocentric authenticity is seen in those who behave in ways that truly reflect what is going on inside of them, but they do so in a way that does not take into consideration what impact their authenticity may have on others. Placing egocentric authenticity on a continuum, this construct is on one extreme with inauthenticity at the other. Thus, this hypothetical continuum ranges from not at all revealing what is truly going on within you (inauthenticity) to sharing too much of what is going on within you without caring about how this authenticity may affect other people.

Other-distorted authenticity can be thought of as being on the "inauthenticity" side of the continuum. When we defer to others in an effort to avoid social disapproval (which is what other-distorted authenticity reflects), we cannot truly be authentic. Between these two extremes is what has been called *balanced authenticity*. This is essentially what it sounds like in the context of the two extremes. Balanced authenticity means that the individual is focused on what is going on internally, but they consider their internal functioning and subsequent expression of their internal experiences in the context of others. Someone with balanced authenticity will not simply act without thinking or without concern for others, nor will they only act based on others. They will find a compromise between their individual needs and desires and how expressing those needs and desires may impact others. Two additional constructs that help to further illustrate the three elements of authenticity are agency and communion.

Agency is a term fully examined by Albert Bandura, a psychologist from the United States who developed social learning theory (or observational learning) and is most well known for his Bobo doll experiment. *Agency*, sometimes also known as *personal agency*, refers to an individual's ability to influence one's self and the world around them. The person believes that their thoughts, feelings, and actions are important and have an impact. *Communion* is often associated with spirituality and refers to being emotionally and cognitively intimate with another person. It is a sharing of one's private thoughts and feelings with another. When someone is functioning with egocentric authenticity, they experience unmitigated agency, which means they are entirely focused on themselves to the exclusion of others. When someone is functioning from the perspective of other-distorted authenticity, they experience unmitigated communion, which means they are entirely focused on others to the exclusion of themselves. True communion involves sharing one's innermost thoughts and feelings; however, in the context of other-distorted authenticity, the communion is distorted such that the individual is interested in a connection with another person but will only share what they perceive to be acceptable to the other person without regard for themselves. Someone who expresses balanced authenticity has a balance between agency and communion. They believe their thoughts and feelings are important, but they also value communion with others and will therefore attempt to strike a balance between one's own agency and communion. They will share their true thoughts and feelings, but they will not intentionally disregard the well-being of another person.

Researchers examining this tripartite conceptualization of authenticity were interested in how each of the three elements of authenticity connect with other psychological concepts, such as social desirability, impression management, empathy, and well-being. Overall, balanced authenticity was found to be associated with well-being, agency, communion, and empathy. Those who had a balanced authenticity were also found to be more likely to have a positive image of themselves than those who had one of the other two types of authenticity; however, they will not please others simply for the sake of getting a positive reaction. When they please others, they do so on purpose because they genuinely care about others, which aligns with their perception of who they are. They do things for other people because they want to not because they are trying to garner favor with that person or others who may observe their "nice" behavior.

Another group of researchers in the United States led by Jake Womick examined the "Dark Tetrad" in the context of authenticity and well-being. The Dark Tetrad consists of Machiavellianism (i.e., unscrupulous, cunning, deceptive), narcissism (i.e., excessive admiration of one's self), psychopathy (i.e., lacking empathy, inability to establish meaningful connections with others), and sadism (i.e., enjoyment from inflicting pain on others). The question these researchers attempted to answer was whether authenticity among those high in these dark traits (i.e., they act according to who they truly are) would score high on measures of well-being because authenticity in general has been routinely linked to high levels of well-being. Their results indicated that although there were some differences between each of the Dark Tetrad traits, overall, being authentically Machiavellian, narcissistic, psychopathic, or sadistic were associated with lower levels of well-being. An interesting twist to their findings was the outcome that those with these Dark Tetrad traits had higher scores on well-being when they acted less authentically. This essentially means that for those with tendencies toward these darker personality traits, being less authentic is, ironically, better for their overall well-being.

Anna Sutton, of New Zealand, examined differences in well-being between being authentic and having a consistent personality (i.e., displaying the same

Signs and Impacts of a Well-Developed Identity 121

traits across situations—meaning that you will "look" the same regardless of the situation you are in or the people you are around). Although previous research has found that consistency in one's personality is linked to positive well-being and inconsistency to negative well-being, subsequent research and theory has shown that it may not be consistency from one situation to the next that predicts overall well-being. In an effort to provide information to help resolve this issue, Sutton examined what was most likely to predict well-being in a person and found that it was being authentic rather than personal consistency that was more likely to result in positive experiences and well-being.

Therefore, knowing who you are and acting in accordance with your internal values and beliefs will lead to greater well-being. Attempting to be the "same person" from one situation to the next was found to be associated with both positive and negative experiences, which further contributes to the notion that personality consistency is complex in terms of how beneficial that is for an individual. This finding may be reflective of balanced authenticity, which is discussed in an earlier section in this chapter. You can still be authentic from one social situation to the next, but when taking into account how an unabashed expression of who you are may impact others, you can still be true to who you are but not be "exactly" the same person in each situation.

In this chapter, we took a look at the importance of constructs such as self-discrepancy, self-reflection, self-esteem, self-concept, authenticity, and other identity-related concepts. The research and theoretical constructs presented in this section in aggregate paint a clear picture. To experience well-being and satisfaction with one's life, one must be true to who one truly is; one must be authentic, with the caveat that we cannot cavalierly reject the impact our authenticity may have on others. In the next chapter, we will examine what happens when you do not have a well-developed identity and therefore cannot be authentic.

CHAPTER SEVEN

Signs and Impacts of a Poorly Developed Identity

As discussed in the preceding chapter, having a clear sense of who one truly is and acting in accordance with one's true identity are beneficial for your psychological well-being. When we are able to be faithful to who we truly are, we are acting authentically and are more likely to experience overall well-being and improved life satisfaction. So what happens when someone does not have a well-developed identity? Is it really that bad for us to not know who we truly are? The sections that follow will examine just that.

A Poorly Developed Identity

One way to describe a poorly developed identity is by using the term *false self*. A person operating from a false self can also be characterized as being inauthentic. Although this may sound somewhat judgmental, the reality is that a false self that leads to inauthenticity usually develops as a protective mechanism early in our lives. Therefore, the false self is initially adaptive because it protects us from pain and discomfort; however, over time, this once helpful self-related construct ultimately does not leave us feeling good about ourselves or our relationships, and it often leaves us with a sense that we do not know who we truly are or what our *real self* is.

James Masterson, a psychiatrist from the United States, authored several books in the area of self-development and how we can become derailed in our identity-related development. He noted that this kind of disruption can lead not only to the development of the false self but also to diagnosable personality disorders. This book will not delve into a discussion of these disorders; however, the fact that there is a particular category of psychiatric disorders known to have roots in late childhood or adolescence that result in maladaptive ways of interacting with one's self, others and the world around us speaks to how damaging the false self can be.

James Masterson and others have stated that the false self develops during childhood due to painful experiences and what he called "negative programming," which primarily occurs during our childhood years. Many readers likely know that when it comes to physical development, brain development is complex and is the last thing in our body to fully mature. The frontal lobe of the brain in particular, which is the part of the brain responsible for things like understanding consequences, the ability to plan, and knowing right from wrong, does not complete its development until our midtwenties. As the brain is responsible for processing all information, including information associated with early childhood experiences, those early experiences are processed by an underdeveloped brain that does not have the capacity to adequately understand what is going on. So, the brain does its best, and the child adapts in a way that promotes psychological (and sometimes physical) survival. One of the factors contributing to the false self is the extent to which we are differentiated or, by contrast, undifferentiated from our parental figures.

Differentiation, as conceptualized by Murray Bowen, a psychiatrist and early pioneer of family therapy, refers to a process that occurs in our relationships with others. Differentiation from others, usually parental figures, is a critical process that involves understanding who you are as separate and distinct from your parental figures. The opposite of differentiation can be considered enmeshment. *Enmeshment* refers to a blurring of boundaries between people that results in not knowing where you psychologically end and the other person begins. This is often experienced between family members or dating partners who feel one another's emotions as though when one person feels an emotion, the other one automatically does as well. Enmeshment fosters an unhealthy dependence on one another and often results in a lack of privacy, being inappropriately "best friends" with a parental figure, a parental figure playing favorites, and so on. In short, enmeshment and a lack of differentiation will contribute to the development of the false self in a child because the child is not provided the opportunity to discover the ways in which they are different and unique from others.

James Masterson suggests we ask ourselves several questions when considering how strongly developed our false self is. These include the following: How much of your identity is truly representative of your own desires and goals in life? How much does your identity reflect the desires and priorities of someone else? Are you following your own path, or are you unconsciously (or consciously) repeating the lives of your parental figures and automatically living according to their values, ideals, and beliefs? He

Signs and Impacts of a Poorly Developed Identity

concluded that most of us are, in fact, compliant with the expectations, beliefs, and values held by our parental figures. He stated that because of this, we will not be able to differentiate (understand how we are separate from them), nor will we realize that we are not living a life of our own making. We are simply following a life recipe handed down to us. In a twist of irony, some of us rebel and do the exact opposite of what we were raised to do, believing that because we are not doing what our parental figures expect of us that we are being true to who we are. However, absent actual exploration and self-reflection, this is another way to foster the development of a false self because we are only choosing to believe ideas or act in ways that are *not* like our parental figures: we are acting this way despite them, not because our behaviors and beliefs truly reflect our innermost beliefs and values.

Both compliance and rebelliousness are architects of the false self, as both are driven by the beliefs, values, and expectations of our parental figures. Doing the work to figure out where your beliefs, values, and preferences begin and your parental figures' end (and where they overlap) is the work of differentiation. This will allow you to figure out what is important to you and what fits with you. This is the process of developing one's real self.

Another distinction that can be made with respect to the false self is that one can craft a "deflated" or an "inflated" false self. The deflated false self is constructed to please others, usually parental figures. Ultimately, all children want to feel love and acceptance from their parental figures. If the only way to get that is to do what others expect of them regardless of whether those expectations are healthy for them, they are likely to ignore what they truly want and need and to assume that when their wants or needs conflict with the expectations of others, there is something wrong with them. Thus, this origin of the false self contributes to forming a version of the self that exists to comply or conform (see also chapter 5). This type of false self is considered to be deflated because this version of the self is accompanied by low self-esteem. By contrast, the inflated false self is accompanied by high self-esteem, but it is a false, fragile sense of esteem that is built on an act rather than who we truly are.

When an inflated false self develops, the child also experiences *conditions of worth* (i.e., parental figures only show love and affection when the child meets their expectations; see also chapter 3), but instead of complying or conforming and feeling like who they truly are is not good enough, the child creates a version of themselves that is seemingly strong, capable, and infallible. This inflated view of one's self is usually grandiose. The person believes they are important in a way that reality does not support, and they expect others to see them the same way they see themselves. In essence, they act like they know who they are and that they feel good about themselves, but underneath that façade, they are someone who is uncertain, scared, and emotionally fragile. What often accompanies this type of false self is the notion that the person believes there is nothing wrong with them and any problems are due to others. The results of one study reflected this notion when the researchers, led by Marisol Perez, found that those with inflated self-esteem were rejected by their peers; however, the person with inflated self-esteem did not detect that there were any problems. This means that when someone like this is told that no one likes them, they are unlikely to see that the problem lies with them. They assume the problem lies with others in terms of their being jealous of who they are or of their successes (either real or imagined).

A related concept to having inflated and therefore manufactured self-esteem is something called the *Dunning-Kruger effect*. The Dunning-Kruger effect is named after its developers, David Dunning and Justin Kruger, who initially conducted several studies to determine why this phenomenon occurs and what mechanisms seem to contribute to it. They sought to study those who make decisions that reflect incompetence and these people's inability to recognize that they are not as competent as they think. Thus, the Dunning-Kruger effect elucidates a type of cognitive bias that leads the less competent individual to conclude that their skills and abilities are far better developed than they are in comparison to others and the highly competent individual to downgrade their abilities because they believe that they are just like everyone else. In short, Dunning and Kruger noted that those who overestimate their abilities have a misunderstanding of themselves, and those who underestimate their abilities have a misunderstanding about others. Each has a view of themselves or others that is erroneous and therefore false, along with an accompanying inability to recognize this falsehood.

A paper authored by Daniel Ames and Lara Kammrath was written to examine people's respective abilities to predict their own competence on a task. They concluded that narcissism (associated with an inflated self-esteem) was a better predictor of a person's self-estimated performance than someone's actual performance. To be clear, those with narcissistic traits were not found to be accurate predictors of their actual abilities. They consistently do poorly at that; however, knowing someone is narcissistic allows researchers to predict that the narcissistic individual will routinely overestimate their competence. Thus, when participants in a study are asked to estimate how they might do on a future task, those who score higher on narcissism are found to significantly overestimate their abilities.

As narcissism can be considered a continuous trait (i.e., narcissism can be placed on a continuum that reflects degrees of narcissism) rather than a dichotomous one (i.e., you either have it or you do not), the conclusions of Joyce Ehrlinger and colleagues, based on their summary of what is known about the Dunning-Kruger effect, are not surprising. They stated that after nearly ten years of research on the Dunning-Kruger effect, the results consistently showed most of us think more highly of our abilities than is warranted,

Signs and Impacts of a Poorly Developed Identity

with an emphasis on those who are objectively unskilled on a particular task having the most skewed view of their actual abilities. The Dunning-Kruger effect and the subsequent research confirming the existence of the phenomenon illustrate how easy it can be to not know one's self, and when we do not know ourselves, we are unable to act authentically. Another way of looking at this type of inflated view of one's self and one's abilities is from the standpoint of *compensation*.

Compensation is a Freudian defense mechanism. Defense mechanisms are believed to protect one's self (more precisely, the ego) from anxiety or discomfort that can arise from any number of sources. Regardless of the source, to provide protection, defense mechanisms distort reality so that the person does not have to deal with uncomfortable things as they actually are. Compensation in this context is the distortion of reality by overachieving in one area of one's life to compensate for actual or imagined deficiencies in another area of one's life. This defense mechanism protects the individual from their own incompetence by focusing on the area in which they are overcompensating. The thing about defense mechanisms, as understood by Freud, is that we do not use them consciously. This means, in the context of compensation, we are unaware of the fact that we feel inadequate in some area of our lives and are desperately trying to make ourselves feel better by overachieving in some other area, such as sports, music, academics, the arts, and charitable giving. More contemporary understandings of compensation suggest that we may compensate consciously (i.e., knowingly) or unconsciously, as Freud suggested. Moreover, since Freud's era, some have suggested there is more than one type of compensation: overcompensation and undercompensation.

Overcompensation, which is essentially what is illustrated by compensation as a defense mechanism, is believed to result in the person wanting to accumulate power and dominance over others. Such an individual has a high degree of self-esteem that reflects an underlying view of their self that is not good (i.e., they appear to think very highly of themselves, but underneath that, they do not feel competent or good about themselves at all). Undercompensation, by contrast, occurs when someone, overtly, does not think highly of themselves and often interacts with the world around them in a helpless manner that reflects a lack of courage and general fear of life.

Regardless of the type of compensation, both reflect a misrepresentation of who one actually is. For example, someone who overcompensates may, in reality, achieve a great deal; however, they pursue this degree of achievement precisely because they view themselves as woefully inadequate elsewhere. As other contemporary research has suggested (as discussed in the preceding paragraphs), there is a high likelihood that the person's sense of incompetence is a misrepresentation and misunderstanding of their own and others' abilities.

Family and Peer Influences on the False Self

Susan Harter and her colleagues, in the mid-1990s, discussed the involvement of parental and peer support and how that impacts false self behavior in adolescents. They were also interested in examining why adolescents engage in false self behavior to begin with. Their model, which their research supported, suggests that when adolescents feel like their parental figures and peers are supportive of them, they are more likely to engage in true/real self behavior, whereas if they do not feel like they are receiving support from their parental figures and peers, they are more likely to engage in false self behavior. Harter and her colleagues further explicated the notion of support from others and indicated that feeling like one has support in general is important, but what also matters is the level and quality of that support. The *level of support* essentially refers to how much support the adolescent receives, and the *quality of support* refers to the extent to which the support feels conditional or unconditional. In other words, does the person providing the support have any conditions placed on that support. For example, a conditional statement would be, "I will support you only if you do what I want you to do." An unconditional statement would be, "I will support you no matter what." Those who have read chapter 3 will recognize similarities between what Harter and her colleagues found in comparison to Carl Rogers's contentions about conditions of worth and unconditional positive regard (see chapter 3 for more information).

Overall Harter and her colleagues found that both parental figures and peers play an important role in true self and false self behavior. Specifically, they found that both the quality and level of support predicted the degree to which the adolescent felt hopeful about receiving support in the future. Hopefulness was identified as a mediator of false self behavior, which means that hope, or the lack thereof, about receiving future support determined whether false self behavior would be evident. As quality and level of support are predictive of hope about future support, Harter and her colleagues concluded that conditional support is experienced by the adolescent as not supportive. They further specifically stated that the adolescents at the highest risk for false self behavior are those who experience conditional support, a low level of support, and hopelessness about receiving future support. While this was found to be the case for both parental figures and peers, the impact of the quality and level of support from parental figures was stronger than that of peers. They concluded that this is likely the case because the consequences of not having support from parental figures may be experienced as a loss of love, whereas with peers, they may merely lose acceptance. Harter and her colleagues also noted that the impact of parental figures may be stronger because one cannot escape from one's parental figures as easily as one can escape from or change peer groups.

Signs and Impacts of a Poorly Developed Identity

When examining the motives for why adolescents engage in false self behavior, Harter and colleagues were able to shed more light on why anyone might divest themselves of their true self in favor of their false self. Those who engaged in the highest levels of false self behavior were those who endorsed the fact that either they or others did not value who they truly were; their true self was devalued. Either they did not or someone else important to them did not like who they really are, and as a result, they engaged in behaviors that would be perceived as more desirable by themselves or others but that ultimately did not reflect who they truly are. This also means that they had very little knowledge of their true self, and they experienced lower levels of self-esteem, were more likely to have a depressed mood, and did not experience hope with respect to their futures.

Interestingly, adolescents who stated that they engaged in false self behavior because they wanted to be accepted by their parental figures or their peers were not as negatively impacted as those who felt like their actual true self was devalued. Most adolescents endorsed this reason (i.e., wanting to be accepted) for their false self behavior and concurrently had some knowledge about who they truly are (i.e., their true self). In addition, these adolescents did engage in some true self behavior. Moreover, these adolescents had higher levels of self-esteem and higher levels of positive feelings, and they experienced higher levels of hope with respect to their futures. The fewest number of adolescents endorsed the reason for their false self behavior as being due to role experimentation (see chapter 3 for more information) and were, by far, the healthiest group psychologically. Role experimenters had greater knowledge and expression of their true self, higher levels of self-esteem, more positive emotions, and higher levels of hope about their future.

It is known, due to extensive scientific study, that conflicts in one's interpersonal relationships are experienced by most of us as highly unpleasant and that these experiences can negatively impact our ability to fulfill our potential and have a meaningful life. Being in conflict with important others (e.g., partner, child, coworkers, family members, roommates, friends) has a more profound impact on being in a bad mood compared to stressors that have nothing to do with relationships (e.g., meeting deadlines). Researchers have noted that being more agreeable and less neurotic will lessen the negative impact of interpersonal conflict. The question then becomes, How does being authentic (i.e., being true to who you truly are) fit into this equation? Researchers from Palo Alto University, led by Robert Wickham, set out to determine whether being authentic reduces the impact of interpersonal conflict.

Wickham and his colleagues identified two aspects of authenticity to study in the context of authenticity and interpersonal conflict: awareness and unbiased processing. *Awareness* refers to how well one knows and ultimately trusts their internal motivations, feelings, desires, and thoughts. *Unbiased processing* refers to a person's ability to evaluate themselves, without bias, and to incorporate that information into their understanding of who they are. This means that all information, good or bad, is incorporated. These researchers found that among the participants studied, those who were the most aware of themselves and were able to critically evaluate themselves in an unbiased manner were not negatively impacted by interpersonal conflict; specifically, they did not experience a reduction in self-esteem or life satisfaction. As such, these researchers characterized authenticity as a protective factor against the negative effects of interpersonal conflicts. This means that the more authentic you are, the more protected you are from feeling bad about one's self and one's life because of an interpersonal dispute. Conversely, the less authentic you are, the more likely you will experience the negative impact of interpersonal conflict and as a result will feel bad about yourself and your life.

Measuring the False Self and What It Can Predict

Kristy Weir and Paul Jose, researchers from New Zealand, developed a measure of false self for adolescents that they called the Perceptions of False Self (POFS). They were interested in how this measure of false self worked with adolescents (i.e., would it, in fact, measure the false self) and how the false self would be related to negative affective states, such as symptoms associated with depression and anxiety. They found that the POFS did measure the false self. They reported that when describing their experiences, adolescents distinguished between their "public self" (what they show other people) and their "private self" (what is personal to them and may not be shared) and the degree to which these two selves overlapped. The less these two selves overlapped, the more likely their public self would represent false self behavior, which adolescents described as "phony" and as not representative of who they truly are. Adolescents also described their false self behavior in terms of "loss of voice," which is characterized as not being able to say what they really think or what they really mean. These researchers also found that the false self can be experienced through one's appearance and how they present themselves to others. Crafting a particular appearance for the purpose of trying to impress others was more representative of the false self.

The false self was also associated with hiding one's true feelings, which is commonly manifested as an adolescent authentically having negative feelings but outwardly expressing positive feelings. This false self experience was associated with higher levels of psychological discomfort. Overall, high levels of false self in adolescents were strongly associated with symptoms consistent with depression and anxiety. Interestingly, these researchers also examined the directionality of the relationship between false self and each element of negative affect. They wanted to know whether false self behavior

Signs and Impacts of a Poorly Developed Identity   131

leads to depression and anxiety or whether depression and anxiety lead to false self behavior; they wanted to know which causes which.

Weir and Jose found that with respect to depressive symptoms, false self behavior did not predict depression in the long term. That is, according to their results, engaging in false self behavior does not make someone depressed; however, they found the reverse to be true. Feeling depressed can lead to higher incidences of false self behavior. With respect to anxiety, they found the relationship to be strong in both directions. False self behavior was found to be predictive of anxiety across time, and anxiety was found to predict engagement in false self behavior over time. Thus, false self behavior seems to cause feelings of anxiety, but feelings of anxiety also seem to cause an increase in false self behaviors. Statistically speaking, the strongest of their results suggest that negative affective experiences such as depression and anxiety lead to false self behavior. This finding, they indicated, is in contrast to typical findings that show false self behavior leads to negative affect. This can, of course, mean that someone may generally know who they are and will usually display their true selves. But when they are actively dealing with depression or anxiety, their false self will become more prominent.

False Self and Identity Statuses

A group of researchers from the United States and Belgium sought to determine what relationship existed between the identity statuses outlined by James Marcia (see chapter 3) and overall psychosocial functioning among emerging-adult college students. This group, led by Seth Schwartz, stated that most of the focus on identity statuses has been to verify that the statuses are correct and what developmental factors may impact one's identity status; however, they noted that what has been missing in the literature was any discussion of what impact each identity status may have on an individual's overall functioning and well-being. Although the original and the expanded identity statuses described in the paragraphs that follow do not explicitly reflect a false self or a true self, the theory and research on these statuses clarifies which statuses reflect a well-developed or coherent self and which statuses reflect a less developed or incoherent self. Although not knowing one's self well does not guarantee that the individual will engage exclusively in false self–related behavior, it does make it more likely because one has to know one's self to engage in true self–related behavior.

The results of the examination of the identity statuses led by Schwartz revealed six different statuses that do not precisely align with James Marcia's original statuses, but they do align with what other researchers have found. The statuses identified that were the same as Marcia's were foreclosure and achievement. As a reminder, Marcia's identity statuses are characterized by the degree of identity-related exploration the person has engaged in and the degree of commitment they have to their identity (see chapter 3 for more information). Someone with the foreclosure status has committed to an identity without having previously explored their options. Someone with the achievement status has engaged in exploration and eventually committed to an identity.

The remaining three statuses diverge from Marcia's original statuses. The searching moratorium status has been identified and verified in myriad other studies and reflects someone who is committed to various aspects of their identity while actively exploring alternatives (Marcia's description of moratorium is someone who is actively in their identity crisis; they are exploring and want to commit to an identity but have not yet done so). Someone who is in searching moratorium will change their identity-related commitment if needed or desired as part of their exploration.

These researchers also identified two forms of diffusion: diffused diffusion and carefree diffusion. Diffused diffusion represents someone who is engaged in minimal identity-related work, but they are in no hurry to engage in active exploration nor to commit to an identity. Carefree diffusion, on the other hand, represents someone who is not engaged in any identity work and shows no indication that they will engage in exploration anytime soon. Finally, the undifferentiated status represents individuals who cannot be clearly categorized in one of the other statuses. The researchers indicate those with this status may show signs of more than one status simultaneously and are therefore classified as undifferentiated.

With respect to psychosocial functioning, the picture is grim for those in either one of the two diffused statuses. Schwartz and his team found that those in the diffused diffusion and the carefree diffusion statuses had the lowest scores on measures of self-esteem, internal locus of control (the belief that how one behaves and the consequences of those behaviors are directly due to our own actions rather than under the control of some external force), life satisfaction, and psychological well-being. Although those classified as diffused diffusion show some indications that they were searching for meaning, their scores were still lower than the other nondiffused statuses and slightly higher compared to those in the carefree diffusion status. In addition, members of both types of diffused status scored the highest on measures of depression, overall anxiety, and social anxiety specifically. One item that distinguished the carefree diffusion status is that members of that group scored the highest of all other statuses on externalizing problems, which means that they were more prone to engage in behaviors such as being aggressive, breaking rules or laws, and generally getting into trouble (internalizing problems tend to be things like sadness, withdrawal, and body aches and pains), all of which can be categorized as reflective of an antisocial personality (i.e., someone who does not care about the rights of others).

Signs and Impacts of a Poorly Developed Identity

Identity achievers scored highest on measures of self-esteem, internal locus of control, life satisfaction, and psychological well-being. Those in the foreclosed status scored similar to achievers on well-being but lower on measures related to having a sense of purpose. The researchers concluded that having a high level of commitment, which differentiates these two statuses from the others, can mean one is satisfied with one's life and content with themselves overall; however, without sufficient exploration (which is what is missing for those in the foreclosed status), the researchers concluded that it is more difficult to find meaning and purpose in one's life. However, an additional comparison of these two statuses revealed that exploration to find one's purpose or meaning in life, as seen with achievers, may result in feelings of anxiety and depression, which suggests that this process is not easy and may cause distress.

Those categorized in either the searching moratorium or the undifferentiated status scored similarly on measures of self-esteem, locus of control, meaning of life, and well-being, with slightly higher scores found among those in searching moratorium. Those classified in the searching moratorium status also scored higher than the undifferentiated status on depression and general anxiety elements, which may lead to higher levels of internalization of symptoms. These researchers also noted that the experiences of the searching moratorium status reveal why this status has been referred to as a "double-edged sword." They stated that along with the higher scores surrounding exploration of the meaning of one's life and finding one's life purpose, there are higher scores on depression and anxiety and some forms of aggression. This suggests that identity exploration is difficult and can cause discomfort to the extent that some people in this status may move to one that feels "safer," such as diffusion or foreclosure.

With respect to behavior that many negatively impact one's physical health, both the foreclosure and achievement statuses scored the lowest on the use of drugs and driving while impaired. As both of these statuses are high in commitment, these findings suggest that committing to an identity, regardless of the amount of exploration completed prior to committing, reduces the likelihood that someone will engage in behaviors that may endanger their health. With respect to the carefree diffusion status, Schwartz and his colleagues reported results that provided additional evidence for antisocial tendencies among those in this category. Those classified as carefree diffused were found to be two to three times more likely than any of the other statuses to engage in dangerous drug- and medication-use behavior (e.g., injecting or inhaling drugs, misuse of prescription medications). Those in this category were also more likely to engage in risky sexual behavior (e.g., sex with a stranger) and other risky behaviors, such as getting in a car with a driver who is intoxicated. Those in the diffused diffusion, searching moratorium, and undifferentiated statuses scored similarly on questionnaires designed to measure the extent to which one engages in health-compromising behaviors. The findings suggest that the carefree diffusion status is the most hazardous to one's health.

Marcia's identity statuses along with the expanded identity statuses studied by Schwartz and colleagues represent varying degrees of a coherent sense of who one is. Not knowing who one is can leave people more susceptible to the influence of others. Therefore, those who have not yet fully explored and fully committed may be at greater risk of engaging in false self behavior. This may be, in part, why these researchers found that the less coherent one's sense of self, the more likely it is that they will encounter negative emotions and engage in potentially health-compromising behaviors.

Displaying One's Self on Social Media

Recent researchers have examined the impact of the presentation of the various versions of one's self on social media and how that may intersect with well-being. Minas Michikyan, Jessica Dennis, and Kaveri Subrahmanyam, out of UCLA, examined the degree to which emerging adults (i.e., those aged eighteen to twenty-five years old) presented their real selves, ideal selves, or false selves on Facebook. These researchers noted that emerging adults are still exploring their identities, and social media platforms have become an integral medium through which young people express themselves and try out new facets of their identity. They found that most people claimed to present their real selves more than their ideal or false selves on this social media platform; however, they also found a particular trend for those who did present their false selves.

Those who presented their false selves on social media were also more likely to have lower self-esteem and a less coherent sense of self. This likely means that these individuals do not know who they truly are and do not feel good about themselves, so they likely present a version of themselves that they think will be perceived favorably. These researchers concluded that younger people's self-exploration and self-presentation through social media is similar to what earlier researchers found when presenting one's self online was not an option and confirms that online platforms are a specific tool used by this age group to facilitate their understanding of themselves.

Loss of Voice

One of the terms often used in the context of self-expression is the concept of *voice*. Readers may be familiar with phrases such as "use your voice" or "find your voice." This refers to finding ways to express your true beliefs and opinions. When people do not have or feel like they do not have a voice, they are more likely to keep their thoughts to themselves. Historically, loss of voice is often understood in the context of adolescent girls who learn what it

Signs and Impacts of a Poorly Developed Identity　　　　　135

means to be a "good" girl: to be seen and not heard. This seemingly insidious message has led myriad researchers and practitioners (e.g., Carol Gillian, Alice Miller, Mary Pipher) to write about how and why girls and young women in particular turn into shy, unassuming people when prior to adolescence, they may have been vibrant, opinionated, and strong-willed. Those who have given attention to this area of study have suggested that girls learn they must make a choice: to be loved and accepted or to be true to who they really are and therefore authentic. Ultimately, choosing to be accepted and loved over being true to one's self is precisely what leads to women putting others' wants and needs ahead of their own and engaging in false self–related behavior. Making sure others are happy and taken care of is believed to be a strong motivator for suppressing one's own voice. Females have long been known to highly value interpersonal relatedness and therefore may sacrifice themselves to establish or maintain relationships with others. The impact of this kind of self-suppression, however, is clear.

Susan Harter and colleagues summarized the views on loss of voice shared by writers such as Carol Gillian and examined what the impact seems to be on suppressing one's voice. First of all, they concluded that the literature supports the notion that girls are more likely to suppress their true thoughts and feelings compared to boys. They further noted that this difference appears to be an artifact of socialization rather than a true difference between the two sexes. That is, girls and boys are shaped to be as they are rather than being born that way. In their review of the literature on this subject, Harter and her colleagues found ample evidence for negative effects associated with loss of voice. They found that when a female does not express her thoughts and opinions, particularly within important relationships, they tend to lose their passion for life and report elevated depressive symptomology. A drop in self-esteem has also been associated with loss of voice. As self-esteem is connected to knowing one's self and accepting one's own thoughts, ideals, beliefs, and opinions, when we suppress our true self by not knowing one's self or by intentionally not expressing one's self, we are effectively turning our back on our true selves and will therefore not feel good about ourselves.

Despite this focus on females, others have contended that males can also be pressured to give up their voice in favor of others' needs and desires. In a scientific study examining, among other things, differences between girls and boys on their experiences with their voice, Harter and her colleagues found that girls and boys scored similarly overall with respect to when or if they use their voice. They did find, however, that when females endorsed identifying with traditionally feminine characteristics, they were more likely to keep their thoughts and opinions to themselves in some relationships but not others, suggesting that femininity rather than being female may be the factor that leads to loss of voice.

Harter and colleagues reported a convergence of the literature with respect to important relationships when it comes to voice support or voice suppression. They noted that lack of support for one's voice early in life, particularly from parental figures, results in both male and female children learning from an early age to keep their true thoughts and feelings to themselves. They echo other theorist's views (e.g., Edward Deci and Richard Ryan's self-determination theory; see chapter 3 for more information) that parental figures who do not value a child as they are but rather try to get the child to fit a particular standard create an environment in which a false self is likely to be created and reinforced. In essence, children and adolescents in a situation like this are experiencing what Carl Rogers called "conditions of worth" (see chapter 3 for more information), which refers to specific conditions in which a child will receive love and support, but only if those conditions are met by the child. Harter and her colleagues further confirmed the relationship between false self-development and lack of support for one's voice when they found that adolescents who reported a lower level of support for self-expression also stated that they did not often express their true thoughts and feelings.

Around the same time Harter and colleagues were researching issues related to voice, Robert Firestone was also focused on the concept of the voice. In his work on the development of the self, he emphasized the critical nature of one's voice so much that he devised a form of treatment he called *voice therapy*. This therapy and the components that contribute to interfering with one's voice and therefore one's self were described in a book he coauthored with Lisa Firestone and Joyce Catlett, *The Self under Siege: A Therapeutic Model for Differentiation*. Readers may recall the term *differentiation* from earlier in this chapter; it refers to the importance of psychologically and emotionally separating from one's parental figures so that the individual can know and listen to their own thoughts and feelings. Firestone and his colleagues agreed that differentiation is a critical process in the development of the self and, ultimately, the development of one's voice.

The authors of *The Self under Siege* note that voice therapy involves identifying destructive thoughts that the individual developed so early in life that they feel like they have always been there. Firestone and his colleagues noted that by becoming aware of these thoughts and the feelings (usually negative feelings), the individual can literally say them out loud, have a conversation with these thoughts, and recognize that these early learned thoughts about one's self are, in fact, alien to who they truly are (i.e., part of the false self). They believe that these alien thoughts about one's self develop during the earliest years of one's life and state that "painful events and negative programming during the developmental years constitute the most serious threat to the evolution of the authentic self." They acknowledge that these alien ideas about one's self develop as a form of defense against pain associated

Signs and Impacts of a Poorly Developed Identity

with one's early relationships (usually with respect to parental figures). In that way, negative, false self–related thoughts (they use the term "anti-self" and "alien system") are adaptive and protective; however, later in life, usually in adolescence and adulthood, these childhood defenses leave us feeling detached from who we truly are, which impacts nearly every aspect of our lives and can lead to serious, diagnosable psychological disorders (e.g., depression, anxiety, personality disorders). By learning to identify these alien or false self–related thoughts and feelings and where they came from, the individual is better able to discern which parts of themselves belong to their real self and which parts were picked up along the way and belong to the false self.

Firestone and his colleagues argued that destructive interactions with parental figures lead to the creation of the anti-self or false self system. Destructive interactions can include misattunement (i.e., the parent misreads or does not understand an infant's various forms of communication; they are therefore not "attuned" to the infant), lack of affection, rejection or neglect of the child, hostility toward the child, or permissiveness of any behavior exhibited by the child. They also noted that factors beyond the child's and parental figures' control can negatively impact a child and contribute to the development of the false self. These include accidents, serious illnesses, and traumatic separation for any reason from a parental figure. Ultimately, when the alien self or false self develops, Firestone and colleagues noted that there are myriad predictable outcomes.

With an active false self, we experience a loss of freedom and a shrinking of personal experience. This means that we do not feel free to think and behave as we truly are, which will also result in the reduction of experiences that reflect who we truly are. Those with a strong false self also have difficulty with anger. Firestone and his colleagues contend that feelings of anger are to be expected. If we do not feel free to be who we truly are, then we are likely, at some level, to feel frustrated, anxious, or even shameful because our true selves do not align with what is expected of us from others (usually parental figures). What happens is that this anger can be hidden and internalized or projected outward. When we internalize this anger, we are likely to self-denigrate, which equates to having very low self-worth and believing that we are not worthy of anyone's time or respect. When this type of anger is projected outward, it means that we operate as though other people are untrustworthy and deserving of skepticism. This means we are more likely to see ourselves as a victim (e.g., everyone has an ulterior motive), and we are more likely to feel paranoid about others' behavior. As the false self is viewed by Firestone and his colleagues as a well-developed defense system, they noted that having a defense system like this results in a poorly integrated sense of self and an accompanying inability to communicate honestly.

When we are unable or unwilling to acknowledge what we truly want or need, we become experts at lying to ourselves and others about our true, authentic motivations. Someone who is passive-aggressive, for example, does not want to follow along with the demands or requests of others; however, instead of honestly acknowledging this, the person acts in ways that indirectly communicate they are not happy (e.g., pouting, procrastinating). Over time, living within this defensive system results in our finding maladaptive ways to self-soothe or self-nourish (e.g., addiction of any kind), which can leave us with overwhelming feelings of guilt. This and other forms of distress develop over time; however, after a long enough period of being disconnected from who we truly are, including what we truly want and need, we become less and less able to determine why we feel distressed. This is one explanation for why someone may feel like they do not know why they are upset—the feelings seem to "come out of nowhere."

The false self has many names. Regardless of the name given to the version of you that does not reflect who you truly are, the results are the same. Those who live primarily within their false self have been unable or have not been allowed to know their true desires, needs, beliefs, and values. Typically, this arises from early childhood experiences that require us to adapt in ways that move us further and further away from our true selves. As a result, we struggle to be honest with ourselves and others, we are more likely to experience significant psychological distress, and our relationships with others will be dissatisfying at best and harmful at worst.

PART 3

Identity and Challenges of the Twenty-First Century

Part 3 explores current sociopolitical and cultural issues that impact all who are living. In this part, we examine significant factors and events that affect us at both the local and global levels. We also explore the impact technology and social media have on us and how we express ourselves through digital media. Before delving into these issues, we examine the differences and similarities that exist between generations that appear to impact how each of us lives and views the world around us, including those belonging to generations younger or older than ourselves.

CHAPTER EIGHT

Millennials and Generation Z

The focus of this chapter is millennials and Generation Z. These two generations will be compared to Generation X, baby boomers, and the Silent Generation, which are other generations that have a significant number of people still living. In addition, members of Generation Z are likely the children of those from Generation X, and millennials are likely the children of baby boomers or those born early in Generation X, with those in Generation X parented by the Silent Generation and to a lesser extent the baby boomers. An internet search for defining the boundaries of each generation will yield multiple results; therefore, the beginning and ending years for each generation will be those used by the Pew Research Center, which is self-described as a "nonpartisan fact tank that informs the public about the issues, attitudes, and trends shaping the world."

The Generations

Before describing each generation from the Silent Generation to Generation Z, it is worth noting that the generation immediately succeeding Generation Z has been named and that there are two named generations that precede the Silent Generation. These generations will be briefly described first.

Generation Alpha (Gen Alpha) is the generation that immediately succeeds Generation Z. Those in Gen Alpha consist of those born in the early 2010s through the mid-2020s—making the oldest possible member of this generation ten years old as of the writing of this book. This generation is so named because they are the first (i.e., alpha) generation to be born entirely during the twenty-first century and are typically the children of those in the millennial generation. This generation will have grown up with an abundance of technology and having regularly used smartphones and tablets as modes of entertainment, education, and "pacifiers."

The two generations that precede the Silent Generation are the Lost Generation and the Greatest Generation (or the G.I. Generation). Members of the Lost Generation were born between 1883 and 1900 and experienced World War I (1914–1918) as a pivotal event during their formative and young adult years. The moniker "Lost" reportedly refers to the fact that those who survived World War I were characterized as having been directionless following the war. There are believed to be no living members of this generation. The Greatest or G.I. Generation, sometimes also known as the World War II Generation, were born between 1901 and 1927. The pivotal events for this generation were the Great Depression (1929–1933) and World War II (1939–1945). The moniker "Greatest Generation" was coined by journalist Tom Brokaw, who wrote a book about this generation and used this name as the book's title. Members of this generation are generally characterized as being tough for having survived two major and difficult world events and as idealistic, since they generally tend to want to do what is "right." There are believed to be just under seventy-five thousand members of this generation still living in the United States, making many of them one hundred or more years old.

Generation Z

Those who are part of Generation Z (Gen Z) fall in between Generation Alpha and the millennials. Although there have been other names used to describe this generation (e.g., iGen, zoomers, digital natives) the Pew Research Center found that Generation Z was, by far, the most widely used term referring to this generation. Members of Generation Z were born between 1997 and 2012. They are likely to be the children of Generation X and early millennials. Like Generation Alpha, members of Generation Z used technology at much younger ages than their parents, but they did not necessarily experience technology such as smartphones until they were older (e.g., late grade school/early middle school). Despite having access to more technology than the generations before them (thus the application of the term *digital natives* to this generation), members of Generation Z are not considered to be particularly digitally literate.

Digital literacy refers to one's ability to use technology in a way that one can find and critically evaluate information and requires the effective use of both cognitive and technical skills (see also "Media and Digital Literacy" in chapter 9). Gen Z has grown up with the ubiquitous availability of wireless networks and cell phones in a post-9/11 world. While many in this generation will have no memory of 9/11, they have grown up with its effects, perhaps the most obvious of which is how the events of that day have permanently impacted airline travel in the United States and around the world. In addition to this threat to safety and security, members of Generation Z also grew up during the time of the Great Recession (2007–2009). Many will have been too young to fully understand what a recession is and why it matters, but they will have grown up with its effects, not the least of which being the impact the recession had on their family, their parental figures in particular. This generation is aware of the financial burden of student loans and is often vocal about whether or not a college education is "worth it" given the substantial debt many previous students (including their parental figures) still have. Contributing to this generation's awareness of the literal cost of things, including the cost of a college education, this fiscal awareness has also likely been influenced by a growing income gap between the wealthiest and the least wealthy while those in the middle class have simultaneously shrunk in number.

Overall, members of Generation Z have been characterized as compassionate, open-minded, thoughtful, responsible, and determined; however, a 2017 report commissioned by the Varkey Foundation, *Generation Z: Global Citizenship Survey*, revealed what those within the generation already know and others have suspected: they do not report high levels of overall well-being. Only 17 percent of the more than twenty thousand members of Generation Z surveyed reported having good physical well-being, and under one-third of this group stated that they have good emotional well-being. Just over half of this group stated that money is a significant source of anxiety, and close to half experienced pressure related to school. Overall, they seem to be a socially progressive group, as nearly 90 percent agreed that men and women should be treated equally, over 60 percent believe same-sex marriage should be legal, and nearly 75 percent believe that transgender people should have equal rights to nontransgender people. While this group of young people generally wants all people to be treated equally (including immigrants and refugees), they see significant problems in the world as direct threats to people's future. Over 80 percent see extremism and terrorism along with war as being the greatest threats to people's futures, and in most countries around the world, more members of Generation Z than not see the world as becoming an increasingly worse place in which to exist.

Millennials

Millennials have also been referred to as Generation Y (Gen Y) because they are the group that follows Generation X; however, *millennial* is the term used almost universally. This group is defined by the birth years 1981 to 1996, and they more likely than not have parents from the baby boomer generation or early Generation X. Millennials are also likely to be the parents of the youngest generation: Generation Alpha.

Like their younger counterparts in Generation Z, millennials have been significantly affected by the economic fluctuations and downturns present in the United States and world economies. They are likely more impacted than those in Generation Z because they have been in the workforce longer and have embarked on their careers, whereas those in Generation Z are just exploring possible career trajectories. Thus, millennials have been highly impacted by the Great Recession (2007–2009) and the current recession due to the coronavirus (2020–present; see also "Economic Insecurity" in chapter 10 and "The Novel Coronavirus Pandemic" in chapter 11), with the greatest impact of the most recent recession being a high rate of unemployment among those in this generation in particular.

Among those aware of their generation's moniker, millennials are the least likely to identify with their generational name compared to baby boomers and Gen Xers. Around 43 percent of those born during the beginning years of this generational age group actually identify as the previous generation: Generation X. Some have referred to this group as the "echo boomers" because they are often the offspring of baby boomers and because they represent a large proportion of the population in comparison to baby boomers, who already represent a large generational group. Some millennials seem to have internalized the less flattering descriptors of their generation and thus self-identify as such. Millennials have been referred to as the most hated generation, and those most likely doing the hating are Gen Xers and baby boomers.

Millennials have been characterized as more confident and assertive compared to their older counterparts, but they have also been called entitled. Millennials tend to have delayed entering into adulthood longer than previous generations, thereby living at home longer than previous generations; however, some suggest that the high cost of living and the high cost of college partly explain this phenomenon rather than being a function of this generation specifically. Millennials who struggle financially more than the older generations have given rise to the "tiny house" movement. Others have suggested that boomers and Gen Xers are less than fond of millennials because millennials remind them of who they once were: bold, having a sense of purpose, and more courageous. Older generations tend not to like being reminded of their past and the fact that they cannot go back. It turns out that the millennials are allegedly surrounded by those who really do not like them, with baby boomers and Gen Xers on one side and members of Generation Z, who have declared that they do not want to be compared to or associated with millennials, on the other.

Although young adults and teenagers are quick to let you know that if you are over the age of forty you are a "boomer," it is no longer true that everyone

Millennials and Generation Z   145

under the age of forty is considered a millennial, as Gen Zers have taken to distancing themselves from their slightly older counterparts. One social media user was quoted in a news story as saying, "Just because you're so old you can't remember the difference, doesn't mean it's OK to lump us all together." Baby boomers, however, were the first to point out the "flaws" of the millennial generation. Baby boomers accused millennials of not being able to be financially independent because of poor spending habits (e.g., the infamous "avocado toast" is often levied at millennials in this context). Ironically, baby boomers are most likely the parents of millennials, which has led many to point out that boomers should perhaps take some ownership of how this generation turned out. Of course, as already mentioned, millennials have experienced two major economic recessions, whereas baby boomers worked and invested their money during the economic expansion of the 1980s.

Generation X

Generation Xers are defined by the birth years 1965–1980 and are most likely the children of the Silent Generation and those born early in the baby boomer generation. This is the generation to which the term *latchkey* was first applied, as Gen Xers enjoyed far less parental or adult supervision compared to earlier, and indeed later, generations. Latchkey kids were typically those who were from divorced homes or homes in which both parental figures worked; therefore, when these children and teens returned home from school, they likely returned to an empty house and had to let themselves in with their own house key. This generation has also been called the MTV Generation, since MTV (i.e., the music television channel on cable television) first appeared during the teenage years of most Gen Xers.

Generally, those from Generation X have been characterized as "disaffected," "cynical," and "slackers," and they were heavily influenced by the music cultures of hip-hop and grunge. Being referred to as disaffected or cynical was partly caused by this generation growing up in the middle of the Cold War and the ever-present threat of mutual nuclear destruction (see "The Silent Generation" section for more information on the Cold War). Those in Generation X are currently the last generation for which going to college made financial sense and for whom getting a college degree resulted in higher-paying jobs that earned them a better way of life—though they are not likely to be as affluent as baby boomers or those from the Silent Generation.

The issues of divorce occurring with much greater frequency and both parental figures entering the workforce—for many women, this occurred postdivorce—has led some to state that Gen X children grew up while their parents focused on themselves and tried to become the best versions of themselves they could. As previously noted, this led to this generation also being known as the "Latchkey Generation" and to a socialization shift, as those in Generation X became more focused on their peers than any generation before them

Pivotal events affecting this generation included the crack epidemic, the AIDS epidemic, the development of home computers, and the passing of Title IX. Crack cocaine, as many readers likely know, is a version of cocaine produced in solid form, like rocks, and smoked. Crack affects the user more quickly than powdered cocaine, but the effects last for a shorter period of time than snorting or injecting cocaine. This can lead to a cycle of use that further increases the likelihood of dependence. During this period of time in the 1980s, the crack epidemic also saw the birth of "crack babies," who were children born to mothers who had been using crack while pregnant. As soon as these babies were born, they went into withdrawal, and they often had long-lasting behavioral and psychological difficulties. The AIDS epidemic occurred during the 1980s and 1990s, when most Gen Xers were in their adolescent years. Although AIDS initially affected the LGBTQ community at much higher rates, particularly among gay males, the fact that a disease that could kill you could be contracted via having sex led Gen Xers to hear the message that having sex can literally kill you.

The early 1980s saw the exponential growth of the number of homes with a personal computer. The most common companies at the time were Commodore, Atari, and Apple. Compared to the computers of today, these were crude devices in appearance and in what they could do, but at the time, they were revolutionary. They paved the way for various methods of storing and sharing files (e.g., floppy discs) and connecting with other computers or people via dial-up modems. These early efforts subsequently paved the way for faster and easier connections, the internet, thumb drives, laptops, tablets, and smartphones, making millennials and all those who follow more "digitally native" than any other preceding generation, including those in Generation X.

Sociopolitically, those of Generation X grew up postsegregation (though some areas of the United States were slower to publicly adopt full integration). At the time, those in Generation X were considered to be the least prejudiced of any previous generation. Similarly, Generation X saw the passing of Title IX, which, among other things, mandated that females should have access to sports in public schools at a rate commensurate with males. Although many readers likely know that full equality in sport (and indeed in many other facets of life) has not been fully achieved, Title IX was pivotal legislation that helped pave the way for today's girls to have access to sports such as ice hockey and football, which have maintained male exclusiveness for longer than most other sports. Other landmark events that occurred when Gen Xers were teenagers or young adults include the demise of apartheid in South Africa, the collapse of the Soviet Union (i.e., the USSR), and the

Millennials and Generation Z 147

fall of the Berlin Wall in 1989, prior to which then president Ronald Reagan famously declared, "Mr. Gorbachev, tear down this wall!" while standing on the West Berlin side of the Brandenburg Gate in June 1987.

Baby Boomers

The baby boomer generation is the only generation officially recognized by the U.S. Census Bureau, in large part due to the "boom" of babies born following World War II and the accompanying decline in the U.S. birthrate following the year 1964. This makes the birth year parameters for baby boomers 1946–1964. Prior to the existence of the millennials, baby boomers had been the largest generation, making it understandable that as this generation aged, more and more resources—including money for research—was devoted to understanding the issues and concerns among the "geriatric" population. As the baby boomers are more likely than not the parents of millennials, it is not surprising that there are quite a few millennials, and as the baby boomers have aged and died, millennials have surpassed this generation as the largest generational group. That being said, seventy-six million baby boomers were born during the parameters of this generation, and sixty-two million millennials were born.

Given their large numbers, baby boomers helped to create an interest in what it means to be from one generation or another. This particular generation was highly influential in the "countercultural" movement of the 1960s, which gave rise to civil rights advocacy and protests around civil rights violations. Baby boomers have historically been associated with privilege, as those of this generation benefited from the World War II and post–World War II economic boom, which included substantial assistance with housing and education (this experience may explain, at least in part, why baby boomers do not understand why millennials struggle financially). Given the fact that most in this generation saw vast improvements in their own lives and the lives of those across the world as a result of the outcome of World War II, baby boomers believed that the world would continue to get better over time. Critics of this generation have stated that their consumerism and self-focus bordering on narcissism were all excessive. In fact, millennials have been some of the more outspoken about baby boomers, perhaps because baby boomers were the first to criticize what they saw in the millennials.

Baby boomers were the first generation to grow up with television, which involved large-sized technology that was bulky and heavy, shows that were only in black-and-white for a time, and a very small number of stations to watch. This generation still relied on radio technology—the transistor radio—so they could listen to nonmainstream music. Although this generation is associated with counterculturalism, civil rights, and feminism, many in this generation were politically more conservative. This paradox is often understood in terms of "early boomers" and "late boomers." Early boomers experienced events such as Beatlemania and Woodstock and Vietnam protests and are more likely to be Democrats, whereas the late boomers experienced the Watergate scandal, the 1970s oil crisis, and the Iran hostage crisis and tend to be Republicans.

Between the late 1970s and the Great Recession (2007–2009), most baby boomers saw their wealth increase, the wealthiest at a rate of 278 percent. By contrast, following baby boomers' graduations from college, the cost of higher education increased by 600 percent. In terms of personal wealth, about one-third of the wealthiest baby boomers planned to give their wealth to charities, holding the opinion that each should earn their own money, including their own children. However, surveys of this generation during what should be their retirement years indicate that not only do baby boomers seem to want to avoid discussing end-of-life issues, but they have also suffered economically due to the substantial economic downturns of recent years. Many baby boomers of retirement age are delaying retirement, with as many as one-quarter of this group claiming they will never retire and are therefore still working.

The Silent Generation

Those in the Silent Generation were born between 1928 and 1945, and they are the generation that immediately precedes the baby boomers. Members of this generation are between the ages of seventy-five and ninety-two years old as of 2020. This generation is smaller compared to other generations due to fewer people (i.e., the parents of members of the Silent Generation) having children because of the Great Depression and World War II. The Silent Generation comprises most of those who fought during the Korean War (1950–1953). They have also been called the "Lucky Few" by sociologist Elwood Carlson, who authored the book *The Lucky Few: Between the Greatest Generation and the Baby Boom.*

Members of the Silent Generation are also referred to as *children of the Depression*, as many of them were very young during this time period. Thus, they grew up watching their parents struggle to support a family during a time of exceptional economic devastation. Some members of this generation were children during World War II, and many of them were old enough to have memories of and to be affected by the war. This means they saw what the Nazis were capable of, and they witnessed the end of Nazism. They also witnessed, during their formative years, the awesome power and destruction of a nuclear bomb.

As this generation aged, they saw the rise in communism, particularly within the Soviet Union, that eventually gave rise to the Cold War, which began in 1947 (two years following World War II, during which both the

Millennials and Generation Z 149

United States and the Soviet Union fought with the Allies) and ended in 1991 (two years following the fall of the Berlin Wall). The *Cold War* essentially refers to the conflict between the United States (along with the Western bloc of Europe) and the Soviet Union (along with the Eastern bloc of Europe). This war was so named because war was never declared on one another, and both sides knew the other had nuclear capability. As a result, war was waged economically and politically instead of with their respective military powers.

The Silent Generation is so called because its members do not express what they think or how they feel publicly. They tended to be characterized as a group in terms of not being risk-takers and embodied the phrase, "Keep your head down, and do your job," which is another way of saying, "Don't cause any trouble" or "Look the other way." This generation is also known for being highly frugal, which is mostly owed to having been raised by Depression-era parents. They tend to use things so that they "get their money's worth" and typically use something to the point that most people would probably not buy it at a garage sale. They tend to save things that can be reused so as not to waste anything, and in some cases, this may reflect hoarding behavior.

Sociopolitically, those belonging to the Silent Generation, in the spirit of not wanting to make waves and cause discomfort, opted for working within a system to make change rather than going outside of the system and demanding change, as the baby boomers did with the civil rights movement. The Silent Generation has been described as generally happy and contented, which is in direct opposition to Gen Xers' dour and bleak view of things— the children of the Silent Generation. The Silent Generation raised their children to be "seen and not heard," reflecting a parent-centric approach. Later, various parenting books were published that changed how the following generation, the baby boomers, viewed parenting, allowing for a more "permissive" approach to child-rearing that those in the Silent Generation found abhorrent.

It was the vast differences in things such as parenting, advocating for civil rights, and between the Silent Generation and the baby boomers that led people to start talking about the differences that exist between different generations. In the 1960s, the term *generation gap* was coined to describe and explain why the baby boomers (the younger of the two generations) seemed to oppose the preferences of those in the Silent Generation at every turn, from music to politics.

The extent to which we identify with the generational label attributed to those who were born during a specific span of years affects our buying habits and what type of managerial style we are more likely to respond to on the job. While these are certainly interesting areas of inquiry, the sections that follow delve into how the generations are the same or different on things such as sociopolitical views, education and family, use of digital resources and social media, and the degree to which those within a particular generation actually identify with the name and characteristics associated with their generation.

Similarities among the Generations

Though there seem to be more differences than similarities between the generations (see the "Differences among the Generations" section that follows), there are some areas in which the generations agree or, at least, overlap.

In terms of how each generation describes itself, millennials, Gen Xers, baby boomers, and those of the Silent Generation generally agree at similar rates that they are entrepreneurial (32%–35%), environmentally conscious (37%–41%), tolerant of others (33%–38%), and rigid (6%–8%). Generation Z and millennials seem to be more aligned in their political views despite each group not wanting to be confused with the other.

In a 2018 study conducted by the Pew Research Center, Gen Z and millennials were similar with respect to their views about various political issues compared to older generations, which included how the current president is doing (lower approval), whether the government should do more to help people and solve problems (higher desire for this), and whether greater diversity with respect to race and ethnicity is a good thing (higher agreement). Generation X and baby boomers are also relatively similar in their views on these same topics but score differently than the two younger generations (higher approval, lower desire, and lower agreement, respectively). Members of Generation Z and millennials are also more likely share the opinion about whether the United States of America is better than all other countries in the world, 14 percent and 13 percent, respectively indicating that a relatively small percentage of these generations see the United States as better than other countries.

Perhaps another way in which the generations are similar is that each is defined by a distinct range of birth years and each having critical historical events that shaped the respective generations during their formative years. In addition, no matter the generation with which each of us identifies, we communicate that we are not like the other generations. In nearly all other ways, the generations are different from one another.

Differences among the Generations

In terms of the overall number of people born to a particular generation, there are differences between the four oldest generations. The fewest born to a generation was the Silent Generation at 47 million. Next were the Gen Xers

Millennials and Generation Z 151

at 55 million. The largest number of births belonged to the baby boomers (which is why this generation has its name) at 71.6 million, but they have since been surpassed by the millennials, as of July 2019, at 72.1 million. One article places the number of members of Generation Z at approximately 72 million, making them the second largest of all generations, and it is predicted that by the year 2026, Generation Z will have the greatest influence on consumer trends than any other generation, outpacing millennials by about 2 million consumers.

There are clearly tensions between the generations. None of them want to be compared to the others, at least not in ways that may imply there are similarities. Millennials, for example, do not like Gen Zers because those who are part of Gen Z have been characterized as seeing themselves as superior, acting puritanical, and wanting to foment insurrection, even if that means entire systems are destroyed. The differences between the various generations seem to largely revolve around how each generation sees itself and the degree to which those born in a particular generation identity with that generation, its label, and subsequent descriptors. This is, not surprisingly, less known about Generation Z because they are still relatively young compared to the other generations, and thus quite a bit more is known in this regard for the older generations: millennials, Gen Xers, baby boomers, and the Silent Generation.

As noted in the section describing millennials, they tend to see themselves in a negative light, which may account for why such a large percentage of those born in this generation do not identity with the label "millennial." A survey of millennials, Gen Xers, baby boomers, and members of the Silent Generation showed dramatic differences in how each generation described itself. Compared to those in the Silent Generation, millennials were, in some cases, eight times more likely to see themselves negatively. Millennials see themselves as self-absorbed (59%), wasteful (49%), greedy (43%), and cynical (31%) compared to those in the Silent Generation, who endorsed those same traits at the rate of 7 percent, 10 percent, 8 percent, and 7 percent, respectively. Gen Xers were more likely than the baby boomers and the Silent Generation but less likely than the millennials to endorse these same traits (30%, 29%, 24%, and 24%, respectively), and baby boomers were more likely to endorse these traits in comparison to the Silent Generation (20%, 20%, 19%, and 16%, respectively).

In a similar vein, members of the Silent Generation were more likely to endorse more positive traits compared to the other generations. Those in the Silent Generation considered themselves to be patriotic (73%), responsible (78%), hardworking (83%), willing to sacrifice (61%), moral (64%), self-reliant (60%), and compassionate (60%). Millennials were the least likely to endorse these same descriptors (12%, 24%, 36%, 15%, 17%, 27%, and 29%, respectively). Gen Xers and baby boomers were in between millennials and the Silent Generation, with baby boomers endorsing these traits at a higher rate than Gen Xers.

Identifying with one's generation can be complex when one considers how a particular generation is viewed by others and, of course, by themselves. An additional factor influencing one's identification with a generational label, or not, includes whether people have heard of the labels ascribed to the various generations. As noted earlier in the section on baby boomers, this is the only generation officially identified by the U.S. Census Bureau, and perhaps this is one reason why baby boomers identify with this descriptor at a rate of 79 percent, which is over 20 percent more than the next generation that identifies strongly with its descriptor: Generation X at 58 percent. Only 40 percent of millennials identify with this name, whereas another 33 percent, of those who are technically millennials, identify with Generation X. Only 18 percent of the Silent Generation identifies with this name; however, another survey indicated that only 27 percent of those in the Silent Generation have ever heard of this term. When all respondents were considered, spanning all generations surveyed, only 15 percent had heard of the Silent Generation. An equal percentage (34%) of those technically in the Silent Generation identity with either the baby boomers or the Greatest Generation (or the G.I. Generation).

Despite the self-described similarity between the generations on whether each group is environmentally conscious (see the previous section, "Similarities among the Generations"), younger generations are more likely to prioritize directing resources to alternative energy sources and are more likely to agree that there is strong evidence for climate change compared to older generations. In terms of political views, as noted in the previous section in this chapter, Generation Z and millennials are similarly minded as are Gen Xers and baby boomers. A 2018 survey conducted by the Pew Research Center found that the greatest difference exists between Generation Z and the Silent Generation. Generation Z approves of how the current president is doing at a rate of 30 percent (millennials are essentially the same at a rate of 29%), whereas members of the Silent Generation approved at a rate of 54 percent. In terms of whether the government should do more to help solve the various problems that exist in the United States, Generation Z, at a rate of 70 percent, endorses this notion, whereas those in the Silent Generation agree at a rate of 39 percent.

Finally, 62 percent of those in Generation Z think the increasing diversity with respect to race and ethnicity is good for society as a whole, whereas only 42 percent of the Silent Generation agree with this statement. When specifically asked about how Black people are treated in this country, those in the two youngest generations (Gen Z and millennials) are more likely to say Black people are not treated fairly compared to White people than the older generations (Gen X, baby boomers, and the Silent Generation). The Pew

Millennials and Generation Z   153

Research Center also reported that Generation Z is the most diverse in terms of race and ethnicity compared to the older generations, which may account, in part, for this generation's endorsement of diversity as being a good thing for the country.

Generation Z and millennials also show differences that are likely the result of the cultural context in which they grew up. While Generation Z and millennials are more likely than the older generations to say they know someone who prefers the use of gender-neutral pronouns, 35 percent of Gen Zers endorsed this compared to only 25 percent of millennials. For the older generations, the percentages of those who know someone who prefers the use of gender-neutral pronouns drops significantly compared to the younger generations at 16 percent for Gen Xers, 12 percent for baby boomers, and 7 percent for the Silent Generation. Similarly, those in Generation Z, at the rate of nearly 60 percent, say nonbinary options related to sex should be included on surveys (i.e., more than simply male or female). Only half of millennials hold this view, and for the older generations, 40 percent or fewer hold this view. As noted in the previous section on Generation Z, members of this generational group are often considered to be digitally illiterate, which may, in part, explain why only 39 percent of this generation think it is bad for society that people get their news from social media outlets, whereas around 50 percent of each of the older generations think this is a bad thing.

With respect to whether the United States is a better country than all other countries in the world, Generation Z and millennials share vastly different sentiments compared to older generations. Generation Z and millennials agree with this at a rate of about 14 percent, whereas 20 percent of Gen Xers, 30 percent of baby boomers, and 45 percent of the Silent Generation endorse the United States as the best country in the world. A similar pattern is revealed when asked whether there are countries that are better than the United States: 30 percent of Gen Zers, 29 percent of millennials, 20 percent of Gen Xers, 12 percent of baby boomers, and 5 percent of the Silent Generation stated they agree that there are better countries than the United States in the world.

When it comes to the two major political parties, Republicans and Democrats, and opinions held among the various generations, Democrats generally agree regardless of which generation they belong to; however, those in Generation Z who identity as Republican are more likely to endorse different ideals compared to their older Republican counterparts. Although Generation Z Republicans still have vastly different political views than Democrats of any generation, they are more likely than Republicans in older generations to say that climate change is due to human activity (54% of Generation Z compared to 38% of the Silent Generation), that the current president at the time of the survey, President Trump, is not doing as good of a job as their older counterparts think (e.g., 90% of Silent Generation Republicans think the current president is doing a good job compared to nearly 60% of Generation Z Republicans), and that the government should do more to solve problems rather than private businesses or individuals (70% of Generation Z Republicans and only 39% of Silent Generation Republicans).

These vast differences on what can be construed as important sociopolitical and cultural topics likely explain why the various generations do not see eye to eye on many things and view generations further removed by age from their own with suspicion and perhaps disdain. The paradox of the generations is found among Generation Z and millennials, who, despite openly expressing dislike for the other group and not wanting to be lumped together, tend to be more similar in values, beliefs, and priorities than any other generational pairing.

Another way in which the generations have distinguished themselves is in terms of whether members of their respective generations have their own households and therefore have started a family. Numbers on this for Gen Z do not exist because many are too early into adulthood for them to have established their own households. According to a survey conducted in 2019 by the Pew Research Center, millennials are not establishing their own family households (defined as living with a spouse and/or children) as early or as often as previous generations. Eighty-five percent of those in the Silent Generation are in a family, whereas only 55 percent of millennials are in a family. Those in Generation X and the baby boomer generation are in families at similar rates: 66 percent and 69 percent, respectively.

This survey also revealed that a correlation between level of education and establishing a household exists for millennials. Millennials without a high school diploma were more likely to establish a family compared to those with a high school education or higher. Interestingly, millennials with a bachelor's degree or higher are more likely, in comparison to those with less education, to live with a spouse and no children. This generation, when in their twenties and thirties, is also more likely than previous generations to live with their parents or other extended family members. This is due, in part, to the Great Recession of 2007–2009; however, the Pew Research Center study revealed this trend continued to increase even after the economy began to recover, with more men (18%) than women (10%) living with their parents.

Finally, confirming what many already likely know, millennials are marrying at later ages than those in previous generations, if they marry at all, and they are also less likely to have children during their early 20s to late 30s. The average age for males who married in 2019 was 30, and for females, it was 28. In 2003, the average ages were 27 and 25, respectively; in 1987, the average ages were 26 and 24, respectively; and finally, in 1968, the average ages were 23 and 21, respectively. In terms of childbearing, the percentage of women in the baby boomer generation who gave birth was 64 percent; for Generation X, it was 62 percent; and for millennials, it was 55 percent. In

2015, the average age at which a female gave birth was 26.4 years old, and in 1980, the average age was 22.7 years old. Moreover, many among the younger generations become first-time mothers in their 40s, which is considered to be a high-risk age group for childbearing.

While there are some similarities and a multitude of differences between the generations, there is no doubt that whatever generation one identifies with becomes part of one's overall identity. Many of us make a point of declaring which generation we are part of and which generations we do not want to be confused with. Some of us may not even know that our generation has a particular label. It is also clear that experiencing economic difficulties directly or indirectly through one's parental figures may affect our ability to afford living on our own, pursuing a college education, or deciding whether to start a family. Regardless of our awareness of the generation we are part of—or whether or not we identify with it—we are undoubtedly influenced by the historically significant events that occurred during our generation's formative years, and they can affect how we view ourselves, the world around us, and the people in it.

CHAPTER NINE

Technology and Social Media

The youngest generations among us (see chapter 8 for more information) have had the greatest access to the most diverse forms of technology. While they may have grown up with the technology and may be able to seemingly effortlessly make new forms of technology work for them, those who use technology may or may not be literate with respect to effectively using technology to access reliable information. In addition, the various forms of technology have given rise to social media, which allows for unique ways of expressing one's identity. This chapter will explore what it means to be media literate and, specifically, digitally literate. We will also examine what is known about how people share themselves online, including the degree to which what we reveal on social media and other platforms reflects who we truly are.

Media and Digital Literacy

Media literacy is a global issue as evidenced by myriad organizations that are designed to educate people on the importance of media literacy and to conduct research in this field. In 1978, the Ontario Association for Media Literacy was formed in Canada. Media education in Russia actually began in the 1920s, but it was halted by the former premier of the Soviet Union, Joseph Stalin. Official programs surrounding media education were eventually implemented in Russia throughout the 1970s to 1990s. Other regions and countries of the world, such as Asia, the Middle East, Australia, Europe, and the United Kingdom, have also formalized media literacy education in schools. Thus, media literacy is believed to have been an area of focus worldwide since the 1970s, with more education and research activity in this field starting in the 1980s and 1990s.

Those with internet access and a computer or another type of device that can access the internet (e.g., smartphone) have massive amounts of data available at their fingertips. Entering almost any term into a search engine (e.g., Google, Firefox) will result in at least hundreds of thousands, if not millions, of hits, which are links to information that include your search term or have a portion of your search term embedded within them. Even without internet access, we still get bombarded by information and messages through other forms of media such as television, newspapers, magazines, and billboards.

Media content impacts our individual perceptions, beliefs, and attitudes about ourselves, others, and the world in general. Given the seemingly ubiquitous nature of the media and how influential it can be, critically thinking about the media messages we are exposed to is a significant skill to develop. Tibor Koltay, a linguist and librarian at Eszterházy Károly University in Hungary, has noted that the field of media literacy is multidisciplinary, and the scientists in the various fields studying media literacy endeavor to see how people "comprehend, interpret, critically analyse and compose" various forms of media. One important element of media literacy is whether we are able to ascertain the degree to which the information we are exposed to is accurate.

Professors of economics Hunt Allcott and Matthew Gentzkow examined the issue of "fake news," particularly as it pertained to the 2016 presidential election in the United States. *Fake news* is described as information that is made up (i.e., fake and therefore not true) but that mimics content one might see from a verified news outlet. Allcott and Gentzkow noted that as technology has allowed for greater and greater ease of creating and disseminating content, the original power of the media, which historically has been to hold those in positions of power accountable (e.g., government officials), has been greatly diminished. They stated that the increase in online news outlets beginning in the early 2000s allowed people greater choice of their source of information, but this also meant that there has been greater opportunity for people to seek out news they wanted to hear or read and to connect with others who share similar beliefs and interests. This results in what Allcott and Gentzkow referred to as "echo chambers" or "filter bubbles," which keep out alternative viewpoints.

In recent years, this concern has focused on social media platforms, where there has been "no significant third party filtering, fact-checking, or editorial judgment." They further noted that almost anyone who posts whatever content they want and who has "no track record or reputation can, in some cases, reach as many readers as Fox News, CNN, or the *New York Times*." The results of their study showed that during the 2016 presidential election in the United States, a typical adult voter consumed and remembered at least one article, possibly several, that was determined to be fake

Technology and Social Media   159

news about a political candidate, and these fake news articles may have been as persuasive as a single campaign advertisement on television.

In addition to things like fake news spread via social media that may have impacted voting behaviors during the 2016 presidential election, Koltay also noted that children and adolescents may be particularly vulnerable to the impact of media messages given the quantities they consume and the importance of all forms of media to promote trends that impact how a child or adolescent is socialized. Perhaps as a direct result of knowing how influential false information can be, an article published in *Science* in 2018 saw sixteen authors from myriad disciplines call upon "interdisciplinary research" to help gatekeeping efforts to reduce the publication and spread of fake news.

There are various forms of media literacy, which itself is an umbrella term that encapsulates literacy of myriad forms of media. In 2001, David Bawden, from the University of Arizona, identified some of the more commonly used literacy-related terms and identified six specific terms that have been widely used in various forums: *information literacy, computer literacy, library literacy, media literacy, network literacy,* and *digital literacy.* Koltay noted that the three forms of literacy that are most widely dissected and studied are media literacy, information literacy, and digital literacy. *Media literacy* has already been defined. *Information literacy* is defined by the Association of College and Research Libraries (a division of the American Library Association) as "a set of abilities requiring individuals to 'recognize when information is needed and have the ability to locate, evaluate, and use effectively the needed information.'" Thus, informationally literate individuals know when they need more information about a topic, they know where to get that information, and they know how to discern whether the information is legitimate and useful. Although he was not the first to use the term, Paul Gilster defined *digital literacy* in 1997, and his definition reflects how the term is understood and used today. He described digital literacy as a set of skills that allow the consumer to seek out digital information from a variety of sources, with the accompanying ability to understand the information and the ability to effectively use that information. He further noted that there are four specific competencies associated with digital literacy: knowledge assembly, internet searching, hypertext navigation, and content evaluation.

In 2008, Bawden wrote about the origins and concepts related to digital literacy. He cited Gilster's four digital competencies and drew upon descriptions of digital and information literacy from international organizations to explicate these competencies. The first digital competency, knowledge assembly, is subdivided into two concepts: presearch knowledge assembly and postsearch knowledge assembly. *Presearch knowledge assembly* is seen in digitally literate people when they recognize the need for information and can determine the type and amount of information required. *Postsearch knowledge assembly,* by contrast, refers to one's ability to organize and synthesize the information to contribute to the existing knowledge base or to create new knowledge. *Internet searching* (i.e., using a search engine such as Google to search for information) and *hypertext navigation* (i.e., exploring links provided on web pages found as a result of one's internet search) are described conjointly as the act of going online and finding the information you need as efficiently as possible. Finally, the *content evaluation* competency reflects the digitally literate person's ability to evaluate not only the credibility of the information discovered but also the source of the information and to select reliable information to incorporate into one's knowledge base. Each of these competencies requires intentional action with an understanding of why one is searching for information to begin with; the process is not a passive one. When taken together, these competencies suggest that the individual who is able to effectively utilize them is likely digitally literate and engaged in critical thinking to weed through unhelpful or inaccurate information to find the most relevant, accurate, and current information available.

Samantha Paige and a group of colleagues in the United States examined how literate people of different ages are with respect to electronic health (eHealth) information. They included members of three different generations: millennials, Generation Xers, and baby boomers/the Silent Generation (the authors combined these two generations). Not surprisingly and consistent with previous published findings, these researchers found that older generations (i.e., Generation X and baby boomers/Silent Generation) are not as literate when it comes to accessing and evaluating eHealth information. They specifically found that members of the younger generation (i.e., millennials) showed that they were more aware of eHealth-related resources online, and they expressed a higher degree of confidence in their ability to find and use such information.

Knowing how to effectively use technology to access digital information of any kind, including health-related information, is more important now than ever. Much of what we do in terms of work and leisure activities involves digital media in some capacity. We send thousands of emails and texts every year, nearly exclusively apply for jobs through online portals, and research information on particular topics via the internet. However, even when one wants to use a library's print resources to assemble information, finding the information you are looking for likely requires your ability to navigate a library-devoted search engine of some kind.

Learning how to effectively navigate these rapidly changing sources of information and modes of communication will serve members of any age or generation well, particularly those who want to be certain they have the most accurate and up-to-date information available. As will be seen in the following section, our ability to effectively navigate and use digital devices and sources of information can impact who we reveal ourselves to be when interacting with others online.

Online Identity

Despite the fact that many people, often those in older generations, have grave concerns about how much children and adolescents use social media and other online forums, there are some benefits when it comes to digitally exploring and establishing one's identity. Researchers from Italy, the United Kingdom, and Spain examined online identity among adolescents aged eleven to sixteen, and their findings seem to concur with the notion that being online is not all bad. They described using social media and having access to various online platforms as playing "an important role in the process of self-presentation and emancipation, providing 'full-time' access to peers and peer culture." As readers will learn later in this section, in many cases, our online identities may be more real compared to how we present ourselves in our face-to-face interactions. Nonetheless, the use of rapidly evolving technologies and various forms of digital media provides a mechanism for members of the younger generations to distinguish themselves from older generations.

Using and Understanding Technology: Differences between Generations

In 2013, Kristen Turner examined the gap between generations when something new is introduced: young people typically embrace such changes with enthusiasm, while older people (not necessarily older adults but simply people of an earlier generation than the "young people") often resist accepting the change. Those in the older generations may actively protest and complain about how terrible the change is. She noted, for example, this occurred when Elvis Presley (the "King of Rock and Roll") burst onto the national scene with the movement of his hips. Young people were excited by the new type of music (and dancing), while older people were horrified by and filled with disdain for Elvis Presley and how he moved his body. This is why in a performance on *The Ed Sullivan Show* in 1956, a year after Elvis's television debut on the same show, home audiences watching his performance on television could only see Elvis from the waist up.

In furthering her explanation of the differences between generations in accepting something new, Turner seemed to turn to elements of Erik Erikson's theory of development (see chapter 3 for more information) by noting that adolescents, or "young people," are focused on carving out not only an individual personal identity but also a more collective identity for their particular generation. Identity exploration and establishment of this kind is typically in full force during our adolescent years, as each generation attempts to establish themselves as unique and different from those who came before them. Thus, the adolescent "subculture" is an attempt to separate themselves from childhood as well as adulthood, essentially declaring, "We're not kids anymore," while simultaneously letting the adults know, "We're not like you." Turner noted that generational gaps have existed throughout history, including the present day, where rapid advances in technology may play a role in widening the gap between existing generations. Growing up with the technology of our times puts us at least one step ahead of the generations older than us because if one did not grow up with various forms of technology or digital media, then one is fairly consistently challenged with learning something new. Given the speed at which technology and various forms of digital media are rapidly changing older generations may fall further and further behind their younger counterparts, thereby further widening the generation gaps that already exist. Another way in which these changes affect and distinguish the younger generations is reflected in a relatively new term used to describe how language conventions are thrown out the proverbial window when younger generations communicate with one another on digital devices: *digitalk*.

Digitalk can be described as conversations that take place online; however, Turner, an English teacher and self-described "grammar guru," indicated that digitalk is "a complex and fascinating combination of written and conventional languages in a digital setting." She noted further that teens' ability to manipulate language in this way displays a certain type of language mastery not fully understood by many (most) adults. Several years after offering this description, she noted that digitalk is a medium through which adolescents tackle the challenges associated with establishing an identity (see "Post-Freudian: Erik Erikson" in chapter 3 for more information). She contends that digitalk serves to distinguish adolescents from the earlier childhood stages they want to leave behind and to differentiate them from the current generations of adults from whom they want to be distinct. One of the ways adolescents distinguish themselves is by how they express their identities and share their lives online.

Expressing Ourselves Online

In 2002, psychologist John Suler, from Rider University, examined how our identities are expressed (or not) in cyberspace (i.e., being online). He noted that we do not have to present ourselves online in the same way we interact with others in person. Our personalities are complex and include myriad facets, all of which we do not necessarily share with everyone we meet. However, Suler suggested that in cyberspace, it is much easier to break our identities into small pieces and only present a very narrow version of ourselves to those we encounter in online forums. He further noted the fact that being anonymous online, or at least not as revealing as one might be in their in-person interactions, reflects a desire to divest one's self from aspects of our identity we do not want others to know about. The motive for this

Technology and Social Media

does not always have to be nefarious (e.g., hiding parts of who we are to deceive others) but may simply reflect a desire to interact with an essentially random group of people on a specific shared interest while keeping other interests, beliefs, or values private. This provides a kind of anonymity that allows people to explore aspects of who they truly are, or who they might be, in a way that feels safer than doing so in person. Like Erikson (see chapter 3), Suler notes that it is critical for these disparate aspects of our identity to be integrated into a coherent whole—our personal identity: "Bringing together the various components of online and off-line identity into one balanced, harmonious whole may be the hallmark of mental health." Having a well-developed sense of who you are is quite literally good for your health.

When we think about the various aspects of who we are, we usually judge those elements as being either positive or negative. Sometimes these judgments are based on personally held beliefs and values (which of course are influenced in our development by our sociocultural experiences), whereas others are based more clearly and solely on the judgments and expectations of others. Suler noted that picking out one piece of our identity to express online may be a way to further explore that element of ourselves and to see how others react to us. But, he noted, it may also be a way to work through, understand, and change aspects of ourselves we do not like. He uses the example of someone who is gay who interacts with an online forum for gay individuals in an effort to further understand and accept this aspect of who they are. Based on the reactions we get from others on the aspects of ourselves we have chosen to reveal, we may make important decisions about what we ultimately include in our identity: whether we will stay true to who we are or focus more on our false selves.

The Real You or the False You Online

As many readers are no doubt familiar, some online forums (often professionally oriented forums) expect that you are who you say you are and that the views you express reflect how you truly feel and think. Other forums require taking on a persona, such as one might find in some gaming environments, particularly those based on role-playing. Still other online forums allow for some mixture of true aspects of one's identity and those that are fabricated. It is possible for some aspects of our identities—those of which we are not fully aware—to surface in fantasy or partially reality-based forums. A character we embody or create may be imbued, possibly unknowingly, with positive or negative elements of who we truly are but have not yet fully (or at all) accepted as part of our identity. This is not unlike daydreams and fantasies that reveal hidden aspects of ourselves.

Ultimately, despite the fact that it is seemingly easier to deceive others with whom we interact online compared to our in-person interactions, we likely reveal more about ourselves than we realize. At the end of his article, Suler wondered about people's choices to use audio only or to use audio and video when online. Much of who we are can be revealed through both; however, limiting one's self to audio only allows for greater opportunity to hide aspects of who we truly are. Of course, it may also mean we did not shower that day and would rather not show up looking unkempt. Some of the choices we make to represent ourselves online are intentionally deceptive. The motive for this is to trick people into entering into some kind of relationship with the false identity we create. This is commonly known as *catfishing*.

The term *catfishing*, as it is currently understood, was used for the first time in a documentary film released in 2010 titled *Catfish*. *Catfishing* refers to creating a fake, usually appealing, online profile for the purpose of tricking someone into getting into a relationship with the fake person. The motive for doing this may be financial gain (i.e., getting the catfished person to trust you and then ask them for financial help) or to embarrass or compromise the victim. Those who catfish may completely conjure an identity out of thin air, and others may steal someone else's online identity and use it to trick whomever is the target of their efforts. As of the mid-2010s, it was estimated that approximately 5 percent of all Twitter accounts were not real (in 2020, 5% of the total number of Twitter accounts was sixty-five million), and over eighty-three million Facebook accounts were identified as fake. Practically speaking, consumers of these social media platforms have more than likely engaged with someone behind a fake profile and not realized it.

When a catfisher takes someone else's actual identity, by using photos and personal details the real person has posted on their own social media accounts, they may damage the reputation of the person whose identity they have stolen by posting comments, photos, or personal information that makes the real person behind the online identity look bad (e.g., posting prejudicial or slanderous remarks, posting embarrassing photos). If the real person behind the identity is not the target of the person doing the catfishing, they may still be harmed by the catfishing behavior because the catfisher's intent, by definition, is never aboveboard. The effect on those who are the targets of catfishing can be extensive. The person may feel shame or embarrassment for having fallen for a scam; however, and more seriously, those who have been catfished may develop serious mental health issues that affect their daily lives and their interpersonal relationships. Those who catfish and are caught may attempt to claim protection under the First Amendment of the United States (freedom of speech); however, not all speech is free from legal ramifications. Legally, those who have done the catfishing can be charged with fraud, causing emotional distress, misappropriation of likeness, invasion of privacy, and FERPA (Family Education Rights and Privacy Act) violations when catfishing occurs in an educational setting.

Technology and Social Media 165

A group of researchers out of Malaysia lead by Chuan Hu examined the motivations used by people when they are constructing or reconstructing an identity online. Drawing from Tory Higgins's self-discrepancy theory (see chapter 6 for more information), these researchers were interested in the extent to which the tripartite configuration of the self applied to an online setting. Higgins stated that we have three selves: true self, ideal self, and ought self. The *true self* is who we and/or others think we are (akin to the self-concept), the *ideal self* represents who we and others think would be good for us to be, and the *ought self* is who we and others think we should be. Hu and his colleagues found that how we interact with others online begins to reveal who we are, and that version of ourselves may be more complete than what we reveal in our in-person interactions. They concluded that we are guided by our ideal and ought selves in our face-to-face interactions as well as a more limited version of our true self: the positive true self; whereas in our online interactions, our self guide is more complete by including not only our ideal and ought selves but also our positive *and* negative true selves. The Malaysian researchers found four distinct reasons to explain why people express more of their true self online. These motivational factors, in order of most frequently cited to least frequently cited reasons, are being anonymous, experiencing fewer restraints online, engaging in online-off-line dissociation, and interacting with others online who will listen.

Anonymity was the most commonly identified reason participants cited for why it was easier to reveal their true self online, particularly with respect to perceived "negative" elements about themselves. One respondent reportedly stated that they can share whatever they want because other people on the internet "can't find me. I can get disappeared whenever I want." The second most commonly cited reason for revealing more of who one is when online was the experience of having fewer restraints online. In real life, people are seemingly more aware of and ultimately adhere to societal expectations, rules, and laws; however, in an online environment, many people feel as though typical expectations of behavior [(il)legal or otherwise] are, at least temporarily, not in effect. Therefore, many respondents felt like they could express more of who they truly are, including negative views, ideals, or behaviors. As one respondent put it, "There is less restraints (sic) on the internet, so there is not much to worry about."

The dissociation between online and off-line identities was the third most commonly cited reason for being more real online. Participants endorsing this motivator indicated that they believe their online presence is more representative of their true self compared to their off-line presentation. They see the online and off-line worlds as not connected (thus the use of the term *dissociation* for this motivator), and when this kind of separation exists, whether real or imagined, people are more likely to feel free to say and do whatever they want because others in their "real life" are not likely to see that behavior.

The final motivator for being more like who they really are online, endorsed by participants in this study, was the fact that they can find people online who will "listen." They noted that they do not have to worry about any consequences of revealing their true self, and one participant stated that it is always possible to find other like-minded people who "understand you, and won't judge you negatively. Expressing my true self to these people makes me feel supported."

The Influence of Others

Christian Roesler, professor of clinical psychology in Germany, examined our understanding of individual/personal identity and how it forms through the lens of various psychological theorists. He relied heavily on psychiatrist Carl Jung (a contemporary of Freud) and how identity formation intersects with cyberspace. He noted that, historically, elements of our identity have been handed to us via cultural traditions, religious tenets, and the expectations of social groups, including our families. Currently, there is a greater opportunity for a less prescribed identity due to the relatively easy access we have to other people and other cultures across the world, which means individuals have the opportunity to craft whatever identity they want. This can be liberating, but it can also lead to feeling overwhelmed by all the possible identities available to us and can leave us stuck in place trying to decide. A term introduced in the 1970s to describe this is *overchoice*, or *choice overload*, which refers to the cognitive process whereby individuals struggle to make a decision or choice because there are too many options available to choose from. Contributing to choice overload are the myriad opinions provided by others about who we should be.

Of course, designing one's own identity does not occur without external influence. There are plenty of people weighing in on who we *should* be or who others may want us to be, but that does not mean these "shoulds" or "wants" are offered up by those who are genuinely interested in our best interests. Even if they are, it does not mean these suggestions are a good fit for us. The result of a struggle to create, from scratch, a personal identity can be a fragmented, nonintegrated patchwork of identity pieces. Roesler questions whether the rapidly changing realities of the world negatively impact our ability to form a well-developed, authentic identity. He noted that being able to witness the world's rapidly changing realities through online access, which requires processing and reprocessing of information as it emerges and new ideas are presented, prevents us from processing and reprocessing our inner worlds in an effort to find out more about who we are. Understanding our inner experiences helps us to refine our understanding of ourselves, but the outer world of people and relationships also matter in terms of how we see and ultimately construct our understanding of ourselves. In that context,

Technology and Social Media

Roesler suggests that the seemingly infinite possibilities of what exists "out there" may serve as a detrimental distraction from the inner work needed to establish a meaningful and coherent identity. Essentially, there may be too much of an outer world focus that leaves precious little time and energy for inner exploration.

Our ability to effectively use digital and other forms of media is referred to as *digital literacy* or *media literacy*, respectively. Knowing how to gather information efficiently while ensuring that the information we gather is also accurate is part of the literacy skill set. Being digitally literate also applies to how we present ourselves online. While it is certainly possible to present a false version of ourselves online—and some do for nefarious and sometimes criminal purposes—some researchers have found that presenting ourselves online allows us to explore facets of ourselves that we might not otherwise do in our face-to-face interactions. Other researchers have concluded that most of us may, in fact, be more "real" online than we are when we are off-line.

CHAPTER TEN

Local Factors

This chapter explores issues that affect a broad spectrum of people but that can be considered local factors as opposed to more global factors. Although many of these local factors may have roots in global issues, such as the 2020 pandemic or social justice issues (see chapter 11 for more information), the issues as discussed in this chapter are intended to take a look at how individuals and families experience the impact of these various factors.

The Economy: Financial (Un)Well-Being

Each of us has differing degrees of economic health that may be affected by job availability; how well our community, our state, and the country are doing; world events that may impact the global economy and trickle down to local economies; and so on. The focus of the following sections is the effects of various factors not only on the economy but on each of us as individuals.

Economic Insecurity

During the 2020 pandemic involving the novel coronavirus (i.e., SARS-CoV-2), many people were furloughed (i.e., temporarily laid off from work), and some were formally let go. One study estimated that over 100,000 small businesses have permanently closed due to the pandemic, and in the month of April 2020 alone, around 560 businesses filed for bankruptcy, which is reportedly up by over 25 percent during the same time the previous year. Although bankruptcy does not mean a company has or will go out of business, it does mean that they have struggled to stay in business. Major companies such as J. Crew, Sears, Blockbuster, RadioShack, Gold's Gym, and Neiman Marcus are among those that have filed for bankruptcy and likely closed their doors temporarily while they restructured the company to fit the demand and expectations of the current economic climate and effects of the pandemic. As of the middle of April 2020, over twenty-three million people in the United States were unemployed, which constitutes a rate of unemployment of 14.7 percent of the workforce. This level of unemployment is the highest it has been since the Great Depression—which at its worst had an unemployment rate of over 25 percent. One year since the high unemployment rate of April 2020 the unemployment rate has dropped significantly and as of April 2021 is 6.1 percent.

As of May 2021, not all are ready to say the United States is out of the economic recession that some economists have indicated began after February 2020 coinciding with the pandemic. Some data suggests the recession lasted only a matter of weeks pointing to economic data such as the decline in unemployment and increase in spending. Regardless of the end date being in an economic recession means that the economy is suffering significantly, employment is lower, and families have less household income. What income families do have is much less likely to be spent on luxury items that they may have previously purchased. By contrast, the effects of an economic depression are more extreme, with unemployment numbers soaring and significant stoppages in economic spending and trading. Recent reports indicate that the effects of the pandemic on the economy have been the worst since the Great Depression of the late 1920s and into the 1930s. Some economists and governmental personnel suggested that if the unemployment rate in the United States exceeds 20 percent and stays there for many months, the country will likely meet the imprecise standard of being in an economic depression, again; the good news is that did not happen. Recessions tend to have a more localized impact on citizens, whereas a depression tends to have a much broader and global impact. The recession may or may not be technically over as of the writing of this book. Even though the economy of the country may have improved since April 2020 the reality is many families may not have recovered from the impact the recession has had on them.

(Un)Employment

One of the important ways we define ourselves and our identity is through our employment (see chapter 2 for more information) or, in the case of those still in school, what we want to become or what we are studying to become. A loss of employment certainly has a significant financial impact on an individual and their dependents; however, one's sense of identity also takes a significant hit when one is no longer employed. In the two most recent economic recessions (prior to the effects of the 2020 pandemic) in the early 1980s and the late 2000s (the recession that occurred between 2007 and 2009 has been referred to as the Great Recession because it was rated as

Local Factors 171

being second only to the Great Depression), rates of suicide substantially increased, particularly among men, who have historically tied more of their identity and self-worth to employment compared to women. Regardless of one's sex or gender, research in the area of identity and threats to aspects of one's identity are clear. When a salient or meaningful aspect of one's identity is threatened or lost, a grieving process is initiated that can result in clinical levels of depression or anxiety.

A recently coined term that has been an area of increased scientific study is *economic insecurity*. Researchers Walter Bossert and Conchita D'Ambrosio defined *economic insecurity* as "the anxiety produced by the possible exposure to adverse economic events and by the anticipation of the difficulty to recover from them." This refers to actually losing one's job, of course, but it also refers to the possibility of losing one's job (even if one never does) along with the concern about how difficult it might be to cope with and ultimately recover from such a loss. Recent research in this area conducted by Daniel Kopasker, Catia Montagna, and Keith Bender found that the effects of economic insecurity can be felt by any member of the workforce and at any point of income distribution (i.e., low income to high income); however, the hardest hit are males, who reportedly experience the greatest negative impact on their mental health. They concluded that the impact on a man's mental health would not be considered small in the sense that the individual would notice the impact and would perceive such a change in their mental health as "harmful." The researchers also pointed out, and is consistent with the definition of economic insecurity, that the effects of economic insecurity can be felt even if there is no job loss or threat to one's job (e.g., rumors of downsizing, possibility of being furloughed). As such, they highlighted the importance of focusing on those who are still employed but who may be experiencing significant distress related to concerns about whether they will remain employed. Finally, these researchers characterized their findings as revealing "a largely hidden welfare loss resulting in psychological distress" (note: *welfare* in this context refers to health and happiness rather than governmental financial support given to those in need).

In the late 1990s, Richard Price, Daniel Friedland, and Anuram Vinokur, from the University of Michigan, examined the literature regarding how the loss of one's job directly impacts one's identity. They noted that the impact of job loss on identity can be experienced in three distinct ways. The first involves one's identity in the context of various role states (e.g., the role of employee, the role of parent), the second has to do with the impact experienced in terms of one's sense of control or mastery, and the third has to do with job loss and the social stigma that may accompany being unemployed.

The first impact identified by the researchers can be considered in terms of one's social identity. As noted in chapter 2, social identity is derived from our perception of the groups we belong to (e.g., family, friend group, teams or clubs). These social groups also help to define and clarify our roles (e.g., someone's child, best friend, team captain, club member). Of course, with respect to employment, our role is usually employee. However, we may attribute other characteristics to this role, such as being the primary breadwinner (i.e., primary or sole income provider for one's household). We may also attribute a certain status to our particular job or profession. For example, we may feel pride and a sense of importance for being the manager of a retail store or for being part of the medical field. Thus, the loss of one's job often has a far-reaching and significant impact on how we view ourselves in terms of who we are and how we feel about ourselves (i.e., self-worth; see chapter 1 for more information).

Price and his colleagues noted that job loss can be considered in terms of a "status passage," indicating a transition from one role state (employed) to another (unemployed). They further noted that job loss affects more than one's role state as an employee, as many of the roles we have in our lives are interconnected. Therefore, the loss of one's job will impact other aspects of one's identity. For example, if you lose your job, do you tell your friends? your family? What if your job was where most of your friendships were established, or the job you just lost was with your family's business? If one has a romantic partner or children, those roles and relationships will also be affected.

Price and his colleagues further noted that the impact on relationships specifically related to the job loss and subsequent economic hardship can place a strain on relationships because the person who lost their job may be irritable and in conflict with others. They further noted that in more extreme cases, when the unemployed person is unable to sufficiently cope with this threat to their financial well-being as well as their sense of identity, the frustration and difficulty associated with job loss can lead to domestic violence. Those who are able to adjust their identity and essentially create a new overall identity that no longer includes the job that was lost may be able to abate the negative psychological, identity-related impact of job loss.

The second way Price and his colleagues noted how identity, mental health, and job loss are related involves one's perception of control and mastery. We tend to feel at our best when we feel like we have control over or at least some influence on our environment. As an example of what this may look like when we feel a loss of control, in the author's psychotherapy practice during the coronavirus pandemic, patients have experienced an increase in clinical symptoms (e.g., depression- or anxiety-related symptoms), and many often talk about how they do not have any control over the fact that there is a pandemic or how it impacts things such as whether and how they work, whether and how they visit friends and loved ones, whether and how they do their shopping, and so on. Price and his colleagues pointed to earlier research showing that when we experience stress in a particular role, we

Local Factors   173

often perceive a lack or loss of control and mastery. This is particularly salient for those roles to which we ascribe a great deal of importance, and for most people, one's job is such a role. Moreover, these researchers noted that if one's job does not allow for self-directed effort (i.e., you do not get to decide what you do and when you do it), those in a job like that are already more likely to experience a lower level of control and mastery related to work. Therefore, losing this job will only exacerbate the psychological effects of not feeling like your efforts make a difference or that you can have an impact on your environment (e.g., not get fired, have your boss listen to you or take you seriously).

The third and final way Price and his colleagues noted that the loss of one's job directly impacts identity and one's mental health involves the social stigma (real or perceived) that comes with losing one's job. They refer to job loss, specifically the status of *unemployed*, as reflecting what Erving Goffman called *spoiled identity*, which simply refers to an aspect of one's identity that leads the individual to feel stigmatized. They noted that the degree of stigma experienced by the unemployed person will vary based on the context of their job loss. They noted, for example, that when unemployment rates are high (e.g., during the Great Depression), the person who lost their job is likely to feel less stigma because so many others are experiencing the same thing. However, if most people are working and someone is fired or furloughed, they may experience more stigma or at the very least fear that they will.

Although, as noted previously in this section, job loss and its impact can occur at any level of income and therefore for anyone in any given socioeconomic status, Price and his colleagues noted that earlier research showed those who have jobs requiring a higher level of education or those who have high-paying jobs are likely to experience a greater impact on their identity than those who have lower-paying jobs and have less education (see also "Professional Identity" in chapter 2 for more information). Moreover, they noted that the degree to which an important loss, such as the loss of a job, is resolved, or not resolved, can have a differential impact on the person's well-being. If one's job loss is successfully resolved either by finding another job or by readjusting one's identity, the long-term impact of the job loss will be small and may be nonexistent. By contrast, however, if the job loss is not resolved and is considered by the person to be a negative event (for some losing their job is welcomed, and therefore the loss may be seen as positive or at the very least neutral), a decline in mental health may continue well into the future.

In her book *Job Loss, Identity, and Mental Health*, Dawn Norris reviewed what is known about this area, and she interviewed many people who had endured a job loss and subsequent extended unemployment. Norris quoted a professional in the broadcasting industry who stated, "I kinda lost my whole music identity . . . so that kinda hurts. It hurts. . . . Now it's all gone." This, of course, speaks to not only the loss of a job in the profession one loves but also how important one's profession may be to one's overall sense of self and well-being. Feeling pain as a result of the loss of an important aspect of identity is what is predicted when a salient aspect of identity is threatened in some way. Another professional quoted in Norris's book was from a director within a nonprofit organization. This professional spoke to the impact of losing his job, how it affects how we may see ourselves, and specifically what it may be like for men. He was quoted as saying, "I think for men especially, you are pretty much your job. If you have a reasonably good job, to dissociate that from who you are I think can make you feel weak and impotent and just at sea in terms of your identity."

Overall, the economy, which is undoubtedly affected by both local and global factors, can have a tremendous impact on one's sense of identity and overall well-being. Downturns in the economy are most acutely felt when one is actually at risk of losing one's job or believes that may happen. Our ability to adjust to such a loss or the threat of such a loss can impact our acute and long-term psychological health.

Bullying: Who Bullies and What Are We Doing about It?

Bullying, particularly in school systems, is something that has been part of our collective consciousness in the United States for many years. Parents talk about their children being bullied and how it is handled both in and outside of school; children and teens talk about bullying and the far-reaching impact that it has on them; social scientists research how prevalent bullying is and examine who gets bullied, who does the bullying, and how to stop it; and lawmakers propose and enact laws to deter bullying and to have a mechanism by which bullies can be held accountable. The Centers for Disease Control and Prevention (CDC) defines *bullying* in the context of our pre-adult years as "any unwanted aggressive behavior(s) by another youth or group of youths, who are not siblings or current dating partners, that involve an observed or perceived power imbalance and is repeated multiple times or is highly likely to be repeated."

In 2011, the U.S. Department of Education accepted a report submitted to them by Victoria Stuart-Cassel, Ariana Bell, and J. Fred Springer entitled *Analysis of State Bullying Laws and Policies*. The report examines individual states' policies and laws, and governmental officials' efforts to curtail bullying in their respective states. In the summary and discussion section, the authors of the report noted that "bullying represents a serious and often neglected youth problem." They further noted that the impact of bullying is substantial and chronic for all involved, including "students who are bullied, their families and their peers, for the students who bully other youths, and

Local Factors

for the social and educational climate of schools." The far-reaching consequences of bullying and the public's growing awareness of the scope of the problem have led all states to enact legislation designed to formally deal with bullying.

As of the publication of the report, nearly all states had laws or a formal policy on bullying; however, as of the writing of this book, all states have anti-bullying laws. The first state to pass school-based anti-bullying legislation was Georgia in 1999. The last state to pass anti-bullying legislation was Montana in 2015. Addressing bullying seems to be solely under the purview of states, as there are no federal anti-bullying laws, although the website StopBullying.org (which is identified as an official site of the U.S. government) notes that discriminatory harassment does overlap with bullying. Harassment based on a protected group (i.e., race, national origin, color, sex, age, disability, religion) is deemed a form a discrimination, which is expressly prohibited in federal law under civil rights laws. Both the U.S. Department of Education (ED) and the Department of Justice (DOJ) enforce Titles IV and VI of the Civil Rights Act of 1964, Title IX of the Education Amendments of 1972, Section 504 of the Rehabilitation Act of 1973, Titles II and III of the Americans with Disabilities Act (ADA), and the Individuals with Disabilities Education Act (IDEA). Each of these pieces of legislation, in one way or another, deals with issues related to equality and the fair treatment of all people.

Siân Jones, Andrew Livingstone, and Antony Manstead wrote in a book chapter entitled "Bully and Belonging" that prior to the 1970s, bullying was considered by some to be important for building character among weaker individuals. In essence, bullying was accepted and considered, to some degree, necessary. They further noted that given how pervasive bullying seems to be, it is a more complex process than one person picking on another. They described an approach to understanding bullying that suggests every child in a classroom plays some role when bullying occurs. They further noted that this approach identifies six separate roles students may play: victim, bully, bully reinforcer, bully's assistant, defender of the victim, and outsider. Within this approach, there is also the understanding that whatever role an individual may play in bullying, networks are formed within the school among those with the same or similar roles. For example, other bullies find other bullies, as do the victims, as do the outsiders, and so on. This fosters bullying behaviors but also serves a protective purpose for nonbullies by ensuring they will not be the target of the bully.

Defenders of victims are characterized as playing a pivotal role in the bullying process, as they are usually individuals who are emotionally stable and have well-developed cognitive abilities, are able to be empathic, and believe that they are capable of defending victims when they are bullied. Defenders of victims are believed to be highly socially skilled, as they are usually well liked among classmates. Moreover, when defenders take action, their efforts have the effect of reducing the overall amount of bullying that occurs in that particular classroom. Overall, Jones and her colleagues concluded that the shift from focusing on the individuals involved in bullying (i.e., bully and victim) toward a social and psychological perspective specifically focused on social identity is a more effective approach to take, as it encompasses children's and teens' sensitivity to the nuances of between-group relationships (i.e., the ways different social groups interact and get along, or not).

Amanda Duffy and Drew Nesdale, from Griffith University in Australia, examined bullying behavior using social identity theory. They noted that some bullies may very well bully regardless of any social group they may or may not belong to, but like Jones and her colleagues noted, the identification with groups—one's social identity—plays a significant role in bullying behavior. They therefore consider bullying to be a "group phenomenon." Duffy and Nesdale found that children who bully usually belong to the same friend groups (i.e., bullies find and interact with other bullies) and that within such groups, not surprisingly, bullying is considered acceptable and a norm of the group. Those who belong to this type of group and those who bully most often in comparison to other group members tend to hold the most central position in the group. The group effectively revolves around this particular person, as they are considered to be engaging the most in the normative behavior of the group: bullying. This also means that as more people in a bullying-normative group engage in bullying, the incidences of bullying by such group members increase. Bullying begets more bullying. Duffy and Nesdale stated that those who are in the same social group related to bullying "are comparable in terms of their direct involvement and support for bullying, their use of behaviors aimed at harming friendships, and the extent of their physical presence during bullying." They further concluded that their findings support a conceptualization of bullying via social identity theory because human beings form social groups to highlight and maximize similarities among group members. Moreover, they indicated that we form social groups to highlight and maximize the differences between members of that group (in-group) compared to members of any other group (out-group).

In an effort to understand the most effective ways to get bullies to stop bullying, Jones and her colleagues used what we know about social identity and how social groups form to illuminate which factors associated with social identity may be most effective in getting bullying behavior to cease. They highlighted the fact that the factors involved in social identity, particularly with respect to how groups form and who makes up a group's members, impact how group members emotionally respond to bullying-based behaviors. The group can dictate how members should feel about bullying and how they should feel about having regret for engaging in bullying (e.g., Should they feel bad about having regret for bullying? Should they feel proud that

Local Factors

they regret bullying?). They noted that research conducted by other scholars found that the more strongly someone identified with a particular group, the more intensely they felt the group-based emotions (i.e., how the group as a whole feels about an event, situation, or behaviors). Jones and her colleagues reported results consistent with this previous research.

Jones and her colleagues identified three different groups to which their study participants belonged. The groups were framed in terms of being a member of the perpetrator's (i.e., the bully) group, a member of the target's (i.e., the person being bullied) group, and a group with members that were not aligned with either the perpetrator or the target. The additional factor they considered was what they referred to as the "normative context" of each group. That is, was the group competitive, cooperative, or neutral in nature? Finally, they also measured each participant's commitment to or identification with the group of which they were a member. Essentially, this refers to how strongly the individual identified with the group itself. These researchers contended that these factors combined to influence how each participant emotionally responded to bullying and what actions the individual would take with respect to bullying. They found that children who experienced a cooperative normative context (i.e., the group expects people to get along and to be kind to one another) were more likely to endorse feeling regret and a lack of pride about bullying. They also found that when an individual strongly identified with the social group of the person who was bullied, they were more likely to feel angry about the bullying and were subsequently more likely to report bullying behavior to an authority figure. They concluded their report by encouraging schools to foster cooperation rather than competition as the overall normative context of a school, which they suggest should lead to more people finding bullying unacceptable as well as more people being more likely to report bullying when it happens.

Of course, schools are not the only place bullying occurs, and children and adolescents are not the only ones doing the bullying. There are myriad places where bullying can occur: at work, out in public, at home, and so on. Anyone is a potential target of bullying, depending on who the bully is and what kind of target they prefer. Jennifer Martin, Martina Sharp-Grier, and Kathleen Piker-King examined what makes people likely to engage in bullying within an academic setting. To be clear, they were not focused on the students; they were focused on understanding bullying among fellow professors. They noted, as others have, that bullying and harassment are separate and distinct concepts. Though the two terms are often used interchangeably and have overlap between them, the reality is that bullying in and of itself is not illegal, but harassment can be. They noted that the distinction is usually not made at institutions of higher learning, as using the more generic term, "bullying," may blind some to the fact that their civil rights have been violated (e.g., being sexually harassed, being harassed based on one's race). An institution and its administration may be more invested in the use of term *bullying* instead of *harassment* as a way of protecting its reputation, which means they would be invested in *not* calling certain behaviors harassment. Targets of bullying tend not to be different than targets of interpersonal aggression found in other settings. Those who are targets are often members of a disenfranchised group (i.e., a group that has diminished social or political status or that is denied some rights). In the context of academia, however, they note that the perpetrator is often dealing with feelings of inadequacy and is therefore likely to target someone who may be seen as vulnerable but who also tends to be high performing and therefore a perceived threat to the perpetrator.

Elizabeth Farrington noted that bullying on university campuses among faculty members may be an issue due to the egos involved. Because colleges and universities seek to hire people who are experts in their fields, that sense of expertise may erroneously extend beyond their academic silo. They may think they are an expert at most things, if not everything. She also noted that, in addition to the known, far-reaching emotional and psychological costs to individuals who are the targets of bullies, there is also a high cost to the institution itself. She reported that around 70 percent of those who are bullied by colleagues leave the institution. This means that the institution has to expend resources on replacing that faculty member, but it may also have to spend $100,000 or more on litigating a formal lawsuit. Therefore, beyond the moral reasons to eradicate bullying, institutions of higher education also have a financial incentive for making sure their faculty members are not on the receiving end of bullying behavior. Farrington states that colleges and universities should take bullying seriously, and they should develop and promote a culture of anti-bullying from the top down that holds everyone accountable.

The effects of bullying are many and varied. Children and adolescents in particular are most vulnerable to the impacts of being bullied, which include an increase in serious mental health issues, such as depression and anxiety. In some cases, depending in part on the severity of the bullying, some may develop the disorder commonly known as post-traumatic stress disorder (PTSD). Although PTSD is often talked about in the context of military veterans, the reality is that anyone who experiences severe injury or a threat or perceived threat to one's life or who witnesses the severe injury, death, or threat of either of someone else is at risk for developing PTSD, the effects of which are often long standing and can be exceptionally debilitating.

Regardless of the nature of the bullying behavior, the target of a bully may also develop physical health problems, even if the bully does not physically harm the person being bullied. Stress and distress are linked to myriad physical health problems, such as gastrointestinal issues and cardiovascular issues. With respect to school-aged children and adolescents, another impact

Local Factors

can be a decline in academic achievement, which can be noted by a drop in GPA, or the target of the bully may withdraw from activities. Being a witness to bullying can also cause measurable distress in bystanders. Bystanders— referring to those who witness bullying but do not do anything about it—are more likely to engage in risky behaviors such as using tobacco, alcohol, or other substances. They may stop going to school for a period of time, and they, too, are at risk for developing mental health issues.

Although there are other local factors that can impact one's identity, such as our relationships with family and friends, the type of culture we live in, and our use of technology, those factors are addressed in other chapters of this book. This chapter discussed the problems of a struggling economy and bullying, which are two major issues that have been ongoing concerns for years, if not decades, and that have extensive empirical evidence for how they affect our overall well-being and our individual identities.

CHAPTER ELEVEN

Global Factors

Whereas chapter 10 examined local factors that can affect one's identity, this chapter explores global factors that can affect identity. Certainly, when you really think about it, if something affects your identity, it affects you locally; however, the topics examined herein are factors that are not unique to your family, city, state, region, or country. They are factors that affect everyone. The impact felt by these factors vary from one country—indeed, one person—to the next, but when considering topics such as social justice issues, terrorism, or a pandemic, these are things that impact everyone.

Globalization: What Is Going On in the World

Globalization is generally defined as a process through which companies and organizations operate internationally and become internationally influential. This broad description, though all encompassing, does not capture the differences between the three main types of globalization that are discussed in this chapter: economic globalization, cultural globalization, and political globalization. Regardless of the subtype of globalization that is the focus of one's attention, globalization generally involves trade policies and agreements, the investment of resources, the movement of people, and the sharing of knowledge on a worldwide scale. Although historical documents show that trade between nations, movement of people, and knowledge sharing have occurred throughout documented world history, the term *globalization* was not used until the mid-1940s and did not become a widely used term and its effects studied until the 1990s.

Economic Globalization

Economic globalization refers to the increasing interdependence of economies throughout the world. Given our ability to rapidly share information, conduct transactions online, and, for many, to travel expediently from one country to another, it is no surprise that there is also an increase in importation and exportation of goods and services, selling and purchasing of technology, and currency trading. With respect to business dealings, specifically, changes in tariffs and taxes to either inhibit or facilitate trade between nations impact the global marketplace. Many readers, for example, have likely purchased something from an online platform that originated in another country. The purchased item may or may not have been manufactured in the country from which it was purchased. Thus, someone in the United States, for example, may find an item online that they would like to purchase from the United Kingdom, but the item itself was manufactured in Taiwan. Several decades ago, one would have been required to physically travel to the United Kingdom to see items available for purchase (which may or may not have been manufactured there).

Cultural Globalization

Cultural globalization reflects the fact that distinct ideas and values associated with a particular culture are shared with other cultures. The recently discovered ancient city of Heracleion (Greek name), also known as Thonis (Egyptian name), located north of Alexandria, Egypt, was known as a thriving port for international trade. Archaeologists have purportedly discovered artifacts among the ruins that can be traced to ancient cultures and countries throughout the Mediterranean. Cultural globalization is certainly facilitated by foreign travel; however, in the current day and age, those with access can be exposed to the traditions and beliefs of nearly any culture in the world through the internet and various forms of and outlets for media.

The field of cross-cultural communication (and the related field of intercultural communication) emerged from our growing understanding of cultural globalization. Cross-cultural communication examines types and patterns of communication used by various cultures to communicate with others from the same culture and to attempt to communicate with others from a different culture. When cultural goods and services, ideas, preferences, religions, and languages spread to other cultures, this is called *cultural diffusion*. Although this certainly allows us to better understand those who grow up and live differently from one another, it can also lead to a reduction in the uniqueness of separate cultures. An example used to illustrate the effect of this type of globalization is the report that Disneyland Paris (formerly known as Euro Disney), located in France, receives more visitors each

Global Factors

year than Paris itself, which is only twenty miles away. Visitors to the theme park reportedly go there to experience various European cultures rather than visiting the countries themselves.

Cultural globalization can be transformative in ways not always welcomed. Religions were among the first elements of culture to be shared with (or imposed upon) foreign cultures. Long-standing traditions can become watered down or fused with traditions from other cultures, which means the "pure" cultural traditions can become lost. Critics of cultural globalization are concerned that Western ways of life (e.g., the United States, the United Kingdom, Europe) have become so widespread and influential that they may impede local cultures from thriving and maintaining their heritage. Not surprisingly, the issues, both beneficial and detrimental, associated with cultural globalization can affect one's cultural identity (see chapter 2 for more information).

Political Globalization

Political globalization has to do with the worldwide political system that has exponentially grown over the years. The system includes national governments, international nongovernmental organizations (NGOs) formed to address social or political concerns, and social movement organizations. The term *multilevel governance* is used to describe the fact that various governmental systems interact with one another and ultimately affect both global politics and the global economy. NGOs have become highly influential over the years in their efforts to provide international humanitarian aid, including providing medical services and vaccinations, and help economically struggling countries with infrastructure (e.g., water, sewer, internet connection).

Additional forms of globalization that do not get as much academic attention as the three primary forms of globalization discussed in the preceding paragraphs include environmental globalization, which involves international agreements on environmental protection, and military globalization, which involves the growing relationships between various security agencies.

Globalization's Impact on Identity

Developing one's identity is never an easy or straightforward endeavor. As detailed in chapters throughout this book, there are myriad theories about how we develop a clear, coherent identity, and there are numerous factors that can help facilitate or impede identity development. Identity development is truly a lifelong process, as our experiences impact how we see ourselves and the world around us.

Lene Jensen, a scholar studying the impact of culture, migration, and globalization, examined the issues surrounding globalization and its impact on identity development in adolescents. She questioned whether it mattered if adolescents experienced and subsequently developed a cultural identity as a result of direct first-person experiences or indirect experiences, such as those through various forms of media. She also contemplated the different paths identity development can take depending on the culture(s) in question, and, finally, she questioned what is gained and what is lost when one's cultural identity is in fact a *multicultural* identity rather than one based on a single culture.

With respect to the initial question, she noted that adolescents do experience direct firsthand contact with other cultures through travel (their own travel or others traveling to where the adolescent lives). Readers who have visited cultures different from their own may recognize that they have taken on spoken phrases or accents of another culture, developed preferences for foods they had never tried before, and incorporated specific cultural traditions into their daily lives. Thus, direct exposure to different cultures can impact how we live and how we perceive ourselves and others. Jensen noted, however, that contemporary adolescents derive most (and in some cases all) of their exposure to different cultures through media (e.g., television, social media, internet searches). An important difference between direct exposure and exposure through the media is that exposure to different cultures through the media provides a greater opportunity for individualization. This means that the individual can easily pick and choose what they want to see and hear. In addition, unless the consumer of media is doing so as part of a group, there is a greater chance that the information is interpreted solely through their own lens. As such, each individual can leave the culture-through-media experience with vastly different interpretations of what they see.

With respect to different developmental paths, Jensen noted examples of how adolescents from different ethnic groups are impacted differently by those around them at differing ages. For example, European American ("American" referring to those in the United States) adolescents are more likely to focus on independence and autonomy during their mid to late teens and then transition to considering their parental figures' point of view in their late teens to early twenties. By contrast, this pattern was reversed for Armenian Americans and Mexican Americans. Korean Americans were found to start and stay focused on their parental figures' point of view. As adolescents are exposed to more and different cultures due to the various forms of globalization, they have to contend with the fact that different cultures value different influences and have different goals. Within that context, adolescents attempt to construct their own cultural identity.

Finally, Jensen noted that globalization can be good and bad in terms of cultural identity development. As adolescents attempt to shape their cultural identity based on their immediate culture's beliefs, values, and traditions and

Global Factors

those of other cultures to which they are exposed, one aspect that may have the greatest impact on how difficult this process can be has to do with how different from one another the various cultures are. Drawing from research conducted on immigration, Jensen noted that the greater the differences between cultures, the greater the difficulties the person may have in feeling like they do not fit in, and they may develop significant psychological difficulties (e.g., substance abuse, various forms of aggression, suicide). Despite this, recent research has shown that acculturation among immigrants is highly complex and can vary in terms of positive and negative adjustment based on the age and gender of the immigrant, their level of education, how much social support they have, and the extent to which they experience discrimination.

Jeffrey Arnett, from the University of Maryland, suggested that cultural identity may be split in two for adolescents growing up in an era of globalization. He indicated that adolescents may end up developing a "local identity" and a "global identity," which would incorporate elements of various cultures, depending on what the adolescent experiences firsthand or, more likely, through the media. Arnett also noted that adolescents may very well experience more identity confusion as a result of this type of exposure. With increased exposure to different cultures, adolescents may feel pulled in multiple directions and ultimately feel as though they do not belong to any particular culture. With their ongoing exposure to traditions, events, and views of disparate cultures, adolescents may reject the narrow, local worldview of their indigenous culture for a more a more global, encompassing perspective. He further pointed to evidence that collectivism, traditionally found in countries such as Japan and China, holds less appeal for young people in those countries. This can, however, lead to identity confusion and difficulty in finding personal meaning, as native collectivist values are starkly contrasted by a global culture characterized by more individualistic and consumer-oriented values.

Another study led by Simon Ozer examined identity development among emerging adults from the North Himalayan region of Ladakh (a territory of India) undergoing acculturation as they studied at universities in Leh (located in the Ladakh region) and Delhi (a territory in India that includes New Delhi, the capital of India). Ozer and his colleagues examined participants' cultural orientation, identity development, and overall psychological well-being. Their results showed that adherence to traditional cultural values had less impact on well-being than identity exploration and commitment to an identity (see James Marcia's identity statuses in chapter 3 for more information). Specifically, Ozer and his colleagues found that participants' endorsement of their traditional cultural values or their endorsement of the cultural values associated with globalization-based acculturation in Delhi was linked to psychological well-being when these cultural endorsements were linked to identity exploration or commitment. Those who maintained connection to and endorsement of their traditional Ladakhi values were classified as having commitment to this aspect of identity and therefore were also found to have positive psychological well-being. In addition, those from Ladakh who endorsed the more globalized values found in Delhi were classified as being in identity exploration, which was found to lead to positive psychological well-being. This reflects the importance of an individual's personal identity when exposed to globalized cultures, as exploration of identity and committing to an identity are processes we engage in "on purpose."

As we saw in the discussion about online identities in chapter 10, competing messages about who we can be and, perhaps, who we should be can come from anyone and anywhere. Globalization contributes to our respective struggles to identify what we want to include within our unique identities due to the myriad competing cultures and ideologies to which we are more easily exposed in this digital age.

The Novel Coronavirus Pandemic

Today, it is relatively quick and comparatively inexpensive to travel from one country to another compared to eras before efficient and relatively affordable forms of mass transportation, and due in part to this, the movement of people between countries continues to increase. Although some people permanently move from one country to another, the bigger issue in the context of a pandemic is the movement of people from one country to another, temporarily, as tourists. In the last few decades, it has become easier to do because fewer and fewer countries require a visa (formal permission to enter and temporarily stay in a foreign country) for international travel, depending on what countries you are traveling to and from. Since both politics and the economy have become globalized, it is also common for politicians and businesspeople to travel internationally to meet with foreign leaders and heads of state and with CEOs of foreign corporations and NGOs. Given the increase in the trade of goods and services and travel for tourism, business, politics, and philanthropy, people have also increased their exposure to diseases with which they may not have otherwise come into contact. Many of these diseases originate in nonhuman animals and are then transmitted to and infect human beings—a process known as *zoonosis*.

The 1918 flu originated in birds and was called H1N1. It impacted one-third of human beings worldwide. Just over ninety years later, another version of the H1N1 flu, its origin found in pigs, was estimated to have killed somewhere between 150,000 and 600,000 people worldwide. The bubonic plague, also known as the Black Death, of the fourteenth century originated in rodents and killed over 20 percent of the world's population at the time. Malaria kills approximately 400,000 people worldwide each year and

Global Factors 187

originates in mosquitoes. Rabies kills approximately 55,000 people worldwide yearly and is usually transmitted to human beings from a dog bite. And HIV (the virus that causes AIDS) originated in chimpanzees. This virus was likely transferred to humans via hunting and consuming these animals, and it ultimately kills hundreds of thousands of people worldwide annually (approximately 770,000 people in 2018). There are myriad other diseases that can be transmitted from a nonhuman species to a human. As of the writing of this book, the latest pandemic continues to impact individuals and nations as we struggle to cope with its effects.

The 2019 novel coronavirus that is believed to have its origins in bats is technically called SARS-CoV-2 and causes the illness commonly known as COVID-19. The first cases are believed to have emerged in late 2019 in China. The World Health Organization (WHO) officially declared COVID-19 a pandemic on March 11, 2020, pointing to how quickly the disease spread between people and its eventual international spread in a matter of weeks. As of May 30, 2021, and according to data from the Johns Hopkins University School of Medicine, over 170 million cases have been confirmed worldwide and over 3.5 million deaths. In the United States, those numbers are over 33 million and nearly 600,000, respectively. Currently, there is no known cure; however, a several different vaccines have been developed and over 1.8 billion vaccines have been administered worldwide.

Effects of a Pandemic on Identity

Researchers and theorists examining how one's identity intersects with epidemic- or pandemic-type diseases have focused on how one's various social identities (see chapter 2 for more information) impact how well they fare during and recovering from an epidemic. Nancy Bristow, a historian out of Washington State, noted that during the 1918 influenza epidemic, families and communities at large were devastated in ways that seemed to reflect discrimination based on gender, class, and race. She noted, of course, that the virus itself was not discriminatory; it did not *only* affect certain segments of the population. However, the degree to which individuals suffered did affect some segments of the population more than other. She suggested that social identity helps to explain why some people suffered more than others.

Those who lost a parent, for example, may not have had a stable home afterward. At the time, if the mother died, the children would have been removed from the care of the father because it was deemed inappropriate for men to live with children without an adult female present. The loss of a father in this respect or due to his own death had a significant financial impact on the remaining family members. In many cases, children were sent to work so that the remaining family had money to live on, all the while grieving the loss of a parent and the loss of their own childhood. Those who were already living in poverty at the time of the epidemic may have found themselves in even more dire straits if the primary wage earner was no longer able to work. Without a financial cushion of any kind, this may have meant starvation, dealing with severe cold without a means of heat during the winter months, and ultimately homelessness.

Bristow also highlighted the impact of Jim Crow–era laws that disenfranchised Black people by denying them things like the right to vote, employment, education, and so on. Anyone who attempted to defy these laws could have been arrested or fined and may have even been met with violence and death. These laws that legalized segregation, Bristow reported, prevented non-White people from accessing adequate and expedient health care that could have saved their lives or improved the quality of their lives. She concludes her paper by stating, "...we would do well to remember the grief, dislocation, and loss such a catastrophe leaves in its wake, and attend with special care to those who might suffer in our midst, even as we guard against the injustices that lurk in the imposition of social hierarchies." Current research suggests that we, perhaps, do not have long enough memories, as we have not mitigated the injustices inherent in various social identities that are not viewed equally.

A group of researchers out of the United Kingdom led by Anne Templeton examined injustices and inequality based on identity processes in the midst of responding to the current SARS-CoV-2 pandemic. They point to previous research conducted by others that echoes the issues revealed during the 1918 epidemic in the United States: when there is an emergency that impacts the public's health, those who have a racial or ethnic identity that is not White are likely to have higher rates of the disease in question and are also more likely to die from the disease. This finding includes what is happening with the SARS-CoV-2 coronavirus pandemic. Additional research on the SARS-CoV-2 pandemic has found that despite guidelines about social distancing and social isolation, those of a lower socioeconomic status, disproportionately populated by disenfranchised racial and ethnic groups, are several times less likely to have jobs that will allow them to work remotely (thereby limiting their contact with others), and they are less likely to be able to self-isolate due to living with myriad other family members, some of whom may be elderly.

Despite the fact that certain social identities (e.g., race, ethnicity, sex, economic class) are disenfranchised, these researchers suggested that it may be important to capitalize on these social identities to ensure all people have access to the support and care they need during a public health crisis. Among other things, they suggested that governmental agencies should provide equal support to all communities and deploy resources designed to empower local groups and local leaders to gain access to resources their specific communities need. In short, they suggested that although some social identities

Global Factors 189

are marginalized and disenfranchised, it is these very social identities that can bring groups of people together, allowing them to effectively advocate for their groups' overall well-being. But, they caution, this will only work if those in positions of power recognize that barriers and inequalities exist in terms of access to resources.

Social Justice Issues

Most readers will be familiar with the term *social justice*, which can be defined as the interactions between an individual and society at large in terms of fair distribution of wealth, opportunities, and privilege. The United Nations notes that social justice represents "an underlying principle for peaceful and prosperous coexistence within and among nations," adding that addressing social justice issues is "at the core of our global mission to promote development and human dignity." Social justice issues have been front and center in the consciousness of many societies and the individuals that live within them. The present and not so distant past have seen an increase in demands related to social issues that affect myriad groups that have all been oppressed or disenfranchised in some way. Despite contemporary efforts to deal with social justice issues that have seemingly exploded in the past few years, the term *social justice* is not a new one.

The term *social justice* was believed to have been coined by a Jesuit priest, Luigi Taparelli, during the 1840s; however, some have claimed that the use of the term may date back to as early as the 1780s. In the early 1900s, social justice issues became an international issue with the establishment of the International Labour Organization (ILO) in 1919 as part of the Treaty of Versailles. The ILO was created "to reflect the belief that universal and lasting peace can be accomplished only if it is based on social justice." This statement implies that there will always be conflict between and among people as long as social justice issues remain unresolved. The events of 2020, in particular the ignition of the Black Lives Matter (BLM) movement and the call to #DefundThePolice, illustrate the unrest predicted by the ILO's statement.

The importance of social justice issues internationally was powerfully illustrated by the United Nations when, in 2007, it established World Social Justice Day, which is observed annually on February 20. Each year, the United Nations identifies a theme. In 2020, the theme was Closing the Inequalities Gap to Achieve Social Justice. Colombian researcher Carlos Andrés Pérez-Garzón stated that when the United Nations declared that World Social Justice Day be observed each year, it "placed social justice as one of the most important issues that it has to promote in order to achieve its original purpose of preserving peace and security in the world."

Social Justice Warriors

Many people worldwide have devoted significant time and resources to fighting social injustices that impact people globally. Such individuals are referred to as *social justice warriors* (SJWs). On the surface, this sounds quite good, and, of course, most efforts addressing social injustices are meant to lead to lasting change for the better. In recent years, however, the term *social justice warrior* has moved from something of a neutral descriptor to being a derogatory term. The term is currently used in reference to the reputation of someone who excessively relies on emotion over logic when debating social justice–related issues and who has been characterized as motivated to seek attention and receive personal validation rather than having a genuine interest in eradicating mistreatment and unfairness. The term first appeared on Twitter in 2011, where it was used in a negative way. In 2014, the term was cemented as a pejorative term when "Gamergate" happened.

Gamergate was a controversial campaign in the online gaming community. Some members of the gaming community targeted female game developers and some female members of the media. The campaign reportedly began with one disparaging blog post from someone who knew one of the female game developers. From there, others used the #gamergate hashtag to attack this female game developer, other female game developers, and female media critics of gaming culture. These hashtag users reportedly made false accusations about some of the women, made death threats, threatened rape, and engaged in doxing, which involves publishing private information online about an individual with the intent of harming that individual. Those involved in #gamergate used the term "social justice warrior" in a negative way to disparage the women who were critical of how females are portrayed in many online and computer-based games. Since then, the term typically refers to those who are committed to social progressivism, cultural inclusivity, or feminism. Those accused of being an SJW are often females or feminists.

Scott Selisker, a professor of English, wrote that SJWs are often characterized as the "stereotype of the feminist as unreasonable, sanctimonious, biased, and self-aggrandizing." He discusses this term in the context of his examination of the Bechdel Test, which is applied to films and other forms of media to determine how feminist or nonmisogynistic the content is. The test involves three interrelated parts: (1) whether there are at least two named female characters within the story/game, (2) who talk with one another, (3) about something other than men. One of the female media critics who was a target of the Gamergaters, Anita Sarkeesian, who has degrees in communication studies and social and political thought, used the Bechdel Test on film award nominees and video games in her efforts to criticize video game culture.

Despite the negative use of the term *social justice warrior* in contemporary society, the fact remains that there are myriad social justice issues that affect

Global Factors 191

people worldwide. Some of these issues include racial discrimination, ageism, sexuality and gender, child welfare, and poverty and economic injustice. As long as these injustices continue, there will always be those who push or fight back in an effort to seek equality and fair treatment.

Racial Discrimination

Racial discrimination is any form of discrimination against another person that is based on their race. The antithesis of this is *White privilege*, which refers to the benefits afforded White people over non-White people, particularly when all else is equal (i.e., they have the same social, political, or economic circumstances). The negative impact on individuals' psychological and physical well-being due to racially based discrimination is well documented. In the United States, those who experience discrimination based on race have higher levels of distress, particularly when one's racial or ethnic identity is of paramount importance to their personal identity. The experience of discrimination based on race has also been linked to myriad health outcomes, including heart disease and cancer, which occur, for example, at the same rates between Black people and White people but that kill more Black than White people.

Critical race theory (CRT), an interdisciplinary field, was developed by scholars of color with the intent of addressing issues related to race in the legal system. It has also been proposed as being useful to include in educational environments to help White students accept and engage in discussions regarding racial inequities. The main tenets of this theory include primarily focusing on race, including racism; recognizing other marginalized identities that intersect with race (e.g., being female and Black, being gay and Latino); challenging the ideals of the dominant culture; learning from and validating the experiences of people of color; using approaches from myriad disciplines to analyze oppression; and having a commitment to social justice. Applying these tenets to non-classroom-based avenues of discourse may be beneficial for members of nondisenfranchised groups to better understand the lived experiences of non-White people.

Research conducted in the United States and led by Karen Suyemoto, from the University of Massachusetts in Boston, examined the effects of a program designed to inform and empower adolescents who identify as Asian American ("American" referring to those in the United States). The purpose of the program was to inform and empower, particularly around the issue of racism. They found that following completion of the program, participants, who prior to participating were found to have limited understanding of race-related identity and racism, developed their own race- and ethnicity-related identities, showed a greater sense of empowerment, felt a greater sense of responsibility for issues surrounding social justice, and increased their engagement in social justice activism. The researchers concluded that experiencing a program like this can be a "powerful intervention for addressing social and psychological challenges . . . by strengthening racial and ethnic identities" due to their increased awareness of race-related issues and the activism in which they were now more motivated to take part.

Although members who identify with or whose appearance may signal being part of a non-White group face discrimination regularly and are likely to suffer the effects of chronic discrimination, perhaps no movement in recent years has been more salient than #BlackLivesMatter, or BLM.

Black Lives Matter

The Black Lives Matter (BLM) movement was founded by Patrisse Khan-Cullors, Alicia Garza, and Opal Tometi, and it is based on the desire for non-violent civil disobedience as a way to protest the disproportionate violence perpetrated by police against Black individuals. BLM began in 2013 when the #BlackLivesMatter hashtag surfaced on social media after George Zimmerman, the neighborhood watch coordinator charged with the shooting death of Trayvon Martin, a seventeen-year-old Black teenager who was walking alone from a convenience store and headed to a family member's home, was acquitted of second-degree murder. At the time of the shooting, Zimmerman reported Trayvon as a suspicious person to the police. Prior to police arriving on scene, there was a fight between Trayvon and Zimmerman, and Trayvon was shot dead. The following year, two additional police-related killings, Michael Brown in St. Louis and Eric Garner in New York City, catapulted the Black Lives Matter movement into the national narrative.

In 2020, the highly publicized killings of George Floyd by police in Minneapolis and Breonna Taylor in Louisville occurred. George Floyd was murdered when police officer, Derek Chauvin, kneeled on Floyd's neck for nine and a half minutes and did not release him despite his declaring, "I can't breathe," and onlookers reportedly imploring police officers to release him because he was no longer moving and appeared unconscious. Nearly a year after Floyd's murder police officer, Derek Chauvin, was found guilty of all charges. The other officers involved (all of whom, including Derek Chauvin, had previously been fired from the Minneapolis police department) have been charged with "aiding and abetting second-degree murder" and will go on trial in March 2022. Breonna Taylor was a twenty-six-year-old emergency room technician who was asleep in her home with her boyfriend when police entered their home with a battering ram and a "no-knock warrant" (this means the police literally did not have to knock on the door of the residence, nor did they have to identify themselves as police officers). Breonna's boyfriend reportedly heard the commotion, got out of bed, and eventually fired his gun at the police (who allegedly had not identified themselves as such). The police

Global Factors

returned fire and shot and killed Breonna, allegedly hitting her several times. None of the police involved have faced any charges in their involvement with Breonna's death. Prior to these deaths and since then, there have been other killings of Black males and females that have contributed to the development of the BLM movement or have fueled the movement since it exploded in 2020.

A study published in 2018 examined fatalities as a result of lethal force used by law enforcement officers. The researchers associated with the Centers for Disease Control and Prevention (CDC) and the University of New York noted that although data exists on such fatalities, very little research has been conducted on this data. Their intent was to examine the data so that effective prevention efforts, risk assessment, and modifications to how law enforcement officers respond to calls can be implemented, with the intended outcome of reducing fatalities due to law enforcement intervention. Sarah DeGue and her colleagues reported that while the majority of victims from their data set were White (52%), there was a disproportionate number of deaths of Black people (32%), noting that the fatality rate of Black people was nearly three times higher than it was for White people. They also found overall that those who died were usually armed (83%) but that Black victims were more likely to be unarmed (14.8%) compared to White (9.4%) or Hispanic (5.8%) victims.

The growing momentum of the Black Lives Matter movement has led to what may appear to be minor decisions by various groups and organizations but that seem to signal an important shift in how the United States views and embraces (or not) Black people. In 2019, NASA changed the name of the street running past their headquarters in Washington, DC, to Hidden Figures Way, after the film *Hidden Figures*, which depicts the lives of three Black female engineers who were pivotal in NASA's work in the 1950s. NASA recently announced that it will rename its headquarters after Mary Jackson, NASA's first Black female engineer. In the world of sports, NFL Commissioner Roger Goodell stated in June 2020, "We were wrong," when commenting on how they have previously handled the peaceful protests by Black and allied NFL players, most notably former NFL quarterback Colin Kaepernick, who famously kneeled during the national anthem as a way to bring attention to violence against Black people by the police. Critics of Goodell's statement have wondered why Kaepernick was not specifically mentioned in the statement, if the statement is truly genuine, and why Kaepernick is not back playing in the NFL. Most recently, NASCAR banned the flying of the Confederate flag at NASCAR events amid the Black Lives Matter protests and following the statement made by one of its drivers, Bubba Wallace, the only Black driver in the sport's top racing series, who implored NASCAR to make the sport welcoming to all people by removing the Confederate flag. Many, though not all, people support and celebrate statements and changes such as these, but they also note there is much more to be done to eliminate systematic and institutionalized racism.

Ageism: Discrimination of the Older Generations

Ageism is understood to represent negative attitudes people have about older adults, usually those aged sixty-five or older. Any "ism" (e.g., ageism, racism) is often based on negative characteristics fueling stereotypes associated with the group in question. Stereotypes about older adults can be positive or negative, which, not surprisingly, may impact how others think or relate to those who are in the older adult age group. Negative stereotypes are often based on ability and health. Those who hold negative stereotypes of older adults often view them as unwell or diseased and that they are impaired in one or more ways (e.g., physically, cognitively).

Researchers from France conducted a series of studies designed to examine how young people aged seventeen to thirty-one viewed older adults. They conducted two studies in which young adult participants were exposed to images of sixty-year-olds or ninety-year-olds, and in a second study, they were exposed to older adults aged sixty-five to seventy-four. Exposure to images of older adults was done under a variety of conditions, including priming participants about their own death (i.e., getting them to be aware of the fact that they will die one day). Overall, the results showed that younger adults tend to not like being reminded of the fact that they will die one day, and older adults serve as such a reminder. As a result, older adults may be treated prejudicially by younger people. Under conditions in which the younger adults were not reminded of their own death, they were able to see the larger group of older adults as more diverse and could identify positive stereotypes that apply to older adults in addition to the negative stereotypes usually associated with this age group. With the reminder of one's own death, young adults rejected the heterogeneity of the older adult population and lumped them all together as people from whom they would like to have a lot of distance, which results in prejudice and, in some cases, discrimination.

Sexuality and Gender

Sexuality refers to one's sexual orientation and how one chooses to express one's self sexually. *Gender* refers to how one identifies in term of being male, female, a combination of the two, or neither.

LGBTQ

LGBT, which stands for lesbian, gay, bisexual, and transgender, is an acronym that has been used since the late 1980s. Prior to this time, the term typically used was *gay community*; however, those involved in the gay community did not feel like that term adequately or accurately reflected all those who were part the community. In the mid-1990s, LGBTQ was first used to include

Global Factors

those who identify as queer or questioning with regard to their sexual identity. Other acronyms, such as LGBTI and LGBTIQ, are used to include those who are intersex. LGBTQIA is used to include those who identify as asexual, and LGBT+ is used to signal inclusion of all on the spectrum of sexuality and gender. There are myriad other letters that are sometimes included in the acronym, including *U* for unsure, *C* for curious, a second *T* for transvestite, *TS* or the number *2* for "two-spirit" people, *P* for pansexual, and *SA* for straight allies, though this last addition has been controversial. Additional controversies have involved the order of the letters in the acronym, how many letters should be included, and what each letter stands for. Regardless of which acronym is used, each is intended to be as inclusive as possible.

Early on in the equality movement of the gay community, in the late 1960s, those who identified as bisexual or transgender were not accepted as belonging to the gay community. They were often accused by others within the gay community as either acting out the gay or lesbian stereotype (associated with those who identified as transgender) or being too afraid to come out as gay or lesbian and so identifying as being sexually attracted to members of both sexes (associated with those who identified as bisexual). To this day, each community (e.g., gay, lesbian, bisexual, transgender, queer, questioning, intersex, asexual) continue to struggle with their community identity and how inclusive the community should be in terms of members of the other communities.

The social justice issues related to sexuality and gender typically focus on women and concerns of the LGBTQ community. The hashtag #LoveWins was used more than seven million times on Twitter on one day, June 26, 2015, the day of the U.S. Supreme Court's decision to allow same-sex couples to legally marry. More recently, on June 15, 2020, the U.S. Supreme Court ruled that the Civil Rights Act of 1964 does, in fact, protect those of any sexual orientation or gender identity from discrimination. According to the *New York Times*, prior to what has been called a landmark decision, more than half of the states in the United States allowed employers to fire employees for being gay, lesbian, bisexual, or transgender.

Researchers led by Darrel Higa, from the University of Washington in Seattle, examined the factors associated with the overall well-being of lesbian, gay, bisexual, transgender, queer, and questioning teens and young adults (ages fourteen to nineteen). They found that well-being is bolstered by several factors, but there was a larger, more pervasive set of factors that negatively impacted these young men and women. Factors associated with well-being included one's identity development, having a peer network, and being actively involved in the LGBTQ community. With respect to identity development, despite the fact that a flexible identity is typically associated with instability and feeling confused, those who participated in this study noted that having a more flexible identity gave them a greater sense of control about how, when, and where they talked about who they are. Many also noted that donning clothing and accessories that clearly signal to others that they are part of the LGBTQ community was also viewed as a positive factor. Negative factors were associated with all domains discussed in the study; however, they were most commonly associated with family, school, religion, and one's community or neighborhood. Generally, the negative factors were associated with fears of possible or actual rejection and feeling like they cannot be true to who they really are. Positive factors were generally associated with feeling supported and accepted.

#MeToo

Use of the #MeToo hashtag went viral in 2017; however, it was originally used on MySpace by Tarana Burke, a Black activist who started the Me Too movement to help empower girls of color enrolled in a program she helped facilitate through her organization Just Be Inc. Me Too was not only used by Tarana Burke to indicate that she had endured sexual abuse and assault but also to signal to other sexually harassed, abused, and assaulted women that they are not alone. Although Burke's work was important and exceptionally valuable, it was not until a well-known actress tweeted about others posting Me Too–related stories to illustrate how many people have been affected by sexual harassment, abuse, and assault that #MeToo went viral. Once other famous celebrities followed suit, the #MeToo hashtag took off in the United States and globally, sparking discussions about the pervasiveness of sexual harassment, assault, and the abuse of women.

The World Health Organization (WHO) interviewed more than twenty-four thousand women, aged between fifteen and forty-nine, in ten different countries and found that up to 21 percent of women had experienced sexual abuse prior to the age of fifteen, up to 61 percent reported having been physically abused at some point in their life; up to 59 percent reported having experienced sexual violence by a partner at some point in their life, and up to 11.5 percent reported experiencing sexual violence by a nonpartner at some point in their lives. Numbers from some countries showed much lower rates of sexual and nonsexual violence. The WHO reported that as many as 24 percent of women stated that their first sexual experience (which occurred during adolescence) was nonconsensual.

An article in the *Washington Post* in 2017 includes data from a poll conducted by the *Washington Post* and ABC News. The data shows that 64 percent of those surveyed view sexual harassment at work as a "serious problem," 54 percent of those surveyed reported receiving unwanted sexual advances from a man, and 23 percent said the unwanted sexual advances were made by a male "who had influence over your work." Moreover, nearly 60 percent of those who endured these experiences *did not* report what happened. The article states that fear of retaliation by the harasser, being shamed by others, and the risk of damage to their career are reasons why women do not report

Global Factors   197

sexual harassment at work. Of the women who indicated they experienced unwanted sexual advances while at work, 94 percent stated that the perpetrator did not receive any consequences for their actions.

Trauma is viewed by many in psychology as something than can disrupt one's identity. Dorthe Berntsen and David Rubin noted that an "unusual, unexpected, and extremely emotional event" is something that interferes with one's schemas (a cognitive framework that allows us to organize and understand information). For example, someone who survives a natural disaster may have any number of schemas disrupted, including those about what it means to be safe, what home is, who one's family is, and so on. This means that when trauma of any kind occurs, one's identity may be disrupted. One of the ways that sexual trauma, specifically, can be disruptive occurs when the individual who endured the trauma reidentifies as a "victim." According to Kaitlin Boyle, of Virginia Tech, the victim identity is one that is associated with powerlessness and is considered to be "deviant." Moreover, when studying the impact of sexual assault on identity, Boyle found that what we understand about ourselves, others, and the world around us gets dramatically, indeed traumatically, violated when one experiences sexual violence or aggression. She further noted that when a survivor of sexual trauma reconfigures their identity in terms of being a "victim," they are more likely to experience ongoing, significant distress. Reconfiguring one's identity as a "survivor," however, can reduce overall distress because the moniker "survivor" is associated with strength and overcoming violence.

Although most #MeToo stories and research conducted on sexual violence focuses predominantly on women as the survivors and men as the perpetrators the reality is males too are survivors and women can also be perpetrators. One study found that males reported sexual abuse or sexual assault at a rate of 1 out of 6 (16.67% of males) prior to age eighteen. Another study found that despite the fact that males who are survivors of sexual assault are much more likely to have significant mental health concerns including thoughts of violence fewer than 15.5 percent of those who are survivors sought help from a mental health professional. One man shared his story with *USA Today* of being raped by a woman and noted that his friends seemed to congratulate him for "scoring" despite the fact that he was intoxicated and unable to consent. In the title of the article he wrote for *USA Today* Jacob Bruggeman noted that the #MeToo movement may help change the "culture of silence" among males who are also survivors of sexual violence.

Protecting Children: Child Labor and Child Welfare

Children have a long history of working in a variety of industries in the United States. In many situations, children were hired along with their parents to do jobs that were more difficult for adults to do (e.g., a child's small stature compared to an adult's allowed them to get into spaces adults could literally not fit into) and to help contribute to the family's income and cover the cost of living expenses. In 1904, the National Child Labor Committee (NCLC) was formed for the purpose of illuminating the issues surrounding child labor, including working conditions, issues related to education, and the overall rights, dignity, and well-being of minors. Within eight years of being established, the NCLC successfully submitted and passed an act that established the United States Children's Bureau housed in the Department of Commerce and Labor, which was signed into law on April 9, 1912, by President Taft. A later effort to ban the shipping of goods using child labor, the Keating-Own Act, was deemed unconstitutional by the U.S. Supreme Court in 1918, two years after it was signed into law by President Wilson, despite including in its decision a statement noting the "evils" of child labor. In 1924, the Child Labor Amendment passed, but to this day, it is short of the required thirty-eight states to ratify the amendment and include it as part of the Constitution. The last state to ratify the amendment, Kansas, did so in the mid to late 1930s. Fifteen state legislatures rejected the amendment.

Sweatshops, also known as *sweat factories*, is the term used for jobs that have terrible and in some cases illegal working conditions, including conditions that are dangerous, employees being underpaid, and work being performed in uncomfortable climates. Essentially, those working in sweatshops work long hours in terrible conditions and without adequate compensation, regardless of laws ensuring adequate pay or overtime pay. In many cases, children are employed for very little money and tasked with working heavy machinery. Typically, when children are working in these sweatshops, they are missing school and working in conditions that are often hazardous to their health.

The anti-sweatshop movement began in the nineteenth century among those who drew parallels between slavery and working in a sweatshop. This is and has been an international concern, with the first law enacted to address sweatshops passed in 1833, the Factory Act of 1833, in the United Kingdom. This act was revised multiple times in later years, with the original act and its subsequent changes intended to address working conditions by limiting the number of hours someone should work and specifically implementing child labor laws. In 1919, the United Nations (at that time, the League of Nations) formed the International Labour Organization (ILO) with the intent of improving working conditions worldwide.

In 2013, the hashtag #WhoMadeMyClothes was first used by the cofounders of the Fashion Revolution. By 2018, the hashtag had nearly one hundred million impressions on Twitter. The purpose was to bring consumers' attention to the brands that they purchased and whether the companies used sweatshops, usually located in poorer countries such as Bangladesh and India, to make their clothes cheaply and sell for a substantial profit. In 2015, the Fashion Revolution released a video on YouTube that shows people depositing

Global Factors   199

two euros to purchase a T-shirt from a vending machine with the option of purchasing the T-shirt or donating their money to charity. When they deposited their money, they were shown a video depicting the working conditions in which the T-shirt was made. Most people chose to donate the money rather than getting the T-shirt.

Critics of the anti-sweatshop movement indicate that making employers pay higher wages in impoverished countries may cause those factories to shut down, eliminating jobs that had been providing income for those who previously had less than what the job provided.

How Aspects of Our Identity That Disenfranchise Us Combine: Intersectionality

Intersectionality refers to the idea that various aspects of one's identity can combine to make one more vulnerable to discrimination or to bestow more privilege. The concept of intersectionality was first identified in the late twentieth century to illuminate the fact that the unique combination of factors an individual has may result in prejudice or discrimination that is different than the sum of discrimination that individuals who only have one factor may experience. For example, a woman of color has an experience that is unique and therefore differentiated from the experiences of oppression experienced by woman in general and the experiences of oppression experienced by individuals of color in general. The sum of those experiences does not encapsulate the specific experience of being a Black woman, an Indigenous woman, or a Hispanic woman. Adding yet another factor, such as sexual orientation or gender identity (e.g., a woman who is Black and a lesbian), creates another unique combination of factors that results in experiences different from those without all three factors.

Researchers Jessica Remedios and Samantha Snyder, from Tufts University, examined the experiences of individuals with multiple stigmatized identities and referred to their discriminatory-based experiences as "intersectional oppression." They found that those who had more than one stigmatized identity (e.g., female, race/ethnicity, sexual or gender identity) reported experiencing more unfair treatment and feeling more invisible compared to those with one or no stigmatized identities. In this context, *invisibility* refers to like the person feeling like they are being ignored or dismissed and that they feel underrepresented compared to those who are nonstigmatized or who have only one stigmatized identity. They noted that when a prototypical individual is identified to represent a particular group, important differences among those who could belong to that particular group are inevitably ignored and therefore are not represented, which leads people to feel invisible. These researchers noted, for example, that the prototypical person of color is usually represented by a male, and the prototypical representation of women is usually White. They concluded that those with identities that include multiple stigmatized aspects live with the expectation that they will be invisible; their experiences will not be adequately represented, if they are represented at all, and as such, they will be overlooked, ignored, and dismissed. They further noted that such individuals experience invisibility as a form of discrimination.

Feeling invisible to those around you can have an impact on how someone sees themself and on their subsequent identity development. Those who do not feel represented or understood by society at large may not fully explore all possibilities when it comes to likes and dislikes, needs and preferences, and so on. This lack of exploration can have a significant impact on identity development (see chapter 3 for more information).

Worldwide Threats: Terrorism

Although there are myriad definitions of *terrorism* (over one hundred), it can be defined as the use of intentional violence or intimidation for political and often religious reasons. In 2004, a report from the United Nations suggested the following definition for *terrorism*: "any act intended to cause the death or serious bodily harm to civilians or non-combatants with the purpose of intimidating a population or compelling a government or an international organization to do or abstain from doing any act." The United States specifically defines *terrorism* as "premeditated, politically motivated violence perpetrated against noncombatant targets by subnational groups or clandestine agents, usually intended to influence an audience."

The first known use of the term *terrorist* was believed to have been in the late 1700s by a French philosopher who was denouncing the regime in France at the time as a dictatorship. Since then, the term has been used to describe individuals and groups both domestically and internationally. In recent years, terrorism has resulted in a large number of deaths worldwide, from a low of 7,827 people in 2010 to a high of 44,490 in 2014. Each year, terrorism typically accounts for approximately 0.01 percent of all deaths, though when looking at specific countries or regions of the world, this percentage can be much higher. In 2017, 95 percent of the terrorism-related deaths that year occurred in the Middle East, Africa, or South Asia; however, that same year, the percentage of worldwide deaths due to terrorism was 0.05 percent.

Terrorist incidents occur with regularity worldwide, and, relatively speaking, few occur on U.S. soil. In 2018, there were over 8,000 terrorist incidents worldwide, and in the United States, there were 67. Although this number is quite low compared to the number of incidents that occur on the world stage, it does represent a significant increase in the number of incidents from 2008, which recorded 18 terrorist events in the United States. Between the years 1970 and 2000, there were just over 2,400 terrorist events in the United

Global Factors

States. Collectively, these incidents resulted in 471 deaths. The year 2001 saw a total of 41 terrorist incidents in the United States, and the total number of deaths was just over 3,000—nearly all of which occurred on September 11, 2001. Although the decades prior to 2001 saw numerous terrorist incidents in the United States, 9/11 forcefully brought terrorism and what terrorist attacks are like to the consciousness of the U.S. population. In the years since 9/11 and through the year 2017, there have been 402 terrorist incidents on U.S. soil that resulted in 302 deaths. The years 2013–2017 have accounted for over half of the incidents (216) and the vast majority of deaths (266).

The terrorist attacks on 9/11 are by far the most deadly of all the terrorist attacks that have occurred in the United States. The second most deadly attack occurred in 1863 and resulted in just over two hundred deaths. The attacks on September 11, 2001, have been identified as the "fourth wave" of terrorism, which has been characterized in terms of being associated with religion, being international, involving "increasingly bloody tactics and weapons, and reliance on technologies of modernity," such as how easy it is to travel from one country to another, the multitude of modes of communication, and the literal wealth some access to finance such incidents. Regardless of the nature of the terrorist incident, it is not unusual to wonder, "Who would do such a thing?"

In an effort to discern why some people are attracted to becoming part of a terrorist organization or group, Donald Taylor and Winnifred Louis examined terrorism in the context of identity in a book chapter entitled "Terrorism and the Quest for Identity." Overall, they concluded that to fully understand those who commit terrorist acts, it is important to let go of the notion that only "psychologically deranged or evil" people commit such acts. This is a similar conclusion that was found as a result of the experiments on obedience conducted in the 1960s by psychologist Stanley Milgram. Milgram had ordinary people deliver increasingly stronger electric shocks to other seemingly ordinary people who answered a question wrong. Unbeknownst to the study participants, they were not actually delivering any electric shock, and those on the receiving end of the fake shock were actors. Milgram found that 65 percent of these ordinary people delivered what they believed to be a fatal shock to another human being merely because they were told by the researcher, someone in a position of authority, that they must continue. The conclusion was that even ordinary people under the "right" conditions will engage in horrific acts.

Taylor and Louis endeavored to identify what it takes for a potentially ordinary human being to engage in terrorist acts beyond other established factors, such as being economically disadvantaged and living within certain political conditions. Their focus on identity made things more personal. They concluded that those who are most effectively recruited to become part of terrorist groups and who may ultimately enact suicide-based terrorist incidents are those without a well-established, clearly articulated cultural or religious collective identity. They noted that such individuals are "psychologically desperate" and find solace in a group that offers a clearly defined collective identity accompanied by religious elements that are usually familiar in some way to those who become involved in terrorist groups. Moreover, such a group and its ideology provide a clearly defined "enemy" and clearly defined expectations for how members of the groups should act. In the simplest terms, those who are desperately searching for belonging and a way to define where they fit in the world are more vulnerable to the tenets of a terrorist group and are more likely to become actively involved with such a group.

Using identity theory, a group of researchers led by Seth Schwartz provided a more in-depth description of the identities of those drawn to terrorist groups. They indicated that such individuals rely on a more collectivist identity (see chapter 5 for more information) that revolves around fundamentalist beliefs tied to a specific religion or culture. There is an in-group/out-group element of such an identity that articulates clear and distinct differences between the group with which one identifies and all other groups, who are perceived as enemies and are therefore threats to the in-group. In terms of the identity statuses, those who identify with a terrorist group tend to be foreclosed (see also chapter 3 for more information), and they tend to be authoritarian (i.e., black-and-white thinking with clear rules that must be followed or there will be harsh punishment).

Andrew Weigert, a sociologist from the University of Notre Dame, discussed terrorism and identity in the context of how we make assumptions about who people are and what they are likely to do when we encounter them, as strangers, in public. We essentially estimate a stranger's identity based on what we can clearly see about their appearance. Based on our quick, nearly instantaneous, read of people, we imbue them with trust that they will act in public as they are "supposed to." Weigert stated that acts of terrorism violate this trust; terrorists, therefore, do not do what they are expected to do. He concluded that such a violation makes us question what we think we know about someone's identity and how they are likely to act. This, he concluded, "threatens public order."

When we are in public at a restaurant, we see the servers, perhaps the cooks, and the other patrons sitting down for their meals. We assume each person is as they seem. The people in the restaurant appear to be taking on specific role-based identities (e.g., server, chef, family out for dinner). We each put out identity cues that signal to others who we are. For example, if someone is dressed casually and pushing a stroller with a baby or young child, these cues likely signal to a stranger that the person pushing the stroller is the parental figure or caretaker of the child. Moreover, interpersonal prompts help to further clue us in as to who the individual is. For

Global Factors

example, the parental-appearing person pushing the stroller who stops to pick up the child and play with them or engages in baby talk with the child is likely to further confirm their parental or caretaker identity. These normal-appearing identities and our collective assumptions that those with whom we interact are as they seem provide a fertile environment for people to hide their true identity as someone who intends to do harm. These assumptions we make about strangers are normal, expected, and, by far, usually correct. Such assumptions about others and their intentions are what help to hold a society together. When these assumptions and the trust we afford one another are violated, public order is threatened.

Focus on the Planet: Climate Change and Sustainability

Climate change and sustainability are two distinct but interrelated concepts. *Climate change* refers to worldwide changes in variables such as temperature, rainfall, wind patterns, sea levels, and decrease in the mass of arctic ice. Those who focus their efforts on understanding climate change and why it is happening suggest that how human beings interact with the world around them has had the greatest impact. Concerns about factors that may be related to climate change, such as pollution, has led many to develop products or procedures that involve *sustainability*, which refers to efforts designed to ensure that the earth can continue to sustain life of all kinds.

Climate Change

Climate change is the term currently used to describe global changes to the environment, including changes in average temperatures, average rainfall, and wind patterns. The term *global warming* had been used universally to refer to the average rise in temperature of the entire earth's climate system. According to the National Aeronautics and Space Administration (NASA), since 1880, the global temperature has risen nearly two degrees, the mass of arctic ice has decreased on average nearly 13 percent every ten years, and level of the earth's seas has risen nearly seven inches over the last one hundred years. Although these numbers may not sound dramatic or even significant, these changes are believed by scientists to be long lasting and potentially devastating to the environment.

Although the terms *global warming* and *climate change* are often used interchangeably, global warming is believed to be a significant contributing factor to climate change itself. Both global warming and climate change are considered controversial in terms of why the climate is changing, whether it truly is changing, whether it matters that the climate may be changing, and perhaps, most importantly, what is causing the climate change. The term *climate change* was seemingly adopted to the international lexicon because some locations on the planet are recording colder winters than ever before, which is often used as refuting evidence of global warming.

In 2013, the Intergovernmental Panel on Climate Change (IPCC) reported that it is reasonably certain (i.e., at least 95% certain) that human beings are the primary contributors to the effects of climate change that have been documented since the 1950s. Scientists involved in the IPCC's conclusions state that without attempts by human beings to change how we interact with the planet, the changes that have been measured to date will continue and will likely accelerate. This is interpreted to mean that we will see changes to the environment occur more and more rapidly. The IPCC predicts rising temperatures worldwide along with increases in average precipitation. Despite consensus among many scientists worldwide that these changes have and will continue to occur, the notion of climate change generally, and global warming specifically, have been and continue to be controversial.

Yale University established the Yale Climate Connections out of the Yale Center for Environmental Communication and has published a series of articles entitled "Common Ground." Among other things, this effort is designed to explicate how and why some people are skeptics of climate change or even dismiss the claims outright compared to people on the other end of the continuum who are significantly concerned to the point of being alarmed by the impact of global warming and the accompanying changes to the world's climate. Psychologists out of Switzerland quoted Presidents Barack Obama and Donald Trump and their views on climate change/global warming to illustrate how dichotomous beliefs between people can be. President Obama was quoted as saying the following on September 23, 2014: "We are the first generation to feel the effect of climate change and the last generation who can do something about it." By contrast, Donald Trump was quoted as saying the following on January 1, 2014 (prior to being elected president): "This very expensive global warming bullshit has got to stop. Our planet is freezing, record low temps, and our GW scientists are stuck in ice." Although people on both sides of the climate change/global warming argument (including those in between) do not often agree, as illustrated by these two qualitatively different quotes, and often wrongly assume how someone from the other camp thinks about climate change and its effects, one area in which people seem to agree is that human beings do negatively impact the earth.

The focus of climate change and global warming and their effects on the well-being of the world in which human beings live, work, and play has led to an additional focus on what human beings do to contribute to or detract from the well-being of the earth. Researchers have recently suggested that figuratively drilling down into the psyche of human beings can help us all understand the motives behind behaviors and beliefs related to climate change. Specifically, these researchers were interested in examining our

Global Factors 205

values as they relate to our own identity, our culture, and our connections to our local and surrounding communities.

Ulf Hahnel and Tobias Brosch, psychologists with the University of Geneva in Switzerland, developed a model to help explain why people diverge so significantly in their beliefs, attitudes, and actions with respect to climate change. They wanted to determine what psychological constructs may need to be included in discussions about interventions related to climate change and how/if they will be accepted by people based on their political group identity. They started with the premise that the "scientific evidence for climate change is robust" and that it is "highly likely that climate change is happening, is caused by humans, and will impact our everyday lives." As such, they were interested in developing a model that would explain differences in perceptions and beliefs so that interventions around climate change could be developed and implemented with these differences in mind. To that end, a significant contributing factor to divergence in climate change beliefs lies in one's political party affiliation.

An individual's political group identity (i.e., the political party with which the individual identifies) plays a significant role in how people judge climate change evidence and subsequently whether they engage in behaviors recommended to help slow the impact of climate change. Hahnel and Brosch noted that an affiliation to a particular political group may be more powerful than the individual's personal political beliefs. They noted that previous research has found that when a political party has issued a statement regarding climate change (or other national or international issues), those who identify with the group that made the statement are more likely to agree with the statement or policy compared to those who identify with a different political group. Those who question the veracity of climate change (usually those identifying as "conservative" politically) and its effects have been found to be more averse to concepts such as complexity, ambiguity, and uncertainty, which tend to be more acceptable concepts to those who do not question climate change (usually those identifying as "liberal" politically). Hahnel and Brosch noted that skepticism to outright denial of climate change has been found to be linked to wanting to protect the current political and economic systems—a desire to keep and support what is familiar. On the other hand, those who believe the evidence showing climate change view initiatives to help slow down its effects see these efforts as innovative and progressive; they accept and perhaps welcome change and exploration.

Facilitating our understanding of climate change and ultimately what we believe about it and how we act in relation to it is what is referred to as the *elite cues hypothesis*. This hypothesis states that we will be selective in where we seek out information and that we tend to rely on sources we trust, particularly when the information we seek is about something that is not clear and is also controversial—like climate change. An interesting pattern of results was revealed when researchers examined previously published studies in this area. They found that our perceptions of local weather-related events may have an impact.

Studies that examined what the air temperature is like in a particular region and how it may or may not have changed found that those whose beliefs are extreme (i.e., politically far left or far right) were less impacted by perceived changes in the weather, but those who identified as more politically conservative were impacted by warmer but not colder temperatures. Thus, those who identify with a more conservative political group, but not to the extreme, and who perceive that the local temperatures are warmer were more likely to have a shift in their beliefs about climate change compared to their more liberal-leaning counterparts. As a result, they concluded that any research on climate change beliefs and actions should include perceptions of climate change (which may also include emotional reactions to climate change) as an important variable in understanding why people believe what they do about climate change and how to encourage people to take protective environmental action.

Hahnel and Brosch further stated that their proposed model for understanding the myriad beliefs around climate change includes identifying someone's political affiliation (i.e., political group identity), that person's perceptions, and ultimately their judgments about climate change and what type of action, if any, should be taken. They specifically noted that political group identity is the factor that can dramatically impact how an individual perceives climate change, which in turn affects their judgment about climate change and the actions they may take.

One of the efforts that seems to have growing support as we grapple with climate change and its effects is sustainability, which can refer to any number of things, but in this context, it refers to behaviors we engage in that help contribute to bolstering the earth's environment so that it can continue to sustain all forms of life for centuries and millennia to come.

Sustainability

Sustainability generally refers to the constant existence of something. The contemporary use of the term typically refers to engaging in efforts that ensure the earth will continue to thrive and have what is necessary to sustain life indefinitely. There are believed to be three dimensions of sustainability: sustainability of the economy, sustainability of society, and sustainability of the environment. Both the sustainability of the economy and society are believed to be limited by the state of the environment. Essentially, this means that the state of the environment will significantly impact the state of the economy and the state of society. For example, when we overfish certain types of sea life (e.g., lobsters, crabs), this can certainly change the ecology of

Global Factors

the ocean, but it will also impact the economy and society at large. The abundance, or lack thereof, of whatever is being fished will impact how much the average consumer pays for it and how much money is funneled back into that particular fishing industry. The more difficult the product is to harvest the more expensive it will be. This impacts who can afford to purchase the catch as well as how much of it they can afford. Moreover, this impacts those businesses that rely heavily on the catch in question, which may further impact whether they can stay in business, which further impacts employment, wages, and so on.

Place identity and *place attachment* are terms used to describe and study the relationship between people and the environment in which they directly live (e.g., the neighborhood, the region). *Place identity* refers to the extent to which a person identifies with where they live and how much of that place is incorporated into their personal identity. One of the most salient ways this can be illustrated is through sports. Sports fans of any kind typically strongly associate with a team (and sometimes specific athletes) that is usually connected to where they live, often where they grew up. It is not uncommon for those who strongly identify with a particular team, when asked who they are as a person, to respond with their name, what they do and where they are from, and they also declare that they are a fan of whatever team/athlete is associated with their area/state of origin.

Place attachment, on the other hand, refers to the emotional connection people have with a particular place. This is an affiliation that can extend over the years regardless of whether or not the person still lives there. This, too, can be seen among sports fans who will vehemently defend their team no matter how they perform and will be devastated emotionally when they lose and elated when they win. Rivalries between sports teams illustrate just how strongly people identify with their team and city/region of residence as well as the strong emotional reactions we may have if our team is ridiculed by a fan of a rival team. Sometimes emotionally charged interactions between fans of different teams will not only criticize the team itself but also the city/area with which the team is affiliated (e.g., Chicago Bears, New England Patriots). The emotional reaction reflects place attachment and is seen among diehard fans even when they no longer live in the area with which their team is affiliated. As readers have no doubt surmised, place identity and place attachment, although distinct concepts, are strongly related to one another. Place identity is believed to reflect a cognitive process, whereas place attachment reflects a more emotional process.

Donelson Forsyth and his colleagues examined the types and strength of identity and how these interact with a commitment to engaging in sustainability-based behaviors throughout the United States. They predicted that when someone's identity is based wholly or even partially on where they live, these individuals will be more likely to engage in sustainability-based behaviors. This means that if we identify with where we live (i.e., place identity), where we live will matter to us more (i.e., place attachment) compared to those who do not identify with where they live. That connection to one's area of residence means that such individuals will be more invested in taking care of the area/region and in helping to ensure that the area/region can continue to sustain people's way of life.

Forsyth and his colleagues described an inherent tension that can exist between an individualistic, self-focused identity and a more community-based sense of identity. The results of their investigation support the notion that when people identify with and feel strongly about some aspect of where they live (e.g., neighborhood, city, state, region), they are more likely to be invested in ensuring the area is environmentally sound. They specifically concluded that government efforts to improve the environment require support from local citizens, which means governmental programs should focus on localized efforts with which citizens can more easily identify and in which they can become more invested. For example, given environmental concerns in various regions throughout the United States, the findings of this and other research indicate that getting support for sustainability-based efforts to improve the environment will be more successful if policy makers focus on how citizens who live and work in the area will benefit from the efforts rather than focusing on how the efforts will "improve the environment" on a more global scale.

Sustainability in Business

Some researchers have examined the extent to which business executives include in their decision-making process how their business-related efforts impact the environment. Complicating such an inquiry is whether or not a business executive's personal values align with what they are asked to do or believe they should do for the betterment of the business itself. This conflict can challenge one's moral identity. *Moral identity* refers to "the desire to act as a moral being" or "the relative importance that is assigned by individuals to being a moral person within their general self-identity." As there are myriad other descriptions of this construct, Carlos Rodriguez-Rad and Encarnacion Ramos-Hidalgo, researchers from Spain, concluded that there is not yet a consensus on how this construct should be defined. Similarly, they reported that there are over seventy definitions of *spirituality* that can be summarized as reflecting one's search for answers to existential questions such as the meaning of things, including one's life, whether or not there is a "higher power," and so on. These researchers reasoned that moral identity and spirituality are distinct but related constructs, and in the context of climate change and sustainability, each plays a different role.

Rodriguez-Rad and Ramos-Hidalgo specifically studied how moral identity may mediate or change the relationship between spirituality and attitudes

Global Factors 209

about unethical behavior as well as spirituality and attitudes about responsible, ethical behavior. They referred to these issues as "doing good" and "recycling practices." They concluded that those who are most likely to engage in sustainability practices themselves and who also patronize companies that do the same are those who have high ethical and moral standards *and* who also include the following characteristics as part of their identity: "caring, compassionate, fair, friendly, generous, helpful, hardworking, honesty and kind." These same individuals were also more likely to support and defend their own and other's efforts for doing good, engage in recycling, and patronize businesses that also engage in similar behaviors.

Overcoming Barriers to Living Sustainably

Researchers from DePaul University in Chicago noted that research on how children in K–12 education learn about the environment is extensive, and less is known about issues related to adults' knowledge of the dynamics of the natural environment. They referred to their sample as "mature-age adult learners" who ranged in age from twenty-five to sixty-three. They were specifically interested in what barriers may exist for adults in this age range to live sustainable lives or to at the very least engage in some sustainability-related behaviors (e.g., recycling, water conservation). They found two overarching themes for the various barriers endorsed by those in this age group: personal relevance and social environmental context.

Kelly Fielding and Matthew Hornsey, from Australia, examined how one's social identity may impact attitudes and behaviors with respect to climate change. They found, perhaps not surprisingly, that one's social identity (see chapter 2 for more information) has a substantial impact on what we think about, how we feel about, and what we do with respect to climate change and the environment in general. As we develop our identities, we do so in the context of our relationships with others, and we eventually affiliate ourselves with various groups. Fielding and Hornsey confirmed that when our social identity aligns with groups of people who are pro-environment, we are more likely to engage in pro-environmental behavior. They offer suggestions on how to develop and capitalize on social identity-based strategies to encourage people to act in pro-environmental ways who may not already be invested in pro-environmental behaviors. Their suggestions include creating a superordinate identity (essentially a shared identity between two otherwise disparate groups) in which members of both groups would be invested and that promotes pro-environmental behaviors and linking one's identity to pro-environmental outcomes. Essentially, the strategy would be to find a way to make pro-environmental behaviors and goals personally relevant because such behaviors would then be embedded into each of our unique identities. Although not specifically noted by these researchers, one cannot help but surmise that tapping into people's place identity and place attachment may also help eliminate barriers to sustainability.

The world in which we live has grown increasingly smaller with advances in technology. Such advances allow for the relative ease of travel between cultures and countries and the ability to access information about other cultures via the internet. The internet allows us to virtually travel anywhere in the world and to virtually meet and interact with people we might not otherwise encounter. There are, undoubtedly, benefits associated with this type of globalism, but along with our increasing understanding of others and the world's cultures comes an awareness of how different from one another we are in ways that can make some psychologically uncomfortable and see those as "different" as being threats and therefore enemies. This can make it more difficult for us to accept one another's differences, of any kind, creating social justice–related problems with respect to equal rights and fair treatment. Differences in beliefs about climate change and the importance of engaging in sustainability-based behaviors have led researchers to identify why these differences exist and what can be done to effectively encourage us all to engage in behaviors that help ensure the planet can sustain life indefinitely.

PART 4

Case Studies

The ten case studies that follow explore various scenarios involving myriad aspects of identity. Some highlight the importance and impact of exploration and commitment, or the lack thereof, and some highlight specific types of identity or specific elements of an identity-related theory. Each case study includes a narrative of what the individual in the scenario is experiencing followed by a brief analysis section that ties elements of the scenario to the ideas and constructs explored in previous chapters in the book.

Stacy Hates Nursing School: The Dangers of Conforming to Other People's Expectations

Stacy is a twenty-year-old college student who has decided to pursue a nursing degree and has been enrolled in her school's nursing program for the past three years. Stacy selected nursing because it was a familiar profession to her and one that seemed to "run in the family." Both her mother and grandmother are nurses who have talked to Stacy throughout her childhood about how much they enjoyed being nurses and helping people in need and also how Stacy should pursue this profession because she would "be good at it."

As a child, Stacy frequently pretended to be a nurse, using her stuffed animals as her patients. Her parents bought her a toy doctor's set that included a surgical mask and stethoscope. She "listened" to her stuffed animals' "hearts" and used the family's bandages to cover up pretend wounds. When she was a bit older, she would take a needle and thread and stitch up her stuffed animals after "surgery." Stacy's mother and grandmother assisted in her "medical practice" by praising her on how well she cared for her "patients" and by gently correcting her if she performed a "procedure" incorrectly.

Throughout high school, Stacy completed as many courses as she could that her mother and grandmother recommended for preparing her for her future nursing education. She shadowed her mother at the hospital where she worked and tried to absorb everything she could about what her mother and the other nurses did all day. She did not really stop to think about whether she liked what she was seeing or if she could imagine herself doing the job of a nurse. Instead, she focused on learning what they did and how they did it so that she would be able to get into a good nursing program. Whenever she thought about exploring another career path, her mother or grandmother would redirect her back to nursing, saying something like, "Oh, you don't want to do that do you? We're both so happy with being a nurse. I know you will be too."

When Stacy first inquired about enrolling in the nursing program at the school that she currently attends, she was asked why she wanted to be a nurse. She replied, "I've always wanted to be a nurse! Besides, it runs in the family. Both my mom and my grandmother are nurses, and I always pretended to be a nurse with my stuffed animals when I was a kid." She was accepted into the highly prestigious nursing program and was excited to begin her studies. She excelled in all the classes she took, but when she had to complete a mandatory general education class in history, she found the subject fascinating. She was excited to read the text and hear the professor's thoughts each class. She thought about enrolling in another history class or two; however, when she expressed this to her family, they smiled and said they were glad she liked it, but taking additional classes in this area would be a "waste of time" and would not help her become a nurse.

Now, three years later, as Stacy reflects on her career choice and the fact that she only has one more year remaining before finishing her degree and sitting for her nursing boards (the required exam all new nurses have to take and pass), she realizes that she does not like what she is studying. She noticed this earlier in her studies (and thought she may have even known this in high school) but just chalked it up to the fact that she had to first learn the basics (e.g., biology, anatomy) before getting into the nursing classes she assumed she would find more enjoyable. She knew it was common for students to struggle to stay motivated when taking required classes that are not exactly in their major and figured her excitement would reemerge after she started taking nursing-specific courses.

Unfortunately, Stacy's excitement never resurfaced, and she struggled to reconcile how she had been so excited and determined to become a nurse as a child with how she was feeling now: dreading taking more nursing classes and dreading the thought of having to complete her clinical experiences at a hospital with actual patients. She was not afraid of performing the duties of a nurse; rather, she felt a great deal of disinterest in what she was being educated to do. Stacy realized the thought of being a nurse for the rest of her working life made her feel depressed and hopeless. She only has one year remaining in her degree program, and changing her major now would mean she would have at least another year and a half to two years to get a bachelor's degree in something else—and she does not even know what that something else would be.

Case Studies   213

Analysis

Stacy had selected a career path that many people choose and to which many often feel a calling. She was certain that being a nurse was essentially "in the blood," as two generations before her were nurses. She never imagined that being a nurse would not be a good fit. She already knew it was a valuable and respected career path and one that not all students could excel in. Stacy never explored other career options prior to entering her degree program, nor did she do much exploration in college. When she had extra classes she could take, Stacy was strongly encouraged by her family to only enroll in classes that would help her with nursing rather than taking classes that may have been purely enjoyable for her.

Stacy decided on a career path and pursued it without engaging in any exploration. In this regard, she would be considered foreclosed in terms of her identity. She seemed to start the process of exploring other areas of interest in college when she realized how much she enjoyed studying history, but further exploration beyond the one required history course was quickly rejected by her family. Therefore, she reoriented her thinking to be sure she stayed focused on nursing. She did not fully realize how much nursing did not fit for her until very late in her studies, which made changing her career path potentially expensive in terms of both time and money. She now has a difficult decision to make: figure out what is truly a good fit for her and pursue that or complete the degree she thought she always wanted and that was fully supported by her family but that she does not like.

Stacy also seems to be experiencing pressure to conform to the wishes of her family. Although they never said they would reject her in any way if she were to pursue any other career path, she was aware of the fact that anytime she expressed an interest in anything other than nursing, she was redirected back to nursing because that is what they thought she should do and that is what they thought would be best for her. She had gone along with their wishes and suggestions and never questioned them, until now, when she was on the brink of launching her professional career.

Alex Struggles to Accept His Own Cultural Heritage: Acculturation Is Not Always the Healthiest Choice

Alex is a twenty-five year-old Latino male. He was born and raised in the United States; however, his family maintains strong connections to their Mexican cultural heritage. Alex's parents and grandparents exclusively speak Spanish, although they have picked up some English over the years. Thus, Alex is bilingual. He had to learn English when he entered the school system in the United States while continuing to speak Spanish when around his family. In addition, Alex's family frequently travels to Mexico to visit friends and family who still live there.

When Alex first entered the school system in the United States, he had to enroll in English as a second language (ESL) courses. Although he was not the only child who required this type of assistance, he was frequently picked on because he did not speak much English and because he had a thick accent when he did speak in English. It was not until the fifth grade that Alex felt like he fit in better with his classmates. His accent diminished, and he was becoming fluent not only with the English language but also the current slang used by his classmates. Although he felt better about fitting in with his peers, he struggled with fully appreciating them because many of them were among those who had teased and bullied him for not speaking English initially and had also made fun of his Mexican heritage.

Alex's middle school and high school were much larger than his elementary school. This meant there was a greater diversity of students, including those from myriad different ethnic and racial heritages. He found that he liked hanging out with these students more than those who were more immersed in mainstream White culture. Many of these fellow students had experienced some of the same struggles that he had dealt with. Many, though not all, had to learn English as part of their schooling, as their respective families only spoke their native language at home. Those in this group of students experienced at least some ostracization for not being White. Of course, there were also many White kids and adolescents who did not care about skin color, accents, native languages, or cultural traditions and were genuinely kind and inclusive. During his teen and preteen years, however, Alex preferred to surround himself with those who had had similar experiences trying to assimilate into the privileged culture. As a result, Alex became more immersed in his family's cultural traditions and struggled to accept and appreciate that which the privileged culture had to offer. This was a shift from his earlier school-aged years, when he was trying hard to fit in and wanted to distance himself from his racial and ethnic roots.

After high school, Alex attended a large university in a big city, which meant that there was a great deal of diversity not only in terms of race and ethnicity but also sexual orientation, religion, socioeconomic status, and so on. Since he had to start over again in terms of meeting people and making friends, he struggled with whether it mattered to him if his friends were from a disenfranchised group of some kind or if he wanted to be more inclusive. By the end of his senior year of college, he had a fairly diverse group of friends, but what tied them together was their common interests with respect to intellectual pursuits and hobbies. Alex did not care about their backgrounds. After being in the workforce for a few years, he came to realize that while his racial and ethnic heritage was important to him, it did not need to be something that prevented him from accepting

Case Studies 215

and appreciating those from other backgrounds, including those from the privileged culture.

Analysis

While Alex has undoubtedly dealt with a variety of issues and concerns throughout his life, what this scenario depicts is Alex's process of racial and ethnic identity development. The various models about identity development in this regard suggest that many people who are part of a disenfranchised group living in a country like the United States often go through a series of stages related to how they accept both their own culture and heritage as well as that of the privileged culture. In many ways, Alex's process is similar to that which would be predicted by these models.

Alex dealt with being ostracized because he did not speak English, and his family was from a culture distinct from the privileged culture of the United States. He initially struggled with trying to fit in, and when he finally did, he struggled with accepting those who had previously bullied him because of his accent and background. He eventually immersed himself in his own culture and surrounded himself with peers who were from the same or a different disenfranchised culture, excluding those who were from the privileged culture. It was not until his college experience that he started to broaden his peer group by finding others who were interested in the same or similar things he was interested in, regardless of their background. Currently, it can be said that Alex is likely in the final stage of most models of racial and ethnic identity development, which suggest that such a person will eventually accept and appreciate both their own cultural heritage as well as that of the privileged culture. During this stage, people surround themselves with others not based on a particular demographic such as race or ethnicity but in terms of who they are as people and what common interests they may share.

Stacey Becomes Steve, and His Family Struggles to Help

Stacey is a ten-year-old who was born a biological female, but as far back as she can remember, she has felt like she fits in better with males. When she thinks about herself, she believes she should be a male.

Stacey was raised as a female, which meant that her parents bought her clothes that girls typically wear and got haircuts for her that kept her hair at a medium length or longer, subsequently having it styled like most girls' hair. When she was still quite young, she asked her mother when her "male parts" would finally grow. Her mother explained that she would not have male parts because she is a girl, and when she gets older, her "girl parts" will develop more fully, which should happen in a few years. Stacey burst into tears and isolated herself. In the days that followed, she continued to isolate herself as often as she could.

A few weeks later, she felt a bit better when she realized she could cut her hair shorter, as a lot of girls have short hair, and wear clothes that boys usually wear. Her parents supported her decision to cut her hair shorter and agreed to buy her more traditionally masculine clothes, but they still shopped in the girl's section of stores, hunting for nonfrilly and not obviously feminine clothing. On one shopping trip, Stacey found the boy's clothing section and picked out several shirts and a few pairs of pants she wanted to get, but her mother told her she needed to shop in the girl's section because she was a girl and boy clothes "wouldn't fit quite right." Stacey burst into tears in the middle of the clothing store, and she and her mother left without buying any clothes. This left Stacey with the more feminine clothes she already had in her closet at home.

Stacey seemed to become more withdrawn and started refusing to go to school, saying she did not fit in and that she would rather die than have to live like a girl anymore. Her parents believed this was a phase that some children go through, but they became worried for her well-being when she declared she would rather be dead. Then Stacey's mother walked in on her in the bathroom crying with her shirt off and a razor blade in her hand held to her chest. She had pressed the blade into her skin, and there was a little bit of blood. Her mother screamed at the sight of her distraught child trying to cut herself and asked what she was doing. Stacey replied, "If I can cut them off now, then they won't grow into girl parts." She was trying to prevent her breasts from developing by cutting them off.

Stacey's mother and father agreed that their daughter needed help, but they did not know what to do or how to handle what their daughter was going through. They called local counselors and psychologists in the area and explained their concerns until they found a counselor who specialized in working with children dealing with gender identity concerns. Although Stacey's parents were not really sure what all her struggles were about, they were not terribly surprised when Stacey, with the help of her counselor, informed her parents that she was transgender. Stacey asked her counselor, with her parents present, what would be involved in becoming a transgender male. She stated that she already had her name picked out and wanted people to start calling her Steve.

Steve's parents sought their own counseling to not only learn about what it means to be transgender but also how to best support him as he transitioned from being their daughter to becoming their son.

Analysis

Steve has a long road ahead of him, as does his family. He is still in school and will have to work with school officials to determine the best way for Steve to effectively adjust to being a male at school and to also help his

Case Studies   217

classmates adjust, as until now they have known him as a girl named Stacey. Steve will work with his counselor and discuss how to best communicate to his friends and acquaintances that he is no longer a girl and that he has a new name. The school may need to ensure that students know their counselors are available should they have questions about Steve's transition as well as if they have difficulty accepting him as he is. Steve will need to continue counseling with someone who is experienced in working with those who are transgender and actively undergoing their transition.

Although it is not clear from this scenario whether Steve plans to undergo a full physical transition via surgery, this would be a long way off because the process of psychologically and physically transitioning from one sex to another takes place over a long period of time. The first part of the process involves what Steve is currently experiencing, which is to get used to living as a male and to be sure that when he is somewhat older, he understands what is involved in fully transitioning. Moreover, part of the transitioning process involves extensive counseling and assessment to ensure that he is psychologically well enough to make such a transition.

Although his parents are struggling to accept these dramatic changes, they know they love their child and are working hard to respect how he feels and what he is going through. They are also working on remembering to use his new name and to refer to him with male pronouns—all of which will take time because they have known Steve as "Stacey" for many years.

David Has No Idea What He Wants to Do with His Life and Does Not Seem to Care

David is an eighteen-year-old high school senior who is just a few months away from graduation. His friends and most of his classmates have either been accepted to college or have plans for work after graduation. He has talked with his friends quite a bit about their plans for not only which colleges they plan to attend but also what they plan to study. When asked what he plans to do, David simply replies, "I don't know. I'll figure it out, I guess." Despite saying that he plans to "figure it out," David has not applied to any colleges or universities, even though he has the capacity to do well in college. He has also not given much thought to what career path he might choose, regardless of whether or not a college-level education would be required.

Growing up, David expressed the stereotypical interests in careers that a lot of children express. At one point, he stated that he wanted to be a firefighter, and at another, he stated that he wanted to be a doctor. In many ways, he has retained his interests in these two career paths, but he has added other possibilities to the list. His parents have weighed in on who he is and who he should become professionally, as have his friends and teachers. When talking to his high school guidance counselor about his career plans, David said he had always wanted to be a doctor but could also see being a veterinarian. When his guidance counselor reflected back that it seems like he has an interest in going into the medical field in some capacity, David replied by saying, "Yeah, but I remember how cool I thought firefighters were when I was growing up. I could see doing that as well. I've even thought about being a taxi driver in a big city. You get to meet a lot of people and get to know the city really well. But, you know, owning my own business would be cool, too."

Given his varied interests and how it did not seem like David was more interested in one type of career or another, his guidance counselor suggested that he take a career interest test that would show how his skills and interests align with those who are already in various careers. His results reflected his expressed interests but also listed some other specific jobs David had not previously mentioned, such as being a counselor or a teacher. When David saw his results and these new career possibilities, he seemed to be as interested in those as he was in the other careers he had mentioned.

Although career interest tests are not designed to definitively indicate which career path someone should choose, the results do tend to help people narrow down their possibilities; however, for David, it seemed to widen his interests. He spent some time at home and at school researching various career paths by searching on the internet for descriptions, pay ranges, and the expectations of various careers, but he seemed to find the information merely interesting rather than informative in helping him direct his interests. Apart from this, he spent most of his free time on various social media platforms looking at what other people were up to, sending and receiving messages from friends, and comparing their lives to his own. He was not, however, motivated to make any kind of decision about what life will be like for him following high school.

Analysis

David seems unconcerned about his lack of direction. Certainly, teenagers and young adults do not have to have their careers and lives figured out before they graduate high school, but they generally have some idea of what they think they would like to pursue. Alternatively, some individuals plan to take time during college to do more exploration to help them decide. David seems disinterested in identifying a career or educational path of any kind. He has not expressed an interest in going to college or in getting a job in which he might be interested. Moreover, he seems unconcerned that his peers are beginning to make plans for their futures while he is not.

According to James Marcia's theory of identity statuses, David is most likely identity diffused. By definition, someone in this identity status has not experienced an identity crisis and is not interested in figuring it out. David has done some exploration with respect to possible careers; however, as noted in the scenario, he seems curious about what people in these professions do,

Case Studies   219

but what he has learned has been fascinating to him rather than instructive in terms of what career path he may take. Someone who is identity diffused, like David, has difficulty deciding on what career to pursue or, more generally, what they want their life to be like. This reflects an identity that is not well developed nor coherent.

Someone with a more well-developed sense of who they are will have some idea about what is important to them and perhaps what they like. They will read a description of a career, such as becoming a veterinarian, and will know to some degree whether they have any personal interest in pursuing that line of work to the exclusion of other career paths. He has been unable to navigate societal expectations, his parents' expectations, or what he wants for himself. It appears that he takes in all information as equally valuable rather than discerning what information may be helpful and what may not be. Until David experiences a crisis that motivates him to seek direction for himself, he will likely continue to spend time on activities that do not help him figure out who he is and what he wants.

Gerald Has Dated Like He Is "Supposed To," but Now He Is Anxious and Depressed

Gerald is a young man currently struggling with his sexual orientation and therefore how he identifies himself sexually. Growing up, he recognized that he was sometimes attracted to females and at other times males. He only ever talked about his attraction to females with his friends and family members because he knew being gay (he had not yet considered that he might be bisexual) would not be accepted by many people with whom he associated. He believed his parents would accept him no matter what, but he had read stories online about people who came out to their parents and were rejected by them. He was terrified the same thing would happen to him, so he decided not to tell anyone about his sexual attraction to males.

Gerald has publicly dated females in the sense that he has gone on group dates and double dates with his guy friends, but only when he was dating a female. He has been comfortable with this and found that he enjoyed the company of the young women he dated and only dated those to whom he was attracted. He has been sexually active with females, but he has not yet engaged in sexual activity or romantic activity (e.g., kissing, holding hands) with a male.

Gerald has never dated a male, secretly or publicly. He has gone on same-sex dating websites but never developed a profile. He started to make a profile on one site, but then he felt too scared to publish it. He was not only afraid that someone he knew might come across it, though admittedly he did not know any gay males and did not think any straight males would look on a gay dating site, but also that if he published a profile someone might actually reach out to him looking for a date. He did not think he was ready for that.

Recently, Gerald has been feeling a combination of anxiety and depression that has been connected to confusion about his dating life. Although the females he has dated have resulted in satisfying relationships while they lasted, he has been feeling like he cannot fully explore all his dating options because he has, to this point, only allowed himself to date females. Recently, while out with friends at a club, he met a young man who he not only found physically attractive but also enjoyed his company. They talked for quite a bit of time while his friends were on the dance floor trying to pick up women. They kept trying to coax Gerald to dance with them and meet the group of young women they were dancing with, but he wanted to stay and talk with his new acquaintance. He did not, however, want his friends to think he was romantically interested in the man he met, even though it seemed obvious to Gerald that this young man was romantically interested in him.

Gerald ultimately decided to literally walk away from this young man to spend time with his friends. He has since strongly regretted that decision, believing that he may have walked away from someone with whom he might have had a satisfying romantic relationship. Since then, he has become aware of growing feelings of depression about the possibility of not finding someone he truly cares about, regardless of their sex, and anxiety about admitting to himself and eventually others that he may be gay. Given his attraction to both males and females, he has also begun to wonder whether he is bisexual.

Analysis

Gerald seems to be confused about his sexual identity. He has allowed himself to acknowledge that he is attracted to those of the same sex, but he also knows that he has been attracted to females as well. He has usually only thought about his and other's sexuality in terms of heterosexuality or homosexuality, but he has recently considered the possibility that he may truly be attracted to both males and females. However, his inability to feel comfortable about acting on his attraction to males has likely contributed to his confusion as well as his declining mental health. His recent abandonment of a possible relationship with a young man that may have had potential seems to have exacerbated his feelings of depression and anxiety.

Gerald has not yet come out to anyone about his sexual attraction to members of the same sex. He has only felt comfortable sharing with others his dating relationships with females. He is admittedly scared that he may lose important relationships to him, including friends and family members, if he were to reveal this secret part of him. Although it may be the case that Gerald would feel better if he came out to those close to him, it is equally important that Gerald come out on his own terms. Moreover, despite the fact that Gerald is clear that he is sexually attracted to both males and females, he has only recently considered the possibility that he may be bisexual.

Case Studies 221

It will likely be important for Gerald to talk with a counselor who has helped other people figure out and come to terms with their sexual identity. Moreover, formal counseling can help him plan if he wants to come out and how and when to do so with those important to him. With the help of a counselor, he can also start to prepare for the possibility that he could lose some important relationships should some in his life reject him because he is not heterosexual. If Gerald realizes that he is, in fact, bisexual, an experienced counselor skilled at helping clients wade through confusion about their sexual identity and coming out may help him navigate the gay, straight, and bisexual communities, as bisexual individuals sometimes feel ostracized by both the gay and straight communities.

Alicia Has Too Many Possibilities for Her Life and Struggles to Narrow Things Down

Alicia is a nineteen-year-old sophomore in college who has not yet picked a major, and she will be required to do so before staring her junior year. Alicia has learned quite a bit about herself while growing up and has moved past wanting to be a teacher, which her six-year-old self wanted, or a chef, which her twelve-year-old self thought would be fun. Working with her guidance counselor in high school helped her to figure out that going to college is a good path to take for her because the jobs that would typically be available to her with a high school diploma were not of interest to her. Since completing a year and a half of college, however, she has not found it any easier to narrow down her interests so that she can pursue one area of study.

Upon recommendation from her college advisor, Alicia enrolled in elective courses that seemed interesting to her as one method of figuring out what area(s) of study may be of interest. She could then learn about the various career paths associated with a degree in that field. When that did not seem to help, her advisor also recommended that she meet with the career counselor on campus who might be able to better help her narrow down her interests. Alicia found this to be helpful, as it became clear to her after seeing her career interest test results and talking in-depth with the career counselor that she wants to go into a career where she can help people. Although realizing this eliminated numerous career paths, it did not sufficiently narrow down her interests in terms of how she might want to help people.

The career counselor recommended identifying a list of possible careers and talking with people in those careers to find what it is really like to be a nurse, or a counselor, or a teacher, or a physical therapist, and so on. Alicia decided that she would start identifying professionals in the careers that were interesting to her and try to meet with them throughout the remainder of the academic year and over the summer. She believed this plan would allow her enough time to make an informed decision about her career path and ultimately declare her major.

Alicia also talked with her parents about how they decided what they wanted to do for the rest of their lives. Both indicated more practical reasons for their career choices. Her father said he picked a career that made a lot of money. He added that Alicia should strongly consider this in her decision-making, thereby eliminating helping careers that, relatively speaking, do not pay very much. Her mother stated that she picked her own career path based on what would give her the most flexible schedule possible so that she could be available to Alicia and her brother while they were growing up. Both of her parents said that she should also think about whether going into a career that requires more education beyond an undergraduate degree (e.g., physical therapy) is a good idea. They added that getting more education will likely mean she has more student loan debt, which can be difficult to pay off, particularly in a struggling economy, which can make finding a good-paying job, regardless of one's education, more difficult. Alicia found these rationales to be valid, but she realized that neither parent said anything about picking a job because it was a good fit in terms of their skills and interests.

Alicia also talked with her friends in college who had already picked a major. She asked them if they knew what they wanted to do with their major after they graduated and how they figured that out. Similar to what she got from her parents, her friends provide myriad answers as to why they picked their majors and career paths. Although Alicia was appreciative of all the advice she received, she still felt lost with respect to what would work for her.

Analysis

Alicia is not alone in her struggle to figure out who she is and what she wants to do with the rest of her life. This is a common struggle for many young adults. Although some of her friends seem to have it figured out and were forthcoming about how they decided on their respective career paths, Alicia was still left feeling like she did not know how to go about figuring this out for herself. Her parents offered her good advice as well, and the career counselor helped her to determine that a possible good fit may be found in a helping career. Despite this assistance Alicia has struggled to reconcile the realities of needing a career that makes enough money, how much education she really wants to get (which can become expensive), and how important her interest and enjoyment in a career path should be. Given her current experiences, Alicia would be identified as being in the moratorium identity status as described by James Marcia.

Those in moratorium are actively struggling to figure out who they are and what they want for their lives, and as such, they are actively in crisis. It is clear that picking a career path matters to Alicia, but she is struggling to figure out how strongly things like the current economy should factor into her decision-making and how much being happy and satisfied in her career

Case Studies 223

should matter. Thus, she has not quite solidified her sense of identity, which can include how important each of these facets of career choice is to her. She knows what is important to her friends and parents and has sought advice from others, but she is struggling to determine which of these ideas makes sense to her and which do not. So, although both Alicia and David (from the identity diffusion scenario) do not have well-developed identities, the difference between them is that Alicia is actively in crisis and exploring her options, whereas David is not in crisis and seems to have a great deal of apathy toward figuring out his life goals.

Jennifer Struggles to Manage Her High Degree of Dedication to Her Sport when She Becomes Injured

Jennifer is a senior in high school and has become an accomplished sprinter in both indoor and outdoor track and field. Her events are the 100 meter dash, the 200 meter dash, and the 4 × 100 meter relay. Her times earned her a spot on the varsity team all four years of high school. By the time Jennifer was a junior, she was expected to not only compete in the state championship meet but also to win the events in which she was entered, thereby earning her a bid to compete in regional and possibly national championship track meets. Her success at the state level garnered the attention of several coaches of collegiate track-and-field teams. She was actively recruited, and these prospective coaches encouraged her to visit their respective universities and stay with a member of the team so that she could get a sense of what life was like for a collegiate track-and-field athlete. She took a few of them up on their offer and was thrilled to have an opportunity to meet potential teammates and to have the opportunity to practice with them. She thoroughly enjoyed her visits and could picture herself devoting all of her nonacademic time and energy to improving her technique and speed.

Growing up, Jennifer earned the nickname "Speedy" because she could usually outrun all the boys and girls at recess when they had races. During middle school, she was able to get a sense of what competing as a sprinter would be like, and she was hooked. She begged her parents to send her to track-and-field camps every summer from middle school through high school. She took every opportunity she could to work out and to compete. Although Jennifer had a fairly diverse group of friends in middle school and during her first year in high school, her friend group narrowed as she became more immersed in track and field. Her nontrack friends did not understand what was so appealing about running around a track, and she found that she simply did not have much else in common with those who were not involved with the sport. By the end of her sophomore year in high school, she was more distant from her nontrack friends and preferred to spend time with her fellow teammates both during and outside of school. She read whatever should could online about successful sprinters ultimately subscribing to numerous online "magazines" devoted to track and field. She always watched collegiate, national, world, and Olympic track-and-field events when they were on TV. On more than one occasion, she commented, "One day that will be me!"

Jennifer had very few injuries, and any injury she did sustain usually healed relatively quickly, in a matter of days. However, it was difficult for her to adhere to the recommendations of her athletic trainer to rest her body so that her injury had sufficient time to heal. She usually rushed to return to practice so that she would be ready for the next competition. Occasionally, she reinjured herself and had to rehabilitate a bit longer. This usually resulted in a marked drop in mood until she was officially cleared to practice and compete again. During these times, Jennifer was irritable and very difficult to be around. Even her track friends, who knew what it was like to be injured, limited their interactions with her because she would snap at them whenever they tried to give her advice or make her feel better.

During her senior year, as she was trying to decide which college she would attend based on which track-and-field program she wanted to be part of, Jennifer found that she was not improving on her times as she had been each previous year. She would occasionally have an outstanding race, but mostly her performances were much less than she and others expected. On many occasions, her times were slower than they had ever been. She worked out harder, including completing workouts above and beyond what her coach expected and what her athletic trainer recommended. This did not help; in fact, it seemed to make things worse, which did not make sense to Jennifer. Both her coach and athletic trainer implored her to rest her body, but Jennifer continued working out more and more with the thought that more training would equal faster times. This did not happen for her, and by the time outdoor track started in the spring, Jennifer's times were still not improving. Frustrated by the lack of results despite all the work she put in, Jennifer started saying things like, "Track is not that important to me anyway. It's just running around in a circle. I can't believe I actually thought I wanted to compete in college!"

Analysis

Jennifer is clearly an athlete who has been highly invested in and committed to running track as soon as she was able to formally compete in middle school. She devoted as much time and energy as she could to the sport and to improving her performances, so much so that her life began to revolve around track and field and seemingly nothing else. Her friend group changed; she was only friends with fellow teammates during the bulk of her high school years. She voraciously read anything related to track-and-field and

Case Studies   225

watched elite-level track athletes compete every chance she got. She even seemed to have long-term aspirations to compete at a high level, as she was actively recruited to compete at the collegiate level and believed that she might be able to compete at the national or international level. Essentially, Jennifer's life revolved around track and field. In this regard, she can be said to have a high athletic identity.

Having a high athletic identity usually looks like Jennifer's life. It typically means that just about everything the person does and everyone they interact with is involved with their sport of choice in some way. In addition, Jennifer's spare time was spent training above and beyond what she needed to do, reading about how to improve her technique, and watching high-level athletes compete on TV. A high athletic identity is also evident in Jennifer's significant drop in mood and increase in irritability when she was not able to practice or compete due to injury. As a result, she started to alienate friends who might have been able to provide some measure of support for her during this time.

Finally, it is not uncommon for those who have a high degree of athletic identity to distance themselves from their sport when they are not performing as they would like or as they think they should. This can be viewed as a protective or defense mechanism because the pain of not being as good as they think they are (or actually are) is so great that it can feel better to distance one's self from the sport by declaring it as something they are not really that interested in.

Carter Has Chosen a Career Path and a Life Partner That Are Both a Good Fit for Him

Carter is a twenty-four-year-old college graduate who has been in law school for over two years and is engaged with plans to marry within the next two to three years. Carter began his initial career exploration during his high school years. During that time, he became aware of his developing interest in issues related to social justice, such as gender, racial, and sexual orientation equality, and was active in his high school student government so that he could help make changes so that all students felt safe and included in school-related activities. He also became aware of the subjects that held little to no interest for him, even though he excelled in nearly every course he took. Throughout high school, he also had a variety of friends; however, the ones who became very good friends were those who held similar perspectives on life and had similar values.

After high school, Carter enrolled in college and became an English major. He knew he did not necessarily want to pursue a career in writing or teaching, but he knew he wanted to master all aspects of the language so that he could communicate as effectively as possible. He also supplemented his degree by taking courses that required making speeches—which included taking a debate course—or that required writing extensive papers. It was through his course in debate that he developed an interest in making sound, logic-based arguments and thought that pursuing a law degree following undergrad would be a good fit for him. Carter was also highly active in non-academic pursuits at his university. He was active in his university's student government and was elected president both his junior and senior years. He joined a few other clubs that tapped into his interests related to social justice issues and debate.

While nearing the end of his college career, Carter was able to intern at two different law offices to determine whether a law degree was what he really wanted and, if so, what type of law he might like to pursue. As a result of his passion for learning about the law and the various types of law in which a lawyer can practice, he developed strong preprofessional connections with a few of the lawyers at different law firms. This allowed him to have more candid conversations about the types of law they each practiced and what they liked and did not like about it, and it allowed him to secure strong letters of recommendation for when he applied to law school.

Carter's friends and family highly supported his decision to become a lawyer, and they often commented on how much money he would be able to make in that career. Although Carter hoped he would make a good living and would not likely turn down a high-paying job if it was offered to him, he already knew that whatever job he took, he wanted to represent those who needed a strong voice on their behalf. He wanted to advocate for them and ensure they were treated fairly.

As Carter's career path became more and more clear to him, his commitment to being able to effectively communicate so that others would listen to what he had to say and understand the exact meaning of what was said was further reinforced. As such, he realized he valued effective communication not only for himself but also in his relationships with others. He also realized that he wanted friends and future dating partners who were also invested in equal rights and fair treatment because there were important pursuits to which he knew he would devote a great deal of time and energy.

Since Carter has been in law school, each class and each experience has confirmed for him the values and interests he has developed over several years. Having this clarity also allowed him to find a dating partner that was a good fit for him. He met his current partner in law school and found that their interests and goals were a good fit for one another. Thus, they planned to marry as soon as they both finished law school.

Analysis

Carter seemed to do a great deal of exploration during his high school years. He was a very good student who got good grades, and he was able to distinguish between being good at something compared to being interested

Case Studies

in something. He seemed to have identified both (interests and abilities) by the time he enrolled in college. Moreover, Carter had a variety of friendships throughout his high school career but was also able to recognize that some relationships were more fulfilling than others. He was able to determine that this was due in large part to the degree to which they shared similar interests and values. Carter's friends and family were supportive of his pursuit of a law degree but not for the reasons he decided to go into law. He was not indifferent to making money, but he knew that his pursuit of a career in law was for reasons that were more meaningful and important to him than money.

Carter can be identified as having the status of identity achievement. Those who attain this status have actively gone through an identity crisis. They have grappled with what interests them, what they are good at, and what others think and have explored their options. This type of exploration helps individuals to find what interests them in terms of a career path and to clarify what values are important to them. Knowing this helps to direct them when seeking a career, deciding what job to ultimately take, and deciding what kind of people are a good fit with who they are. Carter's ability to establish a coherent and well-developed identity has allowed him to choose a career that fits well with who he is and what is important to him and to find a life partner who shares his values. These are indicators of someone who is truly identity achieved.

Stanley Was Adopted as a Baby and Now Has Questions about Where He Came From

Note: When the word *parents* is used without the qualifier *biological*, it refers to Stanley's adopted parents.

Stanley is a sixteen-year-old junior in high school. He was adopted as a two-year-old by parents of the same race and ethnicity as him. He also has a sister who is two years younger who was also adopted as an infant. He is not biologically connected to his sister. Stanley has always known he was adopted and has no memory of the two years he spent with his biological parents. While growing up and to this day, his parents celebrate not only his birthday but also his "coming home" day, which was the day he was brought home to permanently live with his parents.

When Stanley was old enough to understand what being adopted truly meant, he initially struggled with being different from most of his classmates, some of whom teased him for not living with his "real" parents. He occasionally came home from school upset that he was not really his parents' child and that he did not have a family. His parents then sat him down and talked to him about the fact that there are many different kinds of families and that what matters is that every member of the family loves and respects one another. They also assured him that although they are not biologically related to him, he is their son, and they love him as any parent would love their child, regardless of whether or not they are biologically related. At the end of one such conversation, his mother looked at him and said, "We are lucky because we got to pick you and your sister."

As Stanley got older, he began asking questions about his biological mother and father and whether his parents knew who they were. His parents let him know that they had received very little information about his biological relatives because the adoption was "closed," which means that neither the biological nor the adoptive parents know the identity of the other. His parents said they did receive some basic information, such as how old his biological parents were when they had him, what their level of education was at the time of the adoption, and some basic health information, such as his biological family's history of medical illnesses, such as heart disease and cancer. Although he had previously wondered, Stanley finally asked his parents, "How come they didn't want me? What is wrong with me?" His parents reassured him that most biological parents who give their children up for adoption do not do so because there is something wrong with the child or because they do not necessarily want the child. Oftentimes, parents who give their child up for adoption are no longer able to provide adequate care for the child and decide it is best for the child to be adopted by another family who can provide what the child needs. His parents admitted that they did not know the circumstances in which he was given up for adoption because the adoption was closed. They were simply told that the biological parents voluntarily terminated their parental rights.

Over the years since his initial concern about being adopted and what that really meant, Stanley did not think about the fact that he was adopted very much. In fact, he realized it rarely came to mind. Since he has been in high school and studying more advanced topics than he had in middle school and elementary school, he has been wondering about who his biological relatives were, what they were like, and whether he was like them. He does not really have an interest in having a "second family," but he truly wonders whether he looks like either biological parent or is similar in any other way. He asked his parents if they would object to him trying to search for his biological relatives one day. They were supportive and assured him they understood why he would be curious about them and offered to talk with him more about it or to have him talk with a counselor who may be able to better help him sort through the pros and cons of searching for his biological relatives.

Analysis

Stanley is grappling with common issues related to his adoptive identity. Although being adopted is something he has known about as far back as he can remember and therefore has been part of his identity for many years, he continues to struggle with what it means to him to be adopted and what it

Case Studies 229

means that he likely has numerous biological relatives of whom he has no knowledge.

Stanley is fortunate in that he did not find out about his adoption later in life and therefore did not have to reconcile this new piece of important information into his already developing identity. Rather, he has always known he was adopted because his parents told him early on and were able to talk about his adoption openly. Researchers generally indicate that those who have accurate and complete information about their adoption tend to have a more healthy adjustment and development regarding having been adopted. Stanley has the most accurate and complete information available to both him and his parents, but his information nonetheless remains incomplete. He does not know much at all about who his biological parents and relatives are, and he is currently grappling with whether he wants to find out.

Regardless of Stanley's decision about what additional information he wants to have and whether he is able to access additional information because of his adoption being closed, he seems to be getting adequate support from his parents and presumably his friends. This support will allow him to follow his own unique path as he continues to make sense of how being adopted fits in with his understanding of who he is.

Rachel Had a Crisis of Faith and Then an Identity Crisis

Rachel is a twenty-two-year-old living completely on her own for the first time in her life. She was raised in a loving family and maintains regular contact with her parents and two younger siblings. After living with her family throughout her school years, she moved into a dorm at the university she chose and always had a roommate throughout her four years of college. While in college, she attended Sunday Mass each week and went to Mass during the week as often as she could. She only dated Catholic men who were as invested in their faith as she was.

Throughout her time in college, Rachel continued to attend Sunday Mass but not every week. In addition, by the time she graduated, she had stopped attending Mass on additional days of the week altogether. She lost a few friends, and at least one dating relationship ended due to her apparent waning commitment to her faith. While in the midst of her college career, she was confronted by some of her friends who shared her faith about whether she was a "true" Catholic anymore. Rachel vehemently defended her faith and internally vowed to attend Mass with the same frequency she had when she first started college. However, she found that she was not able to sustain that kind of regular attendance and chalked it up to being stressed by the demands of her classes and feeling too tired to get up that early in the morning. She continued to pray daily, kneeling at the side of her bed as she had every night growing up as a child. Rachel became aware that she might, in fact, be having a crisis of faith during her junior year in college when she went home for Christmas break.

Rachel was excited to be with her family again and felt a sense of comfort at the dinner table when her father led the family in prayer before eating. Her concerns about her faith surfaced when the family started talking about attending midnight Mass together on Christmas. Although Rachel had fond memories of attending this important service growing up, she realized she was dreading going. She wondered whether she could feign not feeling well and get out of going, but she ultimately decided she wanted to be with her family and went. Rachel, like most of those in attendance, had the traditional service nearly memorized. They were an hour into the service when she realized she had simply been going through the motions and was not really paying attention to the content of the service nor her responses to it.

Although her parents noted she seemed "distant" and "withdrawn" during the remainder of the Christmas break, Rachel was able to assuage their concerns by saying she was just preoccupied about starting the next semester and reconnecting with her friends. The truth, however, was that Rachel was realizing that she had been lying to herself about why she was not keeping up with her Catholic traditions while away at school. She was not sure whether she believed anymore. She also realized she was starting to question more than simply her family's religious beliefs. She was also questioning other values tied to the faith, such as the emphasis on having and raising children and not having sex before marriage. She realized she felt constrained and desired to feel freer to express her true self, although she simultaneously realized she was not sure who that was.

When she returned to school, Rachel poured herself into the final semester of classes and into applying for jobs. She saw her family again at graduation (she stayed with friends during spring break) but moved from college into her first apartment after having secured a job in her field. She knew she still loved her family and did not want to disappointment or lose them, but she also knew she needed time to figure out who she was and what she truly wanted for herself and her life. This included breaking up with the devout Catholic man she had been dating for over a year rather than moving to wherever he got a job, as they had been talking about.

Analysis

Although *religious identity* was not specifically addressed in chapter 2, it is certainly a type of identity that most readers may recognize within themselves. It is not clear from the scenario whether Rachel's crisis of faith occurred due to exposure to different belief systems in college, through interactions with a diverse group of peers, through some of her coursework, or due to some other reason. Regardless, Rachel recognized that she was not

Case Studies

as involved with her faith at the end of her college career as she had been when she first started. Of course, the demands of college do tend to result in students having to make difficult decisions about how and with whom they spend their time; however, Rachel never would have predicted that not attending Mass would be a result. She had thought her faith was something she would always choose over all else.

Rachel seems to be dealing with differentiation and individuation from her family. It is likely that she had not previously questioned whether Catholicism and other strongly held values in her family were a good fit for her. She, like most children in a family, accepted her family's beliefs, values, and traditions as givens and not anything that should be or even needed to be examined. Now, however, Rachel is finding that that is exactly what she needs to do. We do not know the full impact this has had on Rachel. For some, upending one's long-standing and strongly held belief systems can cause distress and clinical levels of anxiety and depression. It is possible she may question all the choices she has made so far, including her career choice.

Regardless, Rachel's decision to physically and psychologically distance herself from her family may allow what she truly believes to come to the surface. It is entirely possible that she may reject Catholicism and any version of organized religion. She may come to the realization that she is still Catholic or that she is still Christian but not Catholic because the Catholic teachings do not fit with how she has come to see herself, other people, or the world around her. Rachel may benefit from talking with a counselor to help her work through this crisis of faith, which may evolve into a full identity crisis (i.e., not just questioning one's faith but everything about one's self and one's beliefs).

Sources for Further Information

General Resources

Centers for Disease Control and Prevention (CDC): Get the Facts about Coronavirus

www.cdc.gov/coronavirus/2019-nCoV

The mission of the Centers for Disease Control and Prevention (CDC) is to "work 24/7 to protect the safety, health, and security of America from threats here and around the world." The CDC indicates that they are the leading organization that uses science and data to protect the health and well-being of those in the United States. Among many other health-related topics, the CDC's website has a series of web pages devoted to information about the novel coronavirus and COVID-19, the symptoms of COVID-19, how to self-monitor for symptoms, information about who is at increased risk, and what we should do to protect ourselves from spreading or contracting the virus in schools, at work, when we travel, and as we go about our daily lives.

National Association for Media Literacy Education (NAMLE)

namle.net

The Partnership for Media Education launched in 1997. In 2008, the name was changed to National Association for Media Literacy Education (NAMLE), and it officially became a nonprofit organization in 2014. The NAMLE's vision is "to help individuals of all ages develop the habits of inquiry and skills of expression that they need to be critical thinkers, effective communicators, and active citizens in today's world." Its website contains various resources, information about its annual conference, research in the area of media literacy, and information about Media Literacy Week (which last occurred October 21–25, 2020) that also includes a link to resources that can be used at various levels of schooling (e.g., K–12) and within one's community.

Pew Research Center

pewresearch.org
The Pew Research Center originated as a research project called the Times Mirror Center for the People & the Press in 1990. This effort became the Pew Research Center in 2004 and is primarily funded by the Pew Charitable Trusts. Its mission is to "generate a foundation of facts that enriches the public dialogue and supports sound decision-making." It makes a point of noting that it is independent, nonpartisan, and objective. Major tabs on its website include "U.S. Politics," "Media & News," "Social Trends," "Religion," "Internet & Tech," "Science," "Hispanics," "Global," and "Methods." Among other things, there are articles about specific generations (e.g., millennials), the coronavirus, Black Lives Matter, and identity (e.g., racial identity, religious identity, national identity).

Self-Determination Theory (SDT)

selfdeterminationtheory.org
Self-determination theory (SDT) was formally developed by Edward Deci and Richard Ryan in the mid-1980s and describes a set of psychological needs all human beings have that motivate behavior. Those needs include the need for competence, autonomy, and relatedness. Selfdetermination-theory.org was founded to sponsor and disseminate ongoing scholarship designed to advance the theory and to apply our understanding of the theory to people's daily lives. The website illustrates how SDT can be applied to myriad facets of life, including, but not limited to, education, health care, organizations, sport and exercise, and the environment.

Wikipedia

wikipedia.org
Most readers are undoubtedly familiar with Wikipedia, including the fact that you can find information about almost any topic, any major event, and any influential person. Many readers also know that use of this site should be done with an abundance of caution because not all the information contained in the various entries is accurate and it can be edited by nearly anyone. Despite that, when used carefully, Wikipedia, which is hosted by the Wikimedia Foundation, can provide users with good information to learn the basics about whatever one has searched for. Many of the topics, people, and theories contained in this book do not have specific online sources or print sources beneficial to the average reader (i.e., a nonacademic or nonprofessional). To that end, readers of this book may find it helpful to enter various terms (e.g., identity, gender identity), people (e.g., Carl Rogers), or theories (e.g., self-determination theory) contained within this book into Wikipedia's search bar to learn

Sources for Further Information 235

more about these subjects. Read the entries with the assumption that much, if not most, of the information is accurate, but going to the primary sources (i.e., books or scholarly articles often cited within the entries) will yield the most accurate and complete information.

Social Justice Resources

Black Lives Matter (Movement and Website)

https://blacklivesmatter.com
Black Lives Matter (also BLM, #BLM, #BlackLivesMatter) was founded in 2013 by three Black women. It "is an ideological and political intervention in a world where Black lives are systematically and intentionally targeted for demise." The pivotal event that sparked the founding of Black Lives Matter was the acquittal of the person who killed Trayvon Martin. The all-female founders noted that a foundational focus was on the lived experiences of Black women with an emphasis on Black trans women; however, they further stated that Black Lives Matter was founded to support the lives of all Black people. Black Lives Matter is currently a global phenomenon with over forty chapters worldwide.

How to Be an Antiracist (Book)

Ibram X. Kendi
How to Be an Antiracist, published in 2019, is a #1 *New York Times* bestselling book and has been celebrated and identified as an important book by myriad media outlets, including NPR, *Time*, and *Kirkus Reviews*. The author, Ibram X. Kendi, explores obvious and subtle forms of racism and their consequences for those on both sides of racism.

National Center for Transgender Equality (NCTE)

Transequality.org
The National Center for Transgender Equality was founded in 2003 to advocate for the rights of transgender people and to have a voice in the nation's capital, Washington, DC. The mission of the organization is to effect change not only in terms of formal policy but also in terms of the attitudes people have about transgender people for the purpose of increasing others' understanding and acceptance of those who are transgender. The website includes resources to help people learn more about what it means to be transgender and self-help guides for those who are transgender on topics such as getting adequate health coverage, formally changing one's various forms of identification, and legal services devoted to helping transgender people with any legal issues they may encounter due to being transgender.

Recommended Books on Transgender Issues and on Coming Out

https://pflag.org/resource/transgender-reading-list-adults; https://pflag.org/comingoutbooks

The organization PFLAG, which stands for Parents, Family, and Friends of Lesbians and Gays, was founded in 1973 and is currently the largest organization for the families and allies of LGBTQ+ persons. They have curated a list of books addressing transgender issues that can help people understand what it means to be transgender, how to support someone who is transgender, and how to manage the legal issues related to being transgender. There is also a list of recommended books for those coming out. This page notes that "many of the titles listed cover the process both for those who are navigating a new lifetime of being out and proud, and their significant others, friends, families, and allies as well."

Stopbullying.gov

stopbullying.gov

Stopbullying.gov is a website maintained by the U.S. government that focuses on what bullying in general is, who is at risk, and how we can help prevent and respond to episodes of bullying. The site includes a focus on cyberbullying, which has become a significant source of bullying that occurs via digital devices and through texting, social media, and other digital applications. The site also has a substantial resource section that includes information on how to get help, guidelines for media, laws and policies, and sections on "What you can do" and "What teens can do," among other resources.

White Fragility: Why It's So Hard for White People to Talk about Racism (Book)

Robin DiAngelo

White Fragility: Why It's So Hard for White People to Talk about Racism is a *New York Times* best seller that explores why White people struggle to accept that they may be racist and how they tend to respond when challenged on their long-standing beliefs about race and racism. The author of the foreword of the book, Michael Eric Dyson, called the book "vital" and "necessary."

Sustainability

Global Stewards

globalstewards.org/environmental-organizations.htm

The home page of the Global Stewards website is entitled "Green Eco Tips for a Sustainable Lifestyle." This website was created in 1998 and is maintained by Lea Dutton for the purpose of providing "green eco tips" for those who want to live a sustainable lifestyle. The home page shows links to actions people can take, issues affecting sustainability, and quotes related to nature and sustainability. Further down the home page are links to various green eco tips, including reduce, reuse, recycle, and eco gifts, among others, and a list of "green actions," including but not limited to go carbon neutral, stop junk mail, use green business directories, and support environmental and social justice organizations. The web address provided at the start of this entry takes the reader to a page entitled "List of Environmental and Social Justice Organizations."

Recommended Books on Sustainability

https://zerowastememoirs.com/baby-step-10-book-sustainability/
There are hundreds of books written on sustainability and issues related to sustainability. The web page provided here includes a brief description of twenty books on sustainability that cover topics on climate change and recycling as well as the structure of modern cities, what constitutes a "good company," and how to grow your own food.

Glossary

Acculturation
A process of assimilating to another, usually dominant, culture whereby an individual from one culture who moves to another culture may desire or feel pressure to think and behave in ways that align with the new culture.

Actual self
The representation of characteristics you believe you actually have; characteristics you believe others believe you actually have; similar to *self-concept*.

Actualizing tendency
A fundamental principle of Carl Rogers's client-centered theory that states all living things will strive to be the best version of itself it can be.

Ageism
Prejudice or discrimination based on age, usually against older persons.

Agency
The extent to which a person has control over their lives and the decisions they make.

Antisocial
A term typically associated with a diagnosis of antisocial personality disorder and refers to someone who violates or exploits the basic rights of other people, usually without feeling remorse.

Approval-based contingent self-esteem
Feelings of self-worth based on receiving approval from others.

Asexual
Those who have no sexual feelings or do not act on sexual feelings.

Authentic living
Acting according to who you really are; behaving in a way that reflects one's true values and beliefs.

Authenticity
An effort to live based on one's personal needs and desires rather than the demands and expectations of other people or cultural expectations.

Autonomy support
From *self-determination* theory; support from others for one's independence or freedom to make decisions for themselves.

Balanced authenticity
One element of *authenticity* that refers to living according to one's desires and needs while taking into consideration the impact one's decisions may have on others.

Basic strength
Part of Erik Erikson's *post-Freudian* theory; a quality of the ego that emerges from the conflict between the syntonic and dystonic elements of the stage (e.g., the basic strength of the infancy stage is hope).

Bullying
When someone intends to harm, intimidate, or coerce another person who is perceived as vulnerable.

Catfishing
Creating a fictional online profile for the purpose of luring someone into a relationship.

Choice overload
See *overchoice*.

Cisgender
Those whose personal identity and gender align with their sex at birth.

Client-centered
The theory and psychotherapy of psychologist Carl Rogers in which the client is expected to take an active role in their treatment while the therapist provides support to the client and does not direct the content of the session. See also *person-centered* theory.

Climate change
Changes to environmental averages, such as air temperature and amount of rainfall, in a region of the world over a long period of time.

Cognitive dissonance
Occurs when someone experiences conflicting attitudes, beliefs, or behaviors that cause discomfort until the person changes their attitude, belief, or behavior to reduce the dissonance or conflict.

Communion
The sharing of one's thoughts and feelings with another person or group of people.

Glossary

Compensation
A defense mechanism that refers to one's effort to make up for a real or imagined inadequacy.

Conditions of worth
Conditions (actual or imagined) placed on us by other people that we must meet to receive their love and affection; typically associated with the *person-centered* approach of Carl Rogers.

Conformity
A concept of social psychology that reflects the influence we experience from others (e.g., peer pressure) to change or align our beliefs or behaviors to fit into a group.

Congruence
A term associated with Carl Rogers's *person-centered* approach that reflects the overlap between our *ideal self* and our actual experiences; the greater the overlap the better our psychological health, whereas the greater the disparity between the two the greater the psychopathology.

Core pathology
Part of Erik Erikson's *post-Freudian* theory; each of the eight stages has the possibility to be resolved with either a *basic strength* or a core pathology which is disruptive to adequate development (e.g., the core pathology of the infancy stage is withdrawal).

Critical thinking
The process of actively and effectively evaluating information in a clear and rational manner that is informed by evidence.

Cultural globalization
The sharing of ideas and values between world cultures with the intention of expanding social relationships worldwide.

Differentiation of self/self-differentiation
Process by which an individual can identify one's thoughts and feelings as distinguishable from others' thoughts and feelings.

Digital literacy
The ability to find and use various forms of technology to find information or create information that is then evaluated and communicated effectively.

Digitalk
A blending of conversational and written language adapting long-standing conventions used among adolescents.

Discrimination
Unfair and unjust treatment of people based on aspects of their identity, such as, but not limited to race, age, or sex.

Dunning-Kruger effect
The phenomenon involving one's overestimation of one's skills and abilities when one is actually less competent than others or the underestimation of one's skills and abilities despite actually having a higher level of competence compared to others.

Dystonic
Associated with Erik Erikson's *post-Freudian* theory; a disruptive element associated with each stage of development; too much of which can lead to developing the core pathology of the stage.

Economic globalization
Worldwide transmission of goods, money, services, technology, and information; one of three primary dimensions of *globalization*.

Economic insecurity
The uncertainty and anxiety that accompanies the possibility of negative economic events (e.g., unemployment) and how difficult it may be to persevere and recover from them.

Egocentric authenticity
The tendency to value expressing one's self without consideration of the impact of self-expression on others.

Empathy
The ability to understand and experience another's emotional experience from an "as if" perspective (i.e., understanding another's emotional experience *as if* one is experiencing it themselves); a core concept of Carl Rogers's *person-centered* theory.

Enmeshed/enmeshment
Personal boundaries between two or more people in a relationship that are permeable and unclear.

External locus of control
A belief that what you do has no bearing on what happens to you and that one's successes and failures are outside of one's control.

False self
An artificial or fake version of one's self that often forms in our early years as a protective or defensive mechanism against significant distressing relationships; opposite of *true self*.

Fidelity
Used by Erik Erikson to describe the basic strength (or ego quality) of adolescence, during which an individual experiences the conflict related to identity development; the faithfulness one shows to one's identity by thinking, acting, and feeling in ways that reflect what one truly believes and values.

Glossary

Foreclosed/foreclosure
One of James Marcia's identity statuses that is the result of low exploration and high commitment; prematurely committing to an identity without having fully explored all possibilities.

Formative tendency
A fundamental principle of Carl Rogers' *person-centered* theory that states all living things start out simple and evolve into a more complex form, resulting in greater differentiation between individuals within a species.

Fused
Relating to others (usually family members) in a way that helps the individual avoid uncomfortable emotions related to feeling separate; occurs in those without a strong sense of self.

Genuineness
Used by Carl Rogers in his *person-centered* theory and is also known as *congruence*; believed to be one of three cornerstone abilities of the effective therapist in which the therapist reacts outwardly to the client based on what they are feeling internally.

Globalization
The international impact of businesses and organizations.

Heteronomy
Actions that are influenced by external forces.

Ideal self (Higgins)
Part of Higgins's *self-discrepancy* theory; the version of one's self we or others would like us to be.

Ideal self (Rogers)
Part of Carl Rogers's *person-centered* theory; the way we want to or wish we could be.

Identity achievement
One of James Marcia's identity statuses believed to be high in exploration and commitment; identifying one's true self after fully exploring most options available to a person and ultimately selecting which options fit with one's self and which options do not.

Identity cues
The observable facets of someone that signals who they may be (e.g., what clothes they wear, what sex they appear to be).

Identity diffusion
One of James Marcia's identity statuses believed to be low in exploration and commitment; such a person has not identified nor committed to an identity and is not in the process of exploring to figure out their identity.

Inauthenticity
Living in ways that do not represent one's true feelings, beliefs, attitudes, and values; the opposite of *authenticity*.

Independent self-concept
Mental representations of your own traits, attitudes, and preferences.

Informational social influence
Changing an opinion or behavior to conform to others who we think have accurate information; related to *conformity*.

In-group
Belonging to and identifying with a group, particularly when the group is interacting with another group; opposite of *out-group*.

Interdependent self-concept
Mental representations of social norms, group memberships, and the opinions of others.

Internal locus of control
The belief that what you do affects what happens to you; the belief that one's successes and failures are the result of one's own efforts rather than an external force.

Internalize/internalization
Integrating the attitudes, values, and opinions of others into our own identity or sense of self.

Interpersonal prompts
The behaviors we engage in while interacting with others denotes the nature of the interaction or relationship.

Intersectional invisibility
An approach to understanding how those with multiple stigmatized identities (e.g., biological sex, sexual orientation, person of color) are treated and represented.

Intersectionality
Multiple aspects of identity that overlap and influence an individual's experiences.

Intersex
Those who are born with reproductive or sexual organs that do not fit the typical definitions of male or female.

Media literacy
An acquired skill that involves the ability to access, evaluate, create, and share various forms of media.

Glossary

Moratorium
One of James Marcia's identity statuses and is believed to be high in exploration and low on commitment; those with this identity status are actively exploring aspects of their identity but have not yet committed to an identity.

Norm
Something that is typical or normal; in social settings, a typical pattern of behavior expected of a group's members.

Normative social influence
A social psychological term that refers to the impact others have on us so that we conform to others' expectations to be liked and accepted.

Object permanence
Part of Jean Piaget's theory of cognitive development; occurs in infancy during the sensorimotor stage, whereby children understand that just because they cannot see something or someone does not mean it no longer exists.

Organismic self
A term used by Carl Rogers that refers to the whole person, including the internal experiences that we may not be aware of (e.g., automatic biological functions).

Other-distorted authenticity
Foregoing one's true needs and desires in deference to the needs and desires of others; reflects a desire to please others rather than one's self.

Ought self
Part of Higgins' *self-discrepancy* theory; the version of ourselves we or others think we should be.

Out-group
Members of a group who are not members of a specific *in-group* (i.e., the group you are a part of).

Overchoice/choice overload
A cognitive process during which people have difficulty making a decision because there are too many options.

Pansexual
An individual who does not limit their sexual choices with respect to biological sex, gender, or gender identity.

Persona
A term used by psychiatrist Carl Jung to describe the version of yourself you are willing to show others; often visually represented by a mask.

Person-centered theory
Carl Rogers' theory previously known as *client-centered* theory in which he suggests the focus of treatment should be on the client, and the therapist serves as a nonjudgmental guide for the client.

Place attachment
The emotional connection and bond people feel about what surrounds them and the desire to remain connected to that place over time.

Place identity
The extent to which an individual identifies with the place where the individual lives (e.g., neighborhood, state, region) and the extent to which elements of that place are incorporated into the person's personal identity.

Political globalization
One of three highly recognized types of *globalization*; the worldwide political system through which any transaction between countries or regions is regulated; national and international nongovernmental organizations (NGOs) are considered to be watchdogs of governments and help to facilitate resolution of issues that ultimately support the public good.

Positive regard
Associated with Carl Rogers's *person-centered* theory; the acceptance and valuing we receive from other people.

Positive self-regard
Associated with Carl Rogers's *person-centered* theory; Accepting and valuing one's self.

Positivity bias
The tendency for people who already see themselves positively to rate positive traits as reflective of who they are compared to negative traits.

Possible selves
The self-system to include versions of one's self that we might become, we would like to become, we hope not to become, and so on.

Prosocial behavior
Actions an individual voluntarily engages in for the purpose of benefiting or helping another individual or group of individuals; the opposite of *antisocial*.

Psychological well-being
The fulfillment of one's potential and feeling like one's life has meaning.

Real self
Who we actually are; opposite of *false self*.

Role repudiation
Part of Erik Erikson's *post-Freudian* theory; the core pathology of the adolescence stage of development; blocking the ability to synthesize various self-images and values into a coherent identity.

Glossary

Self-alienation
Distancing one's self from one's thoughts, feelings, and behaviors.

Self-complexity
One's knowledge about one's self that reflects myriad distinct aspects of one's self (e.g., parent, sibling, professional, nice person, ambitious, athletic).

Self-concept
The beliefs we have about ourselves and how we evaluate ourselves.

Self-concept clarity
The extent to which one's beliefs about one's self are clearly and confidently defined, making these self-related attributes internally consistent and stable.

Self-control
One's ability to regulate one's own thoughts, emotions, and behaviors regardless of the situation or internal experience.

Self-deceptive enhancement
The tendency to endorse positive, but exaggerated, descriptions of one's self.

Self-determination theory
Developed in 1985 by Edward Deci and Richard Ryan; theory that assumes that people play an active role in their own psychological growth by tackling challenges and incorporating new experiences into an integrated sense of one's self; includes the interrelated basic needs of autonomy, competence, and relatedness.

Self-discrepancy theory
Developed in 1987 by Edward Tory Higgins; states that we engage in comparisons between who we believe we are (*actual self*) to standards representing who we (or others) would like us to be (*ideal self*) and who we (or others) think we should be (*ought self*); self-discrepancy refers to the discrepancy between the actual self and ideal self, or between the ideal self and ought self.

Self-esteem
Confidence in our overall worth and abilities.

Self-evaluation
Assessing or evaluating the data obtained through one's *self-monitoring*; part of the process of *self-regulation*.

Self-guide
Internal representations of one's self used to help with *self-regulation*.

Self-monitoring
Documenting in some way (e.g., written record, log) of one's behavior; part of the process of *self-regulation*.

Self-regulation
Attempts to control one's own behavior by *self-monitoring*, *self-evaluation*, and *self-reinforcement*.

Self-reinforcement
Giving rewards to one's self for engaging in appropriate behavior or reaching a goal; part of the process of *self-regulation*.

Self-respect
Pride in one's self for behaving honorably and with dignity.

Self-worth
The sense of being a good person who deserves to be treated fairly and with respect.

Sibling differentiation
A process that occurs when siblings are more similar to one another genetically and in their experiences; a sibling's attempts to do things differently to clearly declare that they are different from another sibling.

Sibling identification
Vicariously learn from our siblings by watching and imitating what they do.

Social categorization
How we categorize or group people based on their social information such as sex, race, or age. The process by which we categorize ourselves and others into different groups that are usually based on shared characteristics.

Social comparison
Evaluating our own abilities and beliefs in relation or comparison to others; affects self-image and *self-esteem*, depending on how we perceive we compare to others.

Social identification
A process through which a facet of one's self is developed based on the preferences of one's *in-group*; reflects an emotional bond with an *in-group*.

Social justice
Within a given society, fair and equal distribution of wealth, resources, opportunities, and privileges.

Social justice warrior (SJW)
Someone who fights against social injustices.

Socioemotional selectivity theory
Reevaluating and reorganizing our goals as we age based on which ones are more emotionally meaningful to us as opposed to goals that are focused more on the future.

Spoiled identity
A term used by Erving Goffman to describe an aspect of one's identity that leads the person to experiencing stigma.

Glossary

Subjective well-being
Feeling happy overall and as though one has a good life.

Sustainability
Contemporaneously used most often in the context of the natural environment; the ability of something to be maintained at a certain rate or level.

Syntonic
Associated with Erik Erikson's *post-Freudian* theory; refers to a facilitative element that positively impacts development.

Terror management theory
Developed in the 1990s, the theory that all behavior is directed toward keeping one's self alive.

Two-spirit
Those who identify as having both a masculine and a feminine spirit; sometimes used by Indigenous people to reflect their sexual, gender or spiritual identity.

Unconditional positive regard
Part of Carl Rogers's *person-centered* theory; an attitude of nonjudgmental caring expressed toward someone else regardless of their behavior or their own standards about themselves.

Unmitigated agency
Focusing on one's self to the exclusion of others.

Unmitigated communion
Focusing on others to the exclusion of one's self.

Voice
The expression of one's inner thoughts and feelings; often referred to as one's "inner voice."

Voice therapy
A form of psychotherapy developed by Robert Firestone that emphasizes the identification of long-standing (i.e., since childhood) self-destructive thoughts that negatively impact one's *voice* (i.e., self-expression).

White privilege
Benefits given to White people over non-White people, particularly when they are the same in other ways, such as their social, political, or economic circumstances.

Willpower
The ability to resist short-term temptations to meet long-term goals; similar to *self-control*.

Willpower depletion
The inability to resist temptation after one has already repeatedly resisted temptation.

Bibliography

Allcott, H., & Gentzkow, M. (2017). Social media and fake news in the 2016 election. *Journal of Economic Perspectives, 31,* 211–236.

Allison, B. N., & Schultz, J. B. (2001). Interpersonal identity formation during early adolescence. *Adolescence, 36*(143), 509–523.

American Psychiatric Association. (2013). *Diagnostic and statistical manual of mental disorders: DSM-5.* 5th ed. American Psychiatric Publishing.

American Psychological Association. (2012). *What you need to know about willpower: The psychological science of self-control.* American Psychological Association.

Ames, D. R., & Kammrath, L. K. (2004). Mind-reading and metacognition: Narcissism, not actual competence, predicts self-estimated ability. *Journal of Nonverbal Behavior, 28*(3), 187–209.

Anderson, M., Toor, S., Rainie, L., & Smith, A. (2018, July 11). *Activism in the social media age: 2. An analysis of #BlackLivesMatter and other Twitter hashtags related to political or social issues.* Pew Research Center. https://www.pewresearch.org/internet/2018/07/11/an-analysis-of-blacklivesmatter-and-other-twitter-hashtags-related-to-political-or-social-issues/.

Annual Country Reports on Terrorism, 22 U.S. C. § 2656f.

Arena, M. P., & Arrigo, B. A. (2005). Social psychology, terrorism, and identity: A preliminary re-examination of theory, culture, self, and society. *Behavioral Science and the Law, 23,* 485–506.

Arnett, J. J. (2002). The psychology of globalization. *American Psychologist, 57,* 774–783.

Asch, S. (1956). Studies of independence and conformity: A minority of one against a unanimous majority. *Psychological Monographs: General and Applied, 70*(9), 1–70.

Association of College and Research Libraries. (2000). *Information literacy competency standards for higher education.* American Library Association.

Athan, A. (2020). Reproductive identity: An emerging concept. *American Psychologist, 75*(4), 445–456.

Atkinson, D. R., Morten, G., & Sue, D. W. (1998). *Counseling American minorities*. McGraw-Hill.

Baker, Z. G., Tou, R. Y. W., Bryan, J. L., & Knee, C. R. (2017). Authenticity and well-being: Exploring positivity and negativity in interactions as a mediator. *Personality and Individual Differences, 113*, 235–239.

Barroso, A., Parker, K., & Bennett, J. (2020, May 27). *As millennials near 40, they're approaching family life differently than previous generations*. Pew Research Center. https://www.pewsocialtrends.org/2020/05/27/as-millennials-near-40-theyre-approaching-family-life-differently-than-previous-generations/.

Baumeister, R. F. (2019). Social psychologists and thinking about people. In R. F. Baumeister & E. J. Finkel (Eds.), *Advanced social psychology: The state of the science* (pp. 5–24). Oxford University Press.

Bawden, D. (2001). Information and digital literacies: A review of concepts. *Journal of Documentation, 57*, 218–259.

Bawden, D. (2008). Origins and concepts of digital literacy. In C. Lankshear & M. Knobel (Eds.), *Digital literacies: Concepts, policies and practices* (pp. 17–32). Peter Lang Publishing.

BBC. (2020, June 25). *Mary Jackson: NASA to name HQ after first Black female engineer*. Yahoo. https://news.yahoo.com/mary-jackson-nasa-name-hq-094942282.html.

Becker, E. (1973). *The denial of death*. The Free Press.

Berntsen, D., & Rubin, D. C. (2006). The centrality of event scale: A measure of integrating a trauma into one's identity and its relation to post-traumatic stress disorder symptoms. *Behaviour Research and Therapy, 44*(2), 219–231.

Bossert, W., & D'Ambrosio, C. (2013). Measuring economic insecurity. *International Economic Review, 54*, 1017–1030.

Boudjemadi, V., & Gana, K. (2012). Effect of mortality salience on implicit ageism: Implication of age stereotypes and sex. *European Review of Applied Psychology, 62*, 9–17.

Bowen, M. (1985). *Family therapy in clinical practice*. Rowman & Littlefield.

Boyle, K. M. (2017). Sexual assault and identity disruption: A sociological approach to posttraumatic stress. *Society and Mental Health, 7*(2), 69–84.

Boyraz, G., & Kuhl, M. (2015). Self-focused attention, authenticity, and well-being. *Personality and Individual Differences, 87*, 70–75.

Bradford, A. (2017, August 12). *Effects of global warming*. LiveScience. https://www.livescience.com/37057-global-warming-effects.html.

Brewer, B. W., Selby, C. L., Linder, D. E., & Petitpas, A. J. (1999). Distancing oneself from a poor season: Divestment of athletic identity. *Journal of Personal & Interpersonal Loss, 4*(2), 149–162.

Brewer, B. W., Van Raalte, J. L., & Linder, D. E. (1993). Athletic identity: Hercules' muscles or Achilles heel? *International Journal of Sport Psychology, 24*(2), 237–254.

Brewer, M. B., & Chen, Y. (2007). Where (who) are collectives in collectivism? Toward conceptual clarification of individualism and collectivism. *Psychological Review, 114*(1), 133–151.

Bibliography 253

Brinthaupt, T. M., & Lipka, R. P. (Eds.). *Understanding early adolescent self and identity: Applications and interventions*. State University of New York Press.

Bristow, N. K. (2010). "It's as bad as anything can be": Patients, identity, and the influenza pandemic. *Public Health Reports, 125*(3), 134–144.

Broadbent, E., Gougoulis, J., Lui, N., Pota, V., & Simons, J. (2017). *What the world's young people think and feel: Generation Z: Global citizenship survey*. Varkey Foundation.

Bruggeman, J. A. (2019, July 26). For male survivors of sexual assault—like me— #MeToo can help change culture of salience. *USAToday.com*. https://www .usatoday.com/story/opinion/2019/07/26/sexual-assault-among-men -needs-discussed-metoo-column/1807577001/.

Buckner, J. D., & Shah, S. M. (2015). Fitting in and feeling fine: Conformity and coping motives differentially mediate the relationship between social anxiety and drinking problems for men and women. *Addiction Research and Theory, 23*, 231–237.

Bureau of Labor Statistics. (2021, May 7). *The employment situation—April 2021*. U. S. Department of Labor. https://www.bls.gov/news.release/pdf/empsit .pdf.

Business Insider. (n.d.). *Generation Z news: Latest characteristics, research, and facts*. Business Insider. https://www.businessinsider.com/generation-z.

Camacho, T. C., Medina, M., Rivas-Drake, D., & Jagers, R. (2018). School climate and ethnic-racial identity in school: A longitudinal examination of reciprocal associations. *Journal of Community & Applied Social Psychology, 28*(1), 29–41.

Campbell, J. D., Trapnell, P. D., Heine, S. J., Katz, I. M., Lavallee, L. F., & Lehman, D. R. (1996). Self-concept clarity: Measurement, personality correlates, and cultural boundaries. *Journal of Personality and Social Psychology, 70*(1), 141–156.

Carstensen, L. L. (1992). Social and emotional patterns in adulthood: Support for socioemotional selectivity theory. *Psychology and Aging, 7*(3), 331–338.

Catalano, R. F., Berglund, M. L., Ryan, J. A. M., Lonczak, H. S., & Hawkins, J. D. (2004). Positive youth development in the United States: Research findings on evaluations of positive youth development programs. *Annals of the American Academy of Political and Social Science, 591*, 98–124.

Centers for Disease Control and Prevention. (2019, September 25). *Violence prevention: Bullying*. Centers for Disease Control and Prevention. https:// www.cdc.gov/violenceprevention/youthviolence/bullyingresearch /fastfact.html.

Chen, S., Boucher, H., & Kraus, M. W. (2011). The relational self. In S. J. Schwartz, K. Luyckx, & V. L. Vignoles (Eds.), *Handbook of identity theory and research* (pp. 149–175). Springer Science and Business Media.

Chirkov, V., Ryan, R. M., Kim, Y., Kaplan, U. (2003). Differentiating autonomy from individualism and independence: A self-determination theory perspective on internalization of cultural orientations and well-being. *Journal of Personality and Social Psychology, 84*, 97–110.

Chow, D. (2013, September 27). *IPCC climate change report: Experts react.* LiveScience. https://www.livescience.com/40021-ipcc-climate-change-report-reactions.html.

Cicei, C. (2012). Examining the association between self concept clarity and self-esteem on a sample of Romanian students. *Procedia—Social and Behavioral Sciences, 46*(2012), 4345–4348.

Coronavirus Resource Center. (n.d.). *COVID-19 dashboard by the Center for Systems Science and Engineering (CSSE) at Johns Hopkins University (JHU).* Johns Hopkins University of Medicine. https://coronavirus.jhu.edu/map.html.

Cote, J. E., & Levine, C. G. (2016). *Identity formation, youth, and development: A simplified approach.* Psychology Press.

Crocetti, E. (2017). Identity formation in adolescence: The dynamic of forming and consolidating identity commitments. *Child Development Perspectives, 11*(2), 145–150.

Crocetti, E. (2018). Identity dynamics in adolescence: Processes, antecedents, and consequences. *European Journal of Developmental Psychology, 15*(1), 11–23.

Crocetti, E., Branje, S., Rubini, M., Koot, H. M., & Meeus, W. (2017). Identity processes and parent-child and sibling relationships in adolescence: A five-wave multi-informant longitudinal study. *Child Development, 88*(1), 210–228.

Crocetti, E., Prati, F., & Rubini, M. (2018). The interplay of personal and social identity. *European Psychologist, 23*(4), 300–310.

Cross, W. E. (1971). *The Negro-to-Black conversion experience. Black World, 20*(9), 13–27.

Cross, W. E. (1991). *Shades of Black: Diversity in African-American identity.* Temple University Press.

Cucinotta, D., & Vanelli, M. (2020). WHO declares COVID-19 a pandemic. *Acta Bio-Medica: Atenei Parmensis, 91*(1), 157–160.

Deci, E. L., Koestner, R., & Ryan, R. M. (1999). A meta-analytic review of experiments examining the effects of extrinsic rewards on intrinsic motivation. *Psychological Bulletin, 125*(6), 627–668.

Deci, E. L., & Ryan, R. M. (1985). *Intrinsic motivation and self-determination in human behavior.* Plenum Press.

DeGue, S., Fowler, K. A., & Calkins, C. (2018). Deaths due to use of lethal force by law enforcement: Findings from the National Violent Death Reporting System, 17 U.S. States, 2009–2012. *American Journal of Preventative Medicine, 51*, S173–S187.

Diehl, M., Smyer, M. A., & Mehrotra, C. (2020). Optimizing aging: A call for a new narrative. *American Psychologist, 75*(4), 577–589.

Dimock, M. (2019, January 17). *Defining generations: Where millennials end and Generation Z begins.* Pew Research Center. https://www.pewresearch.org/fact-tank/2019/01/17/where-millennials-end-and-generation-z-begins/.

Bibliography 255

Dings, R. (2018). The dynamic and recursive interplay of embodiment and narrative identity. *Philosophical Psychology, 32*(2), 186–210.

Douglass, S., Mirpuri, S., & Yip, T. (2017). Considering friends within the context of peers in school for the development of ethnic/racial identity. *Journal of Youth and Adolescence, 46*(2), 300–316.

Dube, S. R., Anda, R. F., Whitfield, C. L., Brown, D. W., Felitti, V. J., Dong, M., & Giles, W. H. (2005). Long-term consequences of childhood sexual abuse by gender of victim. *American Journal of Preventative Medicine, 28*(4), 430–438.

Duffy, A. L., & Nesdale, D. (2008). Peer groups, social identity, and children's bullying behavior. *Social Development, 18,* 121–139.

Ehrlinger, J., Johnson, K., Banner, M., Dunning, D., & Kruger, J. (2008). Why the unskilled are unaware: Further explorations of (absent) self-insight among the incompetent. *Organizational Behavior and Human Decision Processes, 105*(1), 98–121.

Eliason, M. J., & Schope, R. (2007). Shifting sands or solid foundation? Lesbian, gay, bisexual, and transgender identity formation. In I. H. Meyer & M. E. Northridge (Eds.), *The health of sexual minorities: Public health perspectives on lesbian, gay, bisexual, and transgender populations* (pp. 3–26). Springer Science + Business Media.

Emetu, R. E., & Rivera, G. (2018). After sexual identity disclosure: An ecological perceptive of LGB young adults. *American Journal of Health Behavior, 42*(4), 45–60.

Enjaian, B., Zeigler-Hill, V., & Vonk, J. (2016). The relationship between approval-based contingent self-esteem and conformity is influenced by sex and task difficulty. *Personality and Individual Differences, 115,* 58–64.

Erikson, E. H. (1968). *Identity: Youth and crisis.* Norton.

Farrington, E. L. (2010). Bullying on campus: How to identify, prevent, resolve it. *Women in Higher Education, 19,* 8–9.

Fernandez, M., & Burch, A. D. S. (2020, June 18). George Floyd, from "I want to touch the world" to "I can't breathe." *New York Times.* https://www.nytimes.com/article/george-floyd-who-is.html.

Fielding, K. S., & Hornsey, M. J. (2016). A social identity analysis of climate change and environmental attitudes and behaviors: Insights and opportunities. *Frontiers in Psychology, 7,* Article 121.

Finkenauer, C., Engels, R. C. M. E., Meeus, W., & Oosterwegel, A. (2002). Self and identity in early adolescence: The pains and gains of knowing who and what you are. In T. M. Brinthaupt & R. P. Lipka (Eds.), *Understanding early adolescent self and identity: Applications and interventions* (pp. 25–56). State University of New York Press.

Firestone, R., Firestone, L., & Catlett, J. (2013). *The self under siege: A therapeutic model for differentiation.* Routledge.

Flanders, C. E., Dobinson, C., & Logie, C. (2017). Young bisexual women's perspectives on the relationship between bisexual stigma, mental health, and sexual health: A qualitative study. *Critical Public Health, 27*(1), 75–85.

Forsyth, D. R., van Vugt, M., Schlein, G., & Story, P. A. (2015). Identity and sustainability: Localized sense of community increases environmental engagement. *Analyses of Social Issues and Public Policy, 15*, 233–252.

Galliher, R. V., & Kerpelman, J. L. (2012). The intersection of identity development and peer relationship processes in adolescence and young adulthood: Contributions of the special issue. *Journal of Adolescence, 35*, 1409–1415.

Gecas, V. (1982). The self-concept. *Annual Review of Sociology, 8*, 1–33.

Giacomin, M., & Jordan C. (2017). Interdependent and independent self-construal. In V. Zeigler-Hill & T. Shackelford (Eds.), *Encyclopedia of personality and individual differences* (pp. 2319–2325). Springer.

Giannone, Z. A., Haney, C. J., Kealy, D., & Ogrodniczuk, J. S. (2017). Athletic identity and psychiatric symptoms following retirement from varsity sports. *International Journal of Social Psychiatry, 63*(7), 598–601.

Gibson, C., & Guskin, E. (2017, October 17). A majority of Americans now say that sexual harassment is a "serious problem." *Washington Post*. https://www.washingtonpost.com/lifestyle/style/a-majority-of-americans-now-say-that-sexual-harassment-is-a-serious-problem/2017/10/16/707e6b74-b290-11e7-9e58-e6288544af98_story.html.

Gilster, P. (1997). *Digital literacy*. Wiley.

Globalization and culture. (2003, May/June). Cato Policy Report. https://web.archive.org/web/20121119144402/http://www.cato.org/pubs/policy_report/v25n3/globalization.pdf.

Goffman, E. (1963). *Stigma: Notes on the management of spoiled identity*. Simon and Schuster.

Grotevant, H. D., & Von Korff, L. (2011). Adoptive identity. In K. Luyckx & V. L. Vignoles (Eds.), *Handbook of identity theory and research* (Vol. 2, pp. 585–602). Springer.

Hahnel, U. J. J., & Brosch, T. (2016). Seeing green: A perceptual model of identity-based climate change judgments. *Psychological Inquiry, 27*, 310–318.

Halim, M. L., Ruble, D. N., & Amodio, D. M. (2011). From pink frilly dresses to "one of the boys": A social-cognitive analysis of gender identity development and gender bias. *Social and Personality Psychology Compass, 5*(11), 933–949.

Hamman, D., Coward, F., Johnson, L., Lambert, M., Zhou, L., & Indiatsi, J. (2013). Teacher possible selves: How thinking about the future contributes to the formation of professional identity. *Self and Identity, 12*(3), 307–336.

Hampton, K. (2016). Why is helping behavior declining in the United States but not in Canada? Ethnic diversity, new technologies, and other explanations. *City & Community, 15*, 380–399.

Harter, S., Marold, D. B., Whitesell, N. R., & Cobbs, G. (1996). A model of the effects of perceived parent and peer support on adolescent false self behavior. *Child Development, 67*, 360–374.

Bibliography 257

Harter, S., Waters, P. L., & Whitesell, N. R. (1997). Lack of voice as a manifestation of false self-behavior among adolescents: The school setting as a stage upon which the drama of authenticity is enacted. *Educational Psychologist, 32*(3), 153–173.

Harush, R., Lisak, A., & Erez, M. (2016). Extending the global acculturation model to untangle the culture mixing puzzle. *Journal of Cross-Cultural Psychology, 47*(10), 1395–1408.

Haslam, C., Holme, A., Haslam, S. A., Iyer, A., Jetten, J., & Williams, W. H. (2008). Maintaining group memberships: Social identity continuity predicts well-being after stroke. *Neuropsychological Rehabilitation, 18*(5–6), 671–691.

Haslam, C., Steffens, N., Branscombe, N. R., Haslam, S. A., Cruwys, T., Lam, B. C. P., . . . Yang, J. (2018). The importance of social groups for retirement adjustment: Evidence, application, and policy implications of the social identity model of identity change. *Social Issues and Policy Review, 13*, 93–124.

Hernández, B., Martín, A. M., Ruiz, C., & del Carmen Hidalgo, M. (2010). The role of place identity and place attachment in breaking environmental protection laws. *Journal of Environmental Psychology, 30*, 281–288.

Hickey, C., & Roderick, M. (2017). The presentation of possible selves in everyday life: The management of identity among transitioning professional athletes. *Sociology of Sport Journal, 34*(3), 270–280.

Higa, D., Hoppe, M. J., Lindhorst, T., Mincer, S., Beadnell, B., Morrison, D. M., . . . Mountz, S. (2014). Negative and positive factors associated with the well-being of lesbian, gay, bisexual, transgender, queer, and questioning (LGBTQ) youth. *Youth & Society, 46*, 663–687.

Higgins, E. T. (1987). Self-discrepancy: A theory relating self and affect. *Psychological Review, 94*, 319–340.

History.com. (2019, July 9). *Elvis Presley makes first appearance on "The Ed Sullivan Show."* History.com. https://www.history.com/this-day-in-history/elvis -presley-first-appearance-the-ed-sullivan-show.

Honess, T., & Yardley, K. (1987). *Self and identity: Perspective across the lifespan.* Routledge.

Hu, C., Kumar, S., Huang, J., & Ratnavelu, K. (2017). Disinhibition of negative true self for identity reconstructions in cyberspace: Advancing self-discrepancy theory for virtual setting. *PLoS One, 12*, e0175623.

Iacurci, G. (2020, May 19). *Unemployment in nearing Great Depression levels. Here's how the eras are similar—and different.* CNBC. https://www.cnbc.com /2020/05/19/unemployment-today-vs-the-great-depression-how-do-the -eras-compare.html.

International Labour Organization. (n.d.). *History of the ILO.* International Labour Organization. https://www.ilo.org/global/about-the-ilo/history /lang--en/index.htm.

International Society for Sexual Medicine. (n.d.). *What is the difference between transsexual and transgender.* International Society for Sexual Medicine.

https://www.issm.info/sexual-health-qa/what-is-the-difference-between-transsexual-and-transgender/.

James, W. (1890). *The principles of psychology*. Vol 1. Henry Holt and Co.

Jensen, L. A. (2003). Coming of age in a multicultural world: Globalization and adolescent cultural identity formation. *Applied Developmental Science, 7*, 189–196.

Jetten, J., Haslam, C., Haslam, S. A., & Branscombe, N. R. (2009). The social cure. *Scientific American Mind, 20*, 26–33.

Jetten, J., Haslam, S. A., Iyer, A., & Haslam, C. (2010). Turning to others in times of change: Social identity and coping with stress. In S. Stürmer & M. Snyder (Eds.), *The psychology of prosocial behavior: Group processes, intergroup relations, and helping* (pp. 139–156). Wiley-Blackwell.

Jetten, J., & Pachana, N. A. (2012). Not wanting to grow old: A social identity model of identity change (SIMIC) analysis of driving cessation among older adults. In J. Jetten, A. S. Haslam, & C. Haslam (Eds.), *The social cure: Identity, health and well-being* (pp. 97–114). Psychology Press.

Jetten, J., Postmes, T., & McAuliffe, B. (2002). "We're *all* individuals": Group norms of individualism and collectivism, levels of identification and identity threat. *European Journal of Social Psychology, 32*, 189–207.

Jones, S. E., Bombieri, L., Livingstone, A. G., & Mastead, A. S. R. (2012). The influence of norms and social identities on children's responses to bullying. *British Journal of Educational Psychology, 82*, 241–256.

Jones, S. E., Livingstone, A. G., & Manstead, A. S. R. (2017). Bullying and belonging: Social identity on the playground. In K. I. Mavor, M. J. Platow, & B. Bizumic (Eds.), *Self and social identity in educational contexts* (pp. 70–90). Routledge.

Joshi, A., Dencker, J. C., Franz, G., & Martocchio, J. J. (2010). Unpacking generational identities in organizations. *Academy of Management Review, 35*, 392–414.

Just Be Inc. (n.d.). *Purpose, mission and vision*. Just Be Inc. https://justbeinc.wixsite.com/justbeinc/purpose-mission-and-vision.

Kalenzaga, S., Lamidey, V., Ergis, A.-M., Clarys, D., & Piolino, P. (2016). The positivity bias in aging: Motivation or degradation? *Emotion, 16*(5), 602–610.

Kiefhaber, E., Pavlovich, K., & Spraul, K. (2020). Sustainability-related identities and the institutional environment: The case of New Zealand owner-managers of small- and medium-sized hospitality businesses. *Journal of Business Ethics, 163*, 37–51.

Kim, A. (2014). The curious case of self-interest: Inconsistent effects and ambivalence toward a widely accepted construct. *Journal for the Theory of Social Behaviour, 44*(1), 99–122.

Kirk, K. (2018, April 3). *Finding common ground amid climate controversy*. Yale Climate Connections. https://www.yaleclimateconnections.org/2018/04/finding-common-ground-amid-climate-controversy/.

Bibliography

Klimstra, T. A. (2012). The dynamics of personality and identity in adolescence. *European Journal of Developmental Psychology, 9*(4), 472–484.

Knafo, A., & Schwartz, S. H. (2004). Identity formation and parent-child value congruence in adolescence. *British Journal of Developmental Psychology, 22*(3), 439–458.

Koltay, T. (2011). The media and the literacies: Media literacy, information literacy, digital literacy. *Media, Culture & Society, 33*, 211–221.

Kopasker, D., Montagna, C., & Bender, K. A. (2018). Economic insecurity: A socioeconomic determinant of mental health. *SSM-Population Health, 6*, 184–194.

Koydemir, S., Şimşek, Ö. F., Kuzgun, T. B., & Schütz, A. (2018). Feeling special, feeling happy: Authenticity mediates the relationship between sense of uniqueness and happiness. *Current Psychology: A Journal for Diverse Perspectives on Diverse Psychological Issues.* https://doi.org/10.1007/s12144 -018-9865-z.

Kroger, J. (2007). *Identity development: Adolescence through adulthood.* 2nd ed. Sage.

Kruger, J., & Dunning, D. (1999). Unskilled and unaware of it: How difficulties in recognizing one's own incompetence lead to inflated self-assessments. *Journal of Personality and Social Psychology, 77*(6), 1121–1134.

Krys, K., Zelenski, J. M., Capaldi, C. A., Park, J., van Tilburg, W., van Osch, Y., . . . Uchida, Y. (2019). Putting the "we" into well-being: Using collectivism-themed measures of well-being attenuates well-being's association with individualism. *Asian Journal of Social Psychology, 22*, 256–267.

La Roi, C., Meyer, I. H., & Frost, D. M. (2019). Differences in sexual identity dimensions between bisexual and other sexual minority individuals: Implications for minority stress and mental health. *American Journal of Orthopsychiatry, 89*(1), 40–51.

Lazer, D. M. J., Baum, M. A., Benkler, Y., Berinsky, A. J., Greenhill, K. M., Menczer, F., . . . Zittrain, J. L. (2018). The science of fake news. *Science, 359*, 1094–1096.

Lewandowski, G. W. (2010). The role of self-concept clarity in relationship quality. *Self and Identity, 9*(4), 416–433.

Linville, P. W. (1985). Self-complexity and affective extremity: Don't put all of your eggs in one cognitive basket. *Social Cognition, 3*(1), 94–120.

Linville, P. W. (1987). Self-complexity as a cognitive buffer against stress-related illness and depression. *Journal of Personality and Social Psychology, 52*(4), 663–676.

Liptak, A. (2020, June 15). Civil rights law protects gay and transgender workers, Supreme Court rules. *New York Times.* https://www.nytimes.com /2020/06/15/us/gay-transgender-workers-supreme-court.html.

Live Science Staff. (2020, March 6). *11 (sometimes) deadly diseases that hopped across species.* Live Science. https://www.livescience.com/12951-10-infectious -diseases-ebola-plague-influenza.html.

Long, H. (2020, May 12). Small business used to define America's economy. The pandemic could change that forever. *Washington Post*. https://www.washingtonpost.com/business/2020/05/12/small-business-used-define-americas-economy-pandemic-could-end-that-forever/

Luyckx, K., Klimstra, T. A., Duriez, B., Van Petegem, S., & Beyers, W. (2013). Personal identity processes from adolescence through the late 20s: Age trends, functionality, and depressive symptoms. *Social Development, 22*(4), 701–721.

Macur, J. (2020, June 13). Bubba Wallace thankful for flag ban, but NASCAR's fans might not be. *New York Times*. https://www.nytimes.com/2020/06/13/sports/bubba-wallace-nascar-confederate-flag.html.

Mainiero, L. A., & Gibson, D. E. (2018). The kaleidoscope career model revisited: How midcareer men and women diverge on authenticity, balance, and challenge. *Journal of Career Development, 45*, 361–377.

Mainiero, L. A., & Sullivan, S. E. (2005). Kaleidoscope careers: An alternate explanation for the "opt-out" revolution. *Academy of Management Perspectives, 19*, 106–123.

Marcia, J. E. (1966). Development and validation of ego-identity status. *Journal of Personality and Social Psychology, 3*(5), 551–558.

Markus, H., & Nurius, P. (1986). Possible selves. *American Psychologist, 41*(9), 954–969.

Maroiu, C., & Maricutoiu, L. P. (2017). Self-discrepancies. In V. Zeigler-Hill & T. Shackelford (Eds.), *Encyclopedia of personality and individual differences* (pp. 1–4). Springer.

Martin, J. L., Sharp-Grier, M. L., & Piker-King, K. (2015). Prime targets: Identity markers as the secret rationale for the preponderance of bullying in academe. In M. A. Paludi (Ed.), *Bullies in the workplace: Seeing and stopping adults who abuse their co-workers and employees* (pp. 87–108). Praeger.

Mascheroni, G., Vincent, J., & Jimenez, E. (2015). "Girls are addicted to likes so they post semi-naked selfies": Peer mediation, normativity and the construction of identity online. *Journal of Psychosocial Research on Cyberspace, 9*(1), Article 5.

Masho, S. W., & Anderson, L. (2009). Sexual assault in men: A population-based study of Virginia. *Violence and Victims, 24*(1), 98–110.

Masterson, J. F. (1988). *The search for the real self: Unmasking the personality disorders of our age*. The Free Press.

McAdams, D. P. (2001). The psychology of life stories. *Review of General Psychology, 5*(2), 100–122.

McAuliffe, B. J., Jetten, J., Hornsey, M. J., & Hogg, M. A. (2003). Individualist and collectivist norms: When it's ok to go your own way. *European Journal of Social Psychology, 33*, 57–70.

McConnell, A. R., Strain, L. M., Brown, C. M., & Rydell, R. J. (2009). The simple life: On the benefits of low self-complexity. *Personality and Social Psychology Bulletin, 35*(7), 823–835.

McLean, K. C. (2005). Late adolescent identity development: Narrative meaning making and memory telling. *Developmental Psychology, 41*(4), 683–691.

Bibliography 261

McLean, K. C., & Syed, M. (Eds.) (2015). *The Oxford handbook of identity development.* Oxford University Press.

Meeus, W. (2011). The study of adolescent identity formation 2000–2010: A review of longitudinal research. *Journal of Research on Adolescence, 21*(1), 75–94.

Meeus, W., van de Schoot, R., Keijsers, L., Schwartz, S. J., & Branje, S. (2010). On the progression and stability of adolescent identity formation: A five-wave longitudinal study in early-to-middle and middle-to-late adolescence. *Child Development, 81*(5), 1565–1581.

Merdin-Uygur, E., Sarial-Abi, G., Gurhan-Canli, Z., & Kesapci-Karaca, O. (2019). How does self-concept clarity influence happiness in experiential settings? The role of strangers versus friends. *Self and Identity, 18*(4), 443–467.

Merriam-Webster. (n.d.). *Kaleidoscope.* Merriam-Webster.com. https://www.merriam-webster.com/dictionary/kaleidoscope.

Mesquita, B. (2001). Emotions in collectivist and individualist contexts. *Journal of Personality and Social Psychology, 80,* 68–74.

Micheletti, M., & Stolle, D. (2007). Mobilizing consumers to take responsibility for global social justice. *The Annals of the American Academy of Political and Social Science, 611,* 157–175.

Milgram, S. (1963). Behavioral study of obedience. *Journal of Abnormal and Social Psychology, 67,* 371–378.

Miller, H., & Berk, C. C. (2020, May 15). *JC Penny could join a growing list of bankruptcies during the coronavirus pandemic.* CNBC. https://www.cnbc.com/2020/05/15/these-companies-have-filed-for-bankruptcy-since-the-coronavirus-pandemic.html.

Minas, M., Dennis, J., & Subrahmanyam, K. (2014). Can you guess who I am? Real, ideal, and false self-presentation on Facebook among emerging adults. *Emerging Adulthood, 3*(1), 55–64.

Miranda, A. O., & Umhoefer, D. L. (1998). Depression and social interest differences between Latinos in dissimilar acculturation stages. *Journal of Mental Health Counseling, 20*(2), 159–171.

Mischel, W., & Ebbesen, E. B. (1970). Attention in delay of gratification. *Journal of Personality and Social Psychology, 16*(2), 329–337.

Mischel, W., Shoda, Y., & Peake, P. K. (1988). The nature of adolescent competencies predicted by preschool delay of gratification. *Journal of Personality and Social Psychology, 54*(4), 687–696.

Molleman, E., & Rink, F. (2015). The antecedents and consequences of a strong professional identity among medical specialists. *Social Theory & Health, 13*(1), 46–61.

Morgan, E. M., & Korobov, N. (2012). Interpersonal identity formation in conversations with close friends about dating relationships. *Journal of Adolescence, 35*(6), 1471–1483.

Mpofu, E., & Harley, D. A. (2006). Racial and disability identity: Implications for the career counseling of African Americans with disabilities. *Rehabilitation Counseling Bulletin, 50*(1), 14–23.

Myers, D. G., & DeWall, C. N. (2018). *Psychology.* 12th ed. Worth Publishers.

NASA. (2020, June 18). *Global climate change: Vital signs of the planet.* NASA. https://climate.nasa.gov/.

Natsuaki, M. N., Samuels, D., & Leve, L. D. (2015). Puberty, identity, and context: A biopsychosocial perspective on internalizing psychopathology in early adolescent girls. In K. C. McLean & M. Syed (Eds.), *The Oxford Handbook of Identity Development* (pp. 389–405). Oxford University Press.

Neves, A. (2018, March 7). *It's 2018 and people still hate millennials. Here are 4 reasons why.* Inc.com. https://www.inc.com/antonio-neves/the-real-reason-that-older-generations-hate-millennials-is-not-what-you-think.html.

Noor, P. (2020, June 22). So Gen Z-ers hate millennials now? A handy guide to the generation wars. *The Guardian.* https://www.theguardian.com/us-news/2020/jun/22/gen-z-hate-millennials-handy-guide-generation-wars.

Norris, D. R. (2016). *Job loss, identity, and mental health.* Rutgers University Press.

Oarga, C., Stavrova, O., & Fetchenhauer, D. (2015). When and why is helping others good for well-being? The role of belief in reciprocity and conformity to society's expectations. *European Journal of Social Psychology, 45,* 242–254.

Ohlheise, A. (2015, October 7). Why "social justice warrior," a Gamergate insult, is now a dictionary entry. *Washington Post.* https://www.washingtonpost.com/news/theintersect/wp/2015/10/07/why-social-justice-warrior-a-gamergate-insult-is-now-a-dictionary-entry/.

Oppel, R. A., & Taylor, D. B. (2020, June 24). Here's what you need to know about Breonna Taylor's death. *New York Times.* https://www.nytimes.com/article/breonna-taylor-police.html.

Owens, J. (2020, June 5). *Roger Goodell: NFL admits 'we were wrong' on player protests, says 'black lives matter.'* Yahoo. https://sports.yahoo.com/roger-goodell-nfl-admits-we-were-wrong-on-player-protests-black-lives-matter-224540686.html.

Ozer, S., Meca, A., & Schwartz, S. J. (2019). Globalization and identity development among emerging adults from Ladakh. *Cultural Diversity and Ethnic Minority Psychology, 25*(4), 515–526.

Paige, S. R., Miller, M. D., Krieger, J. L., Stellefson, M., & Cheong, J. (2018). Electronic health literacy across the lifespan: Measurement invariance study. *Journal of Medical Internet Research, 20,* e10434.

Papa, A., & Lancaster, N. (2016). Identity continuity and loss after death, divorce, and job loss. *Self and Identity, 15,* 47–61.

Parker, K., Graf, N., & Igielnik, R. (2019, January 17). *Generation Z looks a lot like millennials on key social and political issues.* Pew Research Center. https://www.pewsocialtrends.org/2019/01/17/generation-z-looks-a-lot-like-millennials-on-key-social-and-political-issues/.

Peets, K., & Hodges, E. V. E. (2016). Authenticity in friendships and well-being in adolescence. *Social Development, 27,* 140–153.

Perez, M., Pettit, J. W., David, C. F., Kistner, J. A., & Joiner, T. E., Jr. (2001). The interpersonal consequences of inflated self-esteem in an inpatient

Bibliography

psychiatric youth sample. *Journal of Consulting and Clinical Psychology, 69*(4), 712–716.

Pérez-Garzón, C. A. (2018). Unveiling the meaning of social justice in Colombia. *Mexican Law Review, 10*(2), 27–66.

Pew Research Center. (2016, September 3). *Most millennials resist the "millennial" label.* Pew Research Center. https://www.pewresearch.org/politics/2015/09/03/most-millennials-resist-the-millennial-label/.

Pew Research Center. (2018, March 1). *The generations defined.* Pew Research Center. https://www.pewresearch.org/st_18-02-27_generations_defined/.

Pew Research Center. (2020, April 28). *Millennials overtake baby boomers as America's largest generation.* Pew Research Center. https://www.pewresearch.org/fact-tank/2020/04/28/millennials-overtake-baby-boomers-as-americas-largest-generation/.

Pew Research Center. (n.d.). *About Pew Research.* Pew Research Center. https://www.pewresearch.org/about/.

Pfeifer, J. H., & Berkman, E. T. (2018). The development of self and identity in adolescence: Neural evidence and implications for a value-based choice perspective on motivated behavior. *Child Development Perspectives, 12*(3), 158–164.

Phys.org. (2019, February 19). *Scientist who popularized the term "global warming" dies at 87.* Phys.Org. https://phys.org/news/2019-02-scientist-popularized-term-global-dies.html.

Podlog, L., Gao, Z., Kenow, L., Kleinert, J., Granquist, M., Newton, M., & Hannon, J. (2013). Injury rehabilitation overadherence: Preliminary scale validation and relationships with athletic identity and self-presentation concerns. *Journal of Athletic Training, 48*(3), 372–381.

Praharso, N. F., Tear, M. J., & Cruwys, T. (2017). Stressful life transitions and wellbeing: A comparison of the stress buffering hypothesis and the social identity model of identity change. *Psychiatry Research, 247*, 265–275.

Price, R. H., Friedland, D. S., & Vinokur, A. D. (1998). Job loss: Hard times and eroded identity. In J. H. Harvey (Ed.), *Perspectives on loss: A sourcebook* (pp. 303–316). Taylor & Francis.

Putnam, M. (2005). Conceptualizing disability: Developing a framework for political disability identity. *Journal of Disability Policy Studies, 16*(3), 188–198.

Pyszczynski, T., Greenberg, J., & Solomon, S. (1997). Why do we need what we need? A terror management perspective on the roots of human social motivation. *Social Inquiry, 8*, 1–20.

Ragelienė, T. (2016). Links of adolescents identity development and relationship with peers: A systematic literature review. *Journal of the Canadian Academy of Child and Adolescent Psychiatry, 25*(2), 97–105.

Ragelienė, T., & Justickis, V. (2016). Interrelations of adolescent's identity development, differentiation of self and parenting style. *Psichologija, 53*, 24–43.

Rathi, N., & Lee, K. (2020). *Does it pay to be authentic? Implications of authenticity for life satisfaction and psychological well-being in a collectivist culture.* Advance online publication. https://doi/10.1007/s10902-020-00223-x.

Remedios, J. D., & Snyder, S. H. (2018). Intersectional oppression: Multiple stigmatized identities and perceptions of invisibility, discrimination, and stereotyping. *Journal of Social Issues, 74*, 265–281.

Ritchie, H., Hasell, J., Appel, C., & Roser, M. (2019, November). *Terrorism.* OurWorldInData.org. https://ourworldindata.org/terrorism.

Roccas, S., Horenczyk, G., & Schwartz, S. H. (2000). Acculturation discrepancies and well-being: The moderating role of conformity. *European Journal of Social Psychology, 30*, 323–334.

Rodriguez-Rad, C. J., & Ramos-Hidalgo, E. (2018). Spirituality, consumer ethics, and sustainability: The mediating role of moral identity. *Journal of Consumer Marketing, 35*, 51–63.

Roesler, C. (2008). The self in cyberspace: Identity formation in postmodern societies and Jung's self as an objective psyche. *Journal of Analytical Psychology, 53*, 421–436.

Rogers, C. (1961). *On becoming a person.* Houghton Mifflin.

Rogers, L. O., & Meltzoff, A. N. (2017). Is gender more important and meaningful than race? An analysis of racial and gender identity among Black, white, and mixed-race children. *Cultural Diversity and Ethnic Minority Psychology, 23*(3), 323–334.

Rosenberg, M. (1976, August 20). *Beyond self-esteem: Some neglected aspects of the self-concept* [conference session]. Annual Meeting of the American Sociological Association, New York.

Ross, S. N. (2009). Critical race theory, democratization, and the public good: Deploying postmodern understandings of racial identity in the social justice classroom to contest academic capitalism. *Teaching in Higher Education, 14*, 517–528.

Ryan, R. M., & Deci, E. L. (2017). *Self-determination theory: Basic psychological needs in motivation, development, and wellness.* Guilford.

Ryan, W. S., & Ryan, R. M. (2018). Toward a social psychology of authenticity: Exploring within-person variation in autonomy, congruence, and genuineness using self-determination theory. *Review of General Psychology, 23*, 99–112.

Salthouse, T. A. (1995). Refining the concept of psychological compensation. In R. A. Dixon & L. Backman (Eds.), *Compensating for psychological deficits and declines: Managing losses and promoting gains* (pp. 21–34). Lawrence Erlbaum.

Santos, C. E., Kornienko, O., & Rivas-Drake, D. (2017). Peer influence on ethnic-racial identity development: A multi-site investigation. *Child Development, 88*(3), 725–742.

Sartor, C. E., & Youniss, J. (2002). The relationship between positive parental involvement and identity achievement during adolescence. *Adolescence, 37*(146), 221–234.

Scabini, E., & Manzi, C. (2011). Family processes and identity. In K. Luyckx & V. L. Vignoles (Eds.), *Handbook of identity theory and research* (Vol. 2, pp. 565–584). Springer.

Bibliography

Schneider, H. (2021, May 4). Is it over yet? Still no recession end date as U.S. economy hums along. *Reuters.* https://www.reuters.com/business/is-it-over-yet-still-no-recession-end-date-us-economy-hums-along-2021-05-04/.

Schutte, N. S., & McNeil, D. G. (2015). Athletic identity mediates between exercise motivation and beneficial outcomes. *Journal of Sport Behavior, 38*(2), 234–252.

Schwartz, S. J., Beyers, W., Luyckx, K., Soenens, B., Zamboanga, B. L., Forthun, L. F., . . . Waterman, A. S. (2011). Examining the light and dark sides of emerging adults' identity: A study of identity status differences in positive and negative psychosocial functioning. *Journal of Youth and Adolescence, 40*, 839–859.

Schwartz, S. J., Dunkel, C. S., & Waterman, A. S. (2009). Terrorism: An identity theory perspective. *Studies in Conflict and Terrorism, 32*, 537–559.

Schwartz, S. J., Klimstra, T. A., Luyckx, K., Hale, W. J. I., Frijns, T., Oosterwegel, A., . . . Meeus, W. H. J. (2011). Daily dynamics of personal identity and self-concept clarity. *European Journal of Personality, 25*(5), 373–385.

Sedikides, C., & Brewer, M. B. (Eds.). (2001) *Individual self, relational self, and collective self.* Routledge.

Selisker, S. (2015). The Bechdel Test and the social form of character networks. *New Literary History, 46*, 505–523.

Shoda, Y., Mischel, W., & Peake, P. K. (1990). Predicting adolescent cognitive and self-regulatory competencies from preschool delay of gratification: Identifying diagnostic conditions. *Developmental Psychology, 26*(6), 978–986.

Slay, H. S., & Smith, D. A. (2011). Professional identity construction: Using narrative to understand the negotiation of professional and stigmatized cultural identities. *Human Relations, 64*(1), 85–107.

Smith, L. R., Smith, K. D., & Blazka, M. (2017). Follow me, what's the harm? Considerations of catfishing and utilizing fake online personas on social media. *Journal of Legal Aspects of Sport, 27*, 32–45.

Smyth, T. (2019, December 9). *"Ok, Boomer": What generational identity means for brands.* Lieberman Research Worldwide. https://lrwonline.com/perspective/ok-boomer-what-generational-identity-means-for-brands/.

Snyder, C., & Lopez, L. (2017, December 13). *Tarana Burke on why she created the #MeToo movement—and where it's headed.* Business Insider. https://www.businessinsider.com/how-the-metoo-movement-started-where-its-headed-tarana-burke-time-person-of-year-women-2017-12.

Statista Research Department. (2020, January 28). *Terrorism—Statistics and facts.* Statista. https://www.statista.com/topics/2267/terrorism/.

Stopbullying.gov. (2017, September 25). *Federal laws.* Stopbullying.org. https://www.stopbullying.gov/resources/laws/federal.

Stuart-Cassel, V., Bell, A., & Springer, J. F. (2011). *Analysis of state bullying laws and policies.* U.S. Department of Education, Office of Planning, Evaluation and Policy Development, Policy and Program Studies Service.

Sue, D. W., & Sue, D. (2012). *Counseling the culturally diverse: Theory and practice.* 6th ed. Wiley.

Suh, E. M. (2002). Culture, identity consistency, and subjective well-being. *Journal of Personality and Social Psychology, 83,* 1378–1391.

Suler, J. R. (2002). Identity management in cyberspace. *Journal of Applied Psychoanalytic Studies, 4,* 455–459.

Sun, T., Horn, M., & Merritt, D. (2004). Values and lifestyles of individualists and collectivists: A study on Chinese, Japanese, British and US consumers. *The Journal of Consumer Marketing, 21,* 318–331.

Sutton, A. (2018). Distinguishing between authenticity and personality consistency in predicting well-being: A mixed method approach. *European Review of Applied Psychology, 68,* 117–130.

Suyemoto, K. L., Day, S. C., & Schwartz, S. (2014). Exploring the effects of social justice youth programming on racial and ethnic identities and activism for Asian American youth. *Asian American Journal of Psychology, 6,* 125–135.

Swann, W., Gómez, A., Conor Seyle, D., Francisco Morales, J., & Huici, C. (2009). Identity fusion: The interplay of personal and social identities in extreme group behavior. *Journal of Personality and Social Psychology, 96*(5), 995–1011.

Tajfel, H., & Turner, J. C. (2010a). An integrative theory of intergroup conflict. In T. Postmes & N. R. Branscombe (Eds.), *Rediscovering social identity* (pp. 173–190). Psychology Press.

Takano, K., & Tanno, Y. (2009). Self-rumination, self-reflection, and depression: Self-rumination counteracts the adaptive effect of self-reflection. *Behaviour Research and Therapy, 47,* 260–264.

Tapper, A. J. H. (2013). A pedagogy of social justice education: Social identity theory, intersectionality, and empowerment. *Conflict Resolution Quarterly, 30,* 411–445.

Taylor, D. M., & Louis, W. (2004). Terrorism and the quest for identity. In F. M. Moghaddam & A. J. Marsella (Eds.), *Understanding terrorism: Psychosocial roots, consequences, and interventions* (pp. 169–185). American Psychological Association.

Templeton, A., Guven, S. T., Hoerst, C., Vestergren, S., Davidson, L., Ballentyne, S., . . . Choudhury, S. (2020). Inequalities and identity processes in crises: Recommendations for facilitating safe response to the COVID-19 pandemic. *British Journal of Social Psychology, 59,* 674–685.

The Women's. (n.d.). *Sexual identity and orientation.* The Women's. https://www.thewomens.org.au/health-information/sex-sexuality/our-sexuality/sexual-identity-and-orientation.

Thomaes, S., Sedikides, C., van den Bos, N., Hutteman, R., & Reijntjes, A. (2017). Happy to be "me"? Authenticity, psychological need satisfaction, and subjective well-being in adolescence. *Child Development, 88,* 1045–1056.

Thompson, D. (2011, September 22). Are today's youth really a lost generation? *The Atlantic.* https://www.theatlantic.com/business/archive/2011/09/are-todays-youth-really-a-lost-generation/245524/.

Bibliography

Torelli, C. J. (2006). Individuality or conformity? The effect of independent and interdependent self-concepts on public judgments. *Journal of Consumer Psychology, 16*, 240–248.

Tsang, S. K. M., Hui, E. K. P., & Law, B. C. M. (2012). Positive identity as a positive youth development construct: A conceptual review. *The Scientific World Journal, 2012*, Article ID 529691.

Tsang, S. K. M., & Yip, F. Y. Y. (2006). Positive identity as a positive youth development construct: Conceptual bases and implications for curriculum development. *International Journal of Adolescent Medicine and Health, 18*, 459–466.

Tucker, H. (2020, May 3). *Coronavirus bankruptcy tracker: These major companies are failing amid the shutdown.* Forbes. https://www.forbes.com/sites/hanktucker/2020/05/03/coronavirus-bankruptcy-tracker-these-major-companies-are-failing-amid-the-shutdown/#7eec99d33425.

Turner, K. H. (2010). Digitalk: A new literacy for a digital generation. *Phi Delta Kappan, 92*(1), 41–46.

Turner, K. H. (2013). The challenge of acceptance: Digitalk and language as conformity and resistance. In F. R. Spielhagen & P. D. Schwartz (Eds.), *Adolescence in the 21st century: Constants and challenge* (pp. 171–185). Information Age.

United Nations. (n.d.). *2020 Theme: "Closing the inequalities gap to achieve social justice."* United Nations. https://www.un.org/en/observances/social-justice-day.

Urick, M. J. (2012). Exploring generational identity: A multiparadigm approach. *Journal of Business Diversity, 12*, 103–115.

Wang, Y., & Li, Z. (2018). Authenticity as a mediator of the relationship between power contingent self-esteem and subjective well-being. *Frontiers in Psychology, 9*, 1066.

Wang, Y. N. (2016). Balanced authenticity predicts optimal well-being: Theoretical conceptualization and empirical development of the authenticity in relationships scale. *Personality and Individual Differences, 94*, 316–323.

Warner, D. F., & Brown, T. H. (2011). Understanding how race/ethnicity and gender define age-trajectories of disability: An intersectionality approach. *Social Science & Medicine, 72*, 1236–1248.

Watzlawik, M., & Clodius, S. (2011). Interpersonal identity development in different groups of siblings: A longitudinal study. *European Psychologist, 16*(1), 43–47.

Webb, R. T. (2015). Suicide, unemployment, and the effect of economic recession. *The Lancet, 2*, 196–197.

Weigert, A. J. (2003). Terrorism, identity, and public order: A perspective from Goffman. *Identity: An International Journal of Theory and Research, 3*(2), 93–113.

Weir, K. F., & Jose, P. E. (2010). The perception of false self scale for adolescents: Reliability, validity, and longitudinal relationships with depressive and anxious symptoms. *British Journal of Developmental Psychology, 28*, 393–411.

Werthner, P., & Orlick, T. (1986). Retirement experiences of successful Olympic athletes. *International Journal of Sport Psychology, 17*(5), 337–363.

Wickham, R. E., Williamson, R. E., Beard, C. L., Kobayashi, C. L. B., & Hirst, T. W. (2016). Authenticity attenuates the negative effects of interpersonal conflict on daily well-being. *Journal of Research in Personality, 60*, 56–62.

Williams, D. R., & Mohammed, S. A. (2009). Discrimination and racial disparities in health: Evidence and needed research. *Journal of Behavioral Medicine, 32*, 20–47.

Womick, J., Foltz, R. M., & King, L. A. (2019). "Releasing the beast within?" Authenticity, well-being, and the Dark Tetrad. *Personality and Individual Differences, 137*, 115–125.

Wong, T. M. L., Branje, S. J. T., VanderValk, I. E., Hawk, S. T., & Meeus, W. H. J. (2010). The role of siblings in identity development in adolescence and emerging adulthood. *Journal of Adolescence, 33*, 673–682.

Wood, A. M., Linley, P. A., Maltby, J., Baliousis, M., & Joseph, S. (2008). The authentic personality: A theoretical and empirical conceptualization and the development of the authenticity scale. *Journal of Counseling Psychology, 55*, 385–399.

World Health Organization/London School of Hygiene and Tropical Medicine. (2010). *Preventing intimate partner and sexual violence against women: Taking action and generating evidence.* World Health Organization.

Xiaoling, S., Xiaowen, L., & Mingzheng, W. (2006). The moderating effects of self-complexity on the relationship between life events and depression in a sample of adolescents. *Acta Psychologica Sinica, 38*(5), 751–761.

Yip, T. (2018). Ethnic/racial identity—A double-edged sword? Associations with discrimination and psychological outcomes. *Current Directions in Psychological Science, 27*(3), 170–175.

Yip, T., Gee, G. C., & Takeuchi, D. T. (2009). Racial discrimination and psychological distress: The impact of ethnic identity and age among immigrant and United States–born Asian adults. *Developmental Psychology, 44*, 787–800.

Index

Acceptance, 48–49, 51–52; unconditional positive regard, 48–49, 128
Accepting external influence, 117–118
Acculturation, 21, 98–99; and global, 21; and globalization, 184–186; and social norms, 98–99
Actualizing tendency, 46–47
Adolescence: and identity statuses, 42–46; and psychosocial development, 38–39
Adoptive identity, 17–18; and assigned identities, 18
Adulthood, and psychosocial development, 41
Ageism. *See* Discrimination, age-based
Agency (aka personal agency), 119–120
Ainsworth, Mary, 68–69. *See also* Attachment
Asch, Solomon, 94–95, 96, 100. *See also* Conformity and Fitting in
Athletic identity, 19–20
Attachment, 68–69, 76
Authentic living, 116–118
Authenticity: and accepting external influence, 117; and adolescence, 114–115; and agency, 119–120; and authentic living, 116–117; and

Authenticity Scale, 116; and authentic self-esteem, 111; and autonomous, 113, 115; and awareness, 129–130; and balanced authenticity, 119–120, 121; and benefits of, 19; and communion, 119; conditions for psychological growth, 47–49; and consistent personality, 120–121; and contingency-based self-esteem, 115; and Dark Tetrad, 120; and ego-centric authenticity, 119–120; and empathy, 120; and happiness, 117–118; and heteronomous, 113, 115; and impression management, 120; and influence of others, 117; and interpersonal conflict, 129–130; and interpersonal relationships, 114; and kaleidoscope career model (KCM), 87; and life satisfaction, 133; and measurement of, 116; and other-distorted authenticity, 119–120; and personal sense of uniqueness, 118; and power contingent self-esteem, 115; and self-alienation, 116; and self-reflection, 112–113; and self-rumination, 112–113; and social-desirability; and unbiased processing, 129–130; and well-being, 112–121

Authenticity Scale, 116–118

Autonomy: and authenticity, 113; and autonomous motivation, 58; and basic psychological needs theory, 56–57; and causality orientations theory, 55; and globalization, 184; and goal contents theory, 57–58; and individualism and collectivism, 103–105; and post-Freudian theory, 36–37; and relationships motivation theory, 58. *See also* Self-determination theory

Autonomy support, 56–57. *See also* Self-determination theory

Baby boomers, 147–148; and differences among generations, 150–155; and digital literacy, 160; and similarities with other generations, 150

Basic psychological needs theory, 56–57. *See also* Self-determination theory

Basic strength, 36

Black lives matter (BLM), 189

Bowlby, John, 68, 76. *See also* Attachment

Bullying, 174–179

Catfishing, 164

Causality orientations theory, 55–56. *See also* Self-determination theory

Child labor and welfare, 197–199

Choice overload, 166

Client-centered theory. *See* Person-centered theory

Climate change, 203–206

Cognitive evaluation theory (CET), 54. *See also* Self-determination theory

Collectivism, 101–106; and authenticity, 113; and autonomy, 105; and globalization, 185; and horizontal collectivism, 105; and

terrorism, 202; and vertical collectivism, 105

Coming out, 30

Commitment: and adolescence, 72–74; and bullying, 177; and false self, 132–133; globalization, 185–186; and parental figures, 76, 78; and peers, 81; and positive identity, 110–111; and racial discrimination, 191; and siblings, 79–81; and sustainability, 207

Communion, 119

Compensation, 127

Competence, 53, 56, 57–58

Condition of worth, 51–52, 125, 128, 136

Conditions for psychological growth, 47–49. *See also* Acceptance; Empathy; Genuineness

Conformity, 94–96, 98–99; and accepting external influence, 117; approval-based contingent self-esteem, 100; and autonomy, 103–105; and conditions for, 95–96; and individualism and collectivism, 103; and informational social influence, 96; and normative social influence, 96; and self-determination theory, 105; and social anxiety (aka social phobia), 100–101; and social norms, 98–99. *See also* Asch, Solomon; Social norms

Congruence, 46, 47, 49, 50, 112, 116; genuineness, 47–48, 112; ideal self, 50–51, 107; self-concept, 6–7

Core pathology, 36

Critical race theory (CRT), 191

Cross, William, 23–24

Cultural globalization, 182–183

Cultural identity, 20–21, 184–185

Dark Tetrad, 120

Deci, Edward, 52–58, 104

Index

Delayed gratification, 12; marshmallow test, 11, 14
Differentiation, 77–78, 124–125, 136
Digital literacy, 142, 157–160
Digitalk, 162
Disability identity, 21–23; political disability identity, 23
Discrimination, age-based, 194
Discrimination, racial, 191–193
Dunning-Kruger effect, 126–127
Dystonic, 36

Early childhood, and post-Freudian theory, 37
Economic globalization, 182
Economic insecurity, 169–170
Egocentrism (cognitive development), 66
Empathy, 48–49, 51–52, 120
Enmeshment, 124
Epigenetic principle, 36
Erikson, Erik, 35–42, 70–71, 72–73, 82–83, 108, 111
Ethnic/Racial identity (ERI), 23–25, 191–192
Exploration: and adolescence, 38, 70–76; and globalization, 185–186; and identity status, 131–133; and paths to identity achievement, 45; and peers, 81–83; and positive identity, 111; and siblings, 79–81; and technology, using, 161
Extrinsic motivation, 54–55. *See also* Self-determination theory

False self, 123–125; and anxiety, 130–131; and depression, 130–131, 135; and family and peer influences, 128–129; and identity statuses, 131–134; and loss of voice, 134–138; and measuring false self, 130; and online, 163–166; and Perceptions of false self scale, 130; and social media, 134
Fidelity, 39, 73, 111
Fitting in, 93–101. *See also* Conformity; Individualism
Five stage model of racial identity development, 23
Formative tendency, 46
Freud, Sigmund, 35

Generation Alpha (Gen Alpha), 141–142
Generation X (Gen X), 145–147; and differences among generations, 150–155; and digital literacy, 160; and similarities with other generations, 150
Generation Z (Gen Z), 142–143; and differences among generations, 150–155; and similarities with other generations, 150
Gender identity, 25–26, 195–196
Genuineness, 47–48, 112; congruence, 46, 47, 49, 50, 112, 116
Global warming. *See* Climate change
Globalization, 181–186
Goal contents theory, 57–58. *See also* Self-determination theory
Greatest generation (G. I. Generation), 142

Heteronomous, 104, 113
Higgins, E. Tory, 108–109, 165. *See also* Self-discrepancy theory

Ideal self, 50–51, 107; congruence, 46, 47, 49, 50, 112, 116
Identity, 3–5; and acculturation, 98; and adolescence, 69–84; and adulthood, 84–92; and attachment, 68–69, 76; and benefits of being true to who you are, 112–121; and birth order, 79–80; and brain

Identity (*cont.*)

activity (adulthood), 92; and brain development (adolescence), 70, 71; and childhood, 62–69; and climate change, 204–206; and commitment, 72–74, 79–80; and conformity, 94–96; and consequences to behavior, 64; and differentiation, 77–78; and digital, 162; and display of emotions, 66; and effect of peers on ethnic/racial identity (adolescence), 81–82; and egocentrism, 66; and exploration, 69, 72–74; 79–80; and family relationships, 67–69; and friendships (adolescence), 81–84; and friendships (adulthood), 91; and generalized core, 4; and globalization, 183–186; and identity status, 83; and intersectionality, 199–200; and intimacy, 82–83; and kaleidoscope, 71–72; and kaleidoscope career model, 86–88; and learning, play and language development, 65–66; and media, 158, 184; and memories, 66–67; and object permanence, 63–64; and occupational changes (adulthood), 86–90; and online identity, 161–167; and pandemic, 187–189; and parental figures (adolescence), 75–78; and parenting style, 76–78; and peers (adolescence), 81–84; and physical changes (adulthood), 84–86; and physical development (childhood), 62–63; and poorly developed, 123–138; and positive identity, 110–112; and positivity bias, 91–92; and principal identity, 4; and puberty, 71; and relationship changes (adulthood), 90–92; and reproductive identity, 85–86; and retirement, 88–90; and romantic relationships (adolescence), 82; and self-complexity, 88; and self-discrepancy, 107–110; and self-recognition, 64–65; and self-reference effect, 66–67; and sensorimotor stage of development, 65; and separation and individuation, 75; and sex of friendships, 83; and sex of siblings, 80; and sexual assault, 197; and sibling differentiation, 79–80; and sibling identification, 79–80; and siblings (adolescence), 78–81; and siblings' place in the family, 80; and sibling type, 80–81; and social identity model of change, 89–90; and social norms, 96–101; and socioemotional selectivity theory, 90–91; and statuses, 76 (*see also* specific identity statuses); and sustainability, 207–208; and sustainability, barriers to, 209–210; and sustainability in business, 208–209; and three-factor identity model, 73–74; and trauma, 197; and understanding connection/separateness from others, 63–64; and unemployment, 170–174; and well-developed, 107–121. *See also specific types of identity*

Identity crisis, 36, 41, 43–44

Identity statuses, 42–46, 76, 83; and anxiety, 132–133; and carefree diffusion, 132–134; and closure, 45; and depression, 132–133; and diffused diffusion, 132–133; and false self, 131–134; and foreclosure, 44, 45, 131–133, 202; and identity achievement, 43, 45, 131–133; and identity diffusion, 43–44, 45; and moratorium, 44, 45; and paths to identity achievement, 45–46; and searching moratorium, 45, 132–133; and self-esteem,

Index

132–133; and undifferentiated, 132–133; and unhealthy behaviors, 132–134

Identity threat, 29

Independent self-concept, 9, 99–100

Individualism, 101–106; and authenticity, 113; and horizontal individualism, 105; and self-determination theory; and vertical individualism, 105. *See also* Collectivism

Infancy, and psychosocial development, 36–37

Information literacy, 159

Informational social influence, 96

Interdependent self-concept, 9, 99–100

Intersectionality, 199–200

Intrinsic motivation, 52–53, 54, 55, 56. *See also* Self-determination theory

Kaleidoscope, 71–72

Kaleidoscope career model (KCM), 86–87

LGBTQ, 194–196

Lost generation, 142

Marcia, James, 42–46, 72–73, 107, 131–134

Marshmallow test, 11, 14; delay gratification, 12

MeToo, 196–197

Media literacy, 157–160

Millennials, 143–145; and differences among generations, 150–155; and digital literacy, 160; and similarities with other generations, 150

Minority identity development model, 24

Multiple identities, 33–34

Narcissism, 126–127

Narrative identity, 26–28; life story model of identity, 26–27

Normative social influence, 96

Object permanence, 63

Observational learning, 97

Old age, and post-Freudian theory, 41–42

Online identity, 161–167

Organismic integration theory, 54–55. *See also* Self-determination theory

Organismic self, 47

Overcompensation, 127

Pandemic, 169–170, 186–189

Parenting style, 76–78

Person-centered theory, 46–52; and acceptance, 48, 51–52; and actualizing tendency, 46–47; and client-centered theory, 46; and conditions of worth, 51–52; and congruence, 46, 49, 50; and empathy, 48–49, 51–52; and enhancement, 47; and formative tendency, 46; and genuineness, 47–48, 51–52; and humanistic, 46; and ideal self, 50–51; and maintenance, 47; and necessary conditions, 47–49; and organismic self/experience, 47, 49; Rogers, Carl, 46–52, 107–108, 116; and self-concept, 50–51

Personal identity, 15–17

Place attachment, 207

Place identity, 207

Play age, and post-Freudian theory, 37

Political disability identity, 23

Political globalization, 183

Positive identity, 110–112

Positive self-regard, 10

Positivity bias, 91–92

Priming, 99–100

Professional identity, 28–29

Prosocial behavior, 97–98; social norms, 96–101

Psychosocial development, 35–42; and adolescence, 38–39; and adulthood, 41; and autonomy, 37; basic mistrust, 36–37; basic strength, 36; and basic trust, 36–37; and care, 41; and competence, 38; and compulsion, 37; and core pathology, 36; and despair, 41–42; and disdain, 42; and dystonic, 36; and early childhood, 37; and epigenetic principle, 36; and exclusivity, 40; and fidelity, 39; and generativity, 41; and guilt, 37; and hope, 37; and identity confusion, 39; and identity crisis, 36, 39; and industry, 38; and inertia, 38; and infancy, 36–37; and inferiority, 38; and inhibition, 37; and initiative, 37; and isolation, 40; and integrity, 41; and intimacy, 39–40; and love, 40; and old age, 41–42; and play age, 37; and purpose, 37; and role repudiation, 39; and school age, 38; and shame and doubt, 37; and stagnation, 41; and syntonic, 36; and will, 37; and wisdom, 42; and withdrawal, 37. *See also* Erikson, Erik

Racial and cultural identity development model, 24–25

Racial identity. *See* Ethnic/Racial identity

Relatedness, 56, 57. *See also* Self-determination theory

Relationships motivation theory, 58. *See also* Self-determination theory

Reproductive identity, 85–86

Retirement, 19–20, 88–90, 148

Rogers, Carl, 46–52, 107–108, 116. *See also* Person-centered theory

Role repudiation, 39, 73

Ryan, Richard, 52–58, 104

School age, and post-Freudian theory, 38

Self-alienation, 116–118

Self-concept, 6–7; and accuracy, 50, 51; congruence, 46, 47, 49, 50, 112, 116; and independent, 9–10, 99; and individualism and collectivism, 103; and interdependent, 9–10, 99; and person-centered theory, 50, 51; and personal identity, 16–17; and self-discrepancy theory, 108–109

Self-concept clarity, 7–9

Self-control, 11–14

Self-determination, 52, 58. *See also* Self-determination theory

Self-determination theory, 52–58; and authenticity, 113, 114; and autonomy, 56, 57, 58, 104–105; and autonomous motivation, 58; and autonomy orientation, 55; and autonomy support, 56–57; and basic psychological needs theory, 56–57; and causality orientations theory, 55–56; and cognitive evaluation theory, 54; and competence, 53, 55, 56, 57–58; and conformity, 105; and controlled orientation, 56; and extrinsic goals, 57; and extrinsic motivation, 54, 55; and goal contents theory, 57–58; and impersonal orientation, 56; and individualism and collectivism, 103–104; and internalization, 55; and intrinsic goals, 57; and intrinsic motivation, 52–53, 54, 55, 56; and mini-theories, 53–58; and organismic integration theory, 54–55; and psychological needs, 55; and relatedness, 55, 56,

Index 275

57; and relationships motivation theory, 58; self-determined competence, 53; and self-esteem, 115; and social norms, 97; *See also* Deci, Edward; Ryan, Richard

Self-discrepancy theory, 107–110; and actual self, 108–110; and agitation-related emotions, 108, 109–110; and dejection-related emotions, 108, 109–110; and domains of the self, 108–110; and ideal self, 108–110, 165; and online identity, 165; and ought self, 108–110, 165; and positive identity, 111–112; and self-concept, 109; and self-guides, 109; and self states, 108; and standpoints of the self, 108; true self (aka actual self), 165

Self-esteem, 10–11; and approval-based contingent, 100; and authentic self-esteem, 111; and contingency-based self-esteem, 115; and Dunning-Kruger effect, 126; and false self, 125–126, 129; and identity statuses, 132; and loss of voice, 135; and overcompensation, 127; and positive identity, 111; and power contingent self-esteem, 115; and self-concept clarity, 7–9; and terror management theory, 10–11; and undercompensation, 127

Self-evaluation, 6

Self-reference effect, 66–67

Self-reflection, 112–113, 125

Self-rumination, 112

Self-schemas, 6

Self-worth, 10, 19, 23, 111, 137, 171–172. *See also* Self-esteem

Separation and individuation, 75

Sexual identity, 29–31, 195–196

School age, and post-Freudian theory, 38

Silent Generation, 148–149; and differences among generations,

150–155; and digital literacy, 160; and similarities with other generations, 150

Social anxiety, 100–101, 132

Social identity, 31–33; and bullying, 176–177; and fused, 33; and pandemic, 187–189; and social categorization, 32; and social comparison, 33; and social identification, 32–33; and sustainability, 209; and unemployment, 171–172

Social identity model of change (SIMIC), 89–90

Social justice, 189–197

Social justice warriors (SJW), 190–191

Social media, 158–159

Social norms, 96–101; prosocial behavior, 97–98

Socioemotional selectivity theory, 90–91

Sustainability, 206–210

Syntonic, 36

Terror management theory, 10–11

Terrorism, 200–203

Transgender, 26, 194–195

Transsexual, 26

Unconditional positive regard, 48–49, 128; acceptance, 48–49, 51–52

Undercompensation, 127

Unemployment, 170–174

Voice, 134–138

Willpower, 12–14

Willpower depletion, 13–14

Young adulthood, and post-Freudian theory, 39–40

Zoomers. *See* Generation Z

About the Author

Christine L. B. Selby, PhD, is a professor of psychology at Husson University, in Bangor, Maine, and a licensed psychologist in part-time private practice. She is a Certified Eating Disorder Specialist with the International Association of Eating Disorder Professionals (IAEDP) and a Certified Mental Performance Consultant-Emeritus with the Association for Applied Sport Psychology (AASP). Much of her clinical work centers around helping patients understand who they truly are so they can make important life decisions that reflect their genuine needs and wishes. She has also designed and teaches a collegiate course entitled The Psychology of Self-Development and Self-Awareness. She is the author of *Chilling Out: The Psychology of Relaxation*, *The Body Size and Health Debate*, *Obesity: Your Questions Answered* and *Therapy and Counseling: Your Questions Answered*.